DELIVER US
FROM DARKNESS

OSPREY
PUBLISHING

DELIVER US
FROM DARKNESS

The Untold Story of Third Battalion 506 Parachute
Infantry Regiment during *Market Garden*

IAN GARDNER
FOREWORD BY MARIO DICARLO

First published in Great Britain in 2012 by Osprey Publishing,
Midland House, West Way, Botley, Oxford, OX2 0PH, UK
44-02 23rd Street, Suite 219, Long Island City, NY 11101, USA

E-mail: info@ospreypublishing.com

OSPREY PUBLISHING IS PART OF THE OSPREY GROUP

A CIP catalog record for this book is available from the British Library

ISBN: 978 1 84908 717 9
ePub ISBN: 978 1 78096 398 3

Page layouts by Myriam Bell Design, UK
Maps by Ian Gardner
Index by Alan Thatcher
Typeset in Bembo
Originated by United Graphics Pte., Singapore
Printed in China through Worldprint Ltd.

12 13 14 15 16 17   10 9 8 7 6 5 4 3 2 1

Osprey Publishing is supporting the Woodland Trust, the UK's leading woodland
conservation charity, by funding the dedication of trees.

www.ospreypublishing.com

Front Cover: Currahee scrapbook.

For my mum and dad, Joan and Dennis

Contents

Foreword

I firmly believe that my service with the Third Battalion, 506th Parachute Infantry Regiment (3/506 PIR), 101st Airborne Division, during World War II, set the standard to which I have adhered for the rest of my life. It turned me from a clueless youth, still wet behind the ears, into a combat veteran able to make split-second decisions that would separate the quick from the dead – although some of our bravest were not quite so fortunate or perhaps lucky.

From the very moment I was ambushed and wounded in Normandy on June 6, 1944, my powers of concentration grew beyond all previous recognition. While I was totally unaware of it at the time, my parents played a huge part in arming me with the attitude and mind-set I would need to cope with the demands of military life. My contemporaries have often been referred to as "The Greatest Generation" but I beg to differ ... to me the greatest generation was the one that preceded, and produced, us. The ones from many different lands and cultures, who came to America to breathe free and climb the financial ladder, through nothing but hard work and a selfless devotion to their new country.

Before immigrating to the USA in early 1917, my father had been wounded and invalided out of the Italian Army during World War I. When he discovered that the quickest route to American citizenship was through the armed forces, he quickly enlisted and by the end of the year, was on his way to face the same old enemy, but this time wearing a different uniform. After being honorably discharged, he married my mother, Anna, who had just arrived in the United States. My parents may have come to America as unschooled immigrants but they brought with them a love for freedom and a work ethic unmatched by any

generation before or since. Multiply Alfonso DiCarlo and Anna Lolli by several millions and one can more fully understand the impact they had on a growing nation.

In 1941, I was graduating Wildwood High School in New Jersey when Pearl Harbor was attacked by Japan. Like most of America's youth, I was anxious to get into the ongoing war and went to Philadelphia, where I enlisted into the fledgling 506th PIR. Suffering from acute acrophobia, I reasoned that this was a sure way to conquer my fear of heights! When I informed my parents of my *fait accompli* I was surprised by their response. Having "been there and done that," my father was lukewarm but my mother, whom I had anticipated would burst into tears, simply kissed me and said, "God be with you and don't dishonor your name."

What follows on these pages accurately describes and explains the trials and accomplishments of 3/506 through its most extended single period of combat during World War II in the Netherlands. With Allied forces solidly entrenched in France, the high command was looking for ways to expand upon their successes and shorten the war. General Bernard Law Montgomery had envisioned, and sold General Dwight D. Eisenhower and the Supreme Headquarters Allied Expeditionary Force (SHAEF), a plan for a bold strike up the Eindhoven–Arnhem highway, to penetrate into the vulnerable factories of the Ruhr and deliver a fatal wound to the Nazi regime.

The plan was to fold the Germans back from the road that became known universally as "Hell's Highway" and throw a steel spear across the Rijn (Rhine). Eindhoven and the bridges at Nijmegen and Arnhem were the keys to that success. In essence, we were to open the road to enable the armor from the British Second Army to speed unimpeded to its intended targets in the Ruhr.

The 3rd Battalion of the 506th started out by successfully attacking and investing Eindhoven and ended up almost 70 days later at the northern end of the Allied penetration, engaging the enemy in the ferociously fought battle for Opheusden. Through the recollections of the remaining veterans and the meticulous research that has been the hallmark of the author, the reader can relive the actual events that occurred – presented with clarity and a passion for the facts that is not often encountered in military histories.

As I write this, it occurs to me that we were all members of two separate but inseparable families: the one we were born into and the one we voluntarily joined in a time of national peril. Our obligation and commitment to each aspect was total. Yet one was centered on life and growth and the other dealt with death and destruction. Despite the disparity in goals the core of our innermost conviction was the unspoken willingness to imperil our very existence to preserve the continuation of the lives of other members of both our families. I never heard any of our guys say it out loud but I think their actions under fire prove my thesis.

Our regimental commander, Colonel Robert F. Sink, showed his pride in our performance when he said about us in the attack, "When they fell, they fell face forward." Scared witless or not, we did what had to be done, even when we really didn't want to do it, and, as I recall, there were times when we really *didn't* want to do it. But we did it anyway. The one immutable fact is that the young boys who marched so blithely off to war in 1942 bore little resemblance to the weary men who came home in 1945.

Read and enjoy.

Mario "Hank" DiCarlo – July 2010
Fort Washington, Pennsylvania, USA

Preface

My relationship with the Netherlands began in the late 1980s, when as a British paratrooper and member of 10th Battalion, the Parachute Regiment (V), I first took part in the annual parachute drop – north of the Neder Rijn (Lower Rhine), near Oosterbeek – commemorating the battle of Arnhem. At the time, I was completely unaware of the American struggle that had taken place just a few miles away in the Betuwe, an area on the southern bank of the river also known as "the Island."

Nearly 20 years later, in 2005, when I was researching my first book, *Tonight We Die As Men*, I arranged to spend the day with 3/506 veteran Bill Galbraith. At the time, Bill was visiting the Netherlands on a tour for the "Remember September" celebrations, while I was on a pilgrimage to Arnhem with a group of friends from 10 Para. Bill made special arrangements with the Dutch Airborne Friends for me to join him in Eindhoven.

However, the plan began to unravel when I was late for the coach rendezvous, due to an unexpected party the night before in Belgium! After spending three hours hungover on a train, I finally arrived in Eindhoven, where Bill's hosts, Jenny and Jan van Hout, kindly picked me up. Despite the fact that they had sacrificed most of the morning's events, Jenny and Jan graciously accepted my apology and drove me to Sint Oedenrode, where the tour had stopped for a late lunch. It was wonderful to see Bill, who introduced me to his family, and another historian, John Klein, who was a close friend and neighbor back in the States.

After the celebrations, I should have caught the train back to Arnhem but Jenny invited me to her house for dinner, along with the Galbraiths, John Klein, and fellow Dutch airborne friend Wim Klerkx. Like Bill, my hosts had also experienced the liberation of Eindhoven and during the course of a wonderful evening I began to understand what September 18, 1944, really meant for them. That night I stayed at Wim's with Bill and the following day instead of going back to the boys, elected to stay with the Galbraiths and their Dutch airborne friends. I have no regrets because over the last six years, Jenny has not only become my "Dutch mum" but also my powerbase in Eindhoven, and it is mainly down to her incredible enthusiasm that this book has become a reality.

It was through the Van Houts, that I grew to know Geurt van Rinsum, a retired police officer from Zetten who has been instrumental in helping me understand and record the social history of the island. Since we first met in Sint Oedenrode, John Klein has also become a close friend, whose generosity and loyalty over the last few years has been truly humbling. In June 2009, when John came to Normandy with Bill Galbraith and Manny Barrios to help myself and Roger Day launch *Tonight We Die As Men*, he unwittingly introduced me to a pair of Dutch historians, Tom Timmermans and Tom Peeters, who later became my research team in Eindhoven. Despite having busy careers and their own historical websites – www.battledetective.com and www.battleatbest.com – both men are a joy to work with and have helped me shape this book into a profound and meaningful historical record, that I hope everyone who reads will understand and appreciate.

Ian Gardner – September 2011

Acknowledgments

As usual this section has been one of the hardest parts of the book to compile, as I am anxious not to forget any of my many contributors. If anyone's name has been overlooked I hope you will accept my sincere apologies. Individual thanks are extended, by country, to the following.

United States of America and Canada: Jannie Anderson (née Arnoldussen), Kathleen "Tachie" Anderson, Fred Bahlau (HQ Co), Rick Bahlau, Sam Bailey (442nd TCG), Michael Baldinger, Mark Bando, Manny Barrios (I Co), Ralph Bennett (H Co), Derwood Cann (Co HQ), Merrick O'Connell, Joan Chincarini, Landon Cozad (442 TCG), Joe Doughty (G Co), Bob Dunning (81mm Mortar Ptn), Teddy Dziepak (I Co), Bill Galbraith (Co HQ), John Gibson (Medical Detachment), Kenneth Glassburn (442 TCG), Ben Hiner (HQ Co), Ken Johnson (H Co), Hendrik de Jong, Brenda Kightlinger, Walter Lukasavage (I Co), Pat McCann, Karen McGee, Ross McLachlan (RCAF), George McMillan (I Co), James Martin (G Co), James Melhus (MG Ptn), Eugene and Vada Montgomery, Carolyn Packert, Judson Wright Pittam (442 TCG), Rich Riley, Bobbie Rommel (MG Ptn), Bob Saxvik, Seymour Shapiro (442 TCG), Ray Skully (Co HQ), Elsie and Nathan Spurr, Harold Stedman (I Co), Tom Stedman, John Sushams, Ann Tanzy, Kathy Tozzi, Lou Vecchi (H Co), Bob Webb Jnr, Chad Weisensel.

The Netherlands: Dick Bakker, Henk Beens, Frits Berens, Hans den Brok, Michel Clements, Jo van Dongen (née van der Water), Gerda den Hartog, Johannes van den Hatert, Peter Hendrikx, Piet van den Heuvel, Erwin Janssen, Wim and Jos Klerkx, Steph Leenhouwers, Vic van Lijf, Peter van der Linden, Frans Mientjes, Ronald Ooms, Wan van Overweld, Johannes Peerbolte, Clazien van Rinsum (née Hermse),

Albert Roxs, Frits van Schaik, Jaap van Schaik, Ronald Stassen, Willemien van Steenbergen, Jurgen Swinkels, Noud Stultiens, Dirk van Tintelen, Frenk Derks van de Ven, Peter van de Wal.

United Kingdom: Robert Dudley (my literary agent), Bob Hilton, Monique Jones, Peter Mills, Rosemary and Sarah Pinches, Francis Wyndham.

I would like to extend a special gratitude to the following people, Dave Berry (Pathfinder Historian), David Bevis, Donald van den Bogert, Mario "Hank" DiCarlo (H Co), Mark Durivage (for his invaluable help with the 442nd Troop Carrier Group), Bernard Florissen, Judy Gamble, Gido Hordijk, Jan and Jenny van Hout (neé Soons), George Koskimaki, Geurt van Rinsum, Frank and Chantal Slegers, Bob Smoldt (for Robert Harwick's personal letters), Daan Viergever, Aaron Walser, Bill Wedeking (MG Ptn), Kate Moore, John Tintera, Emily Holmes, Ruth Sheppard, and the creative team at Osprey, and my father, Dennis, Tom Timmermans, Tom Peeters, Geurt van Rinsum, and Jenny and Jan van Hout for proofreading the manuscript. Once again Ed Shames (I Co, 3/506 CO HQ, 506 RHQ, and 2/506) continues to be a huge influence and supporter of my work and it is almost impossible for me to calculate just how much our regular visits to the Netherlands over the last few years have helped towards the success of this project. Last but not least, I would like to thank Roger Day for showing me the way and my long-suffering wife, Karen, for allowing me to stumble along it.

Since I started work on *Deliver Us From Darkness* the following veterans have passed away: Tom Bucher, Derwood Cann, Teddy Dziepak, John Gibson, Ross McLachlan, Spencer Phillips, Harold Stedman, and Dirk van Tintelen. I would like to dedicate this book to the memory of S/Sgt "Hank" DiCarlo who died on September 30, 2010, after a long battle with diabetes and cancer: "How I wish I was a child again, when time was still my friend."

Introduction

Deliver Us From Darkness is the sequel to my first book, *Tonight We Die As Men*, co-written with Roger Day, which told the story of the 3rd Bn 506th Parachute Infantry Regiment (PIR) and its actions during the invasion of Normandy. For those unfamiliar with the actions of 3rd Bn 506th PIR in this period, here follows a brief summary of events leading leading up to the Allied invasion of the Netherlands in September 1944.

During the long, hot summer of 1942, those young volunteers who passed the rigors of selection training for the 506th at Camp Toccoa, Georgia, were blazing a trail that would make America sit up and listen. This "new breed" of soldier, most barely out of their teens, came from a wide range of social backgrounds and brought with them a level of intelligence and motivation that had never been seen before in the US Army. The 506th PIR was the first airborne unit to be directly recruited from the civilian population and the men had a lot to prove but prove themselves they did. Out of the 7,000 who originally applied for Col Robert Sink's new "super unit," only 2,000 made it through to become qualified military parachutists.

The regiment was divided into three battalions. The 1st was commanded at the time by LtCol William Turner; the 2nd by LtCol Robert Strayer; and the 3rd by LtCol Robert L. Wolverton. Wolverton was universally loved by his men because he put them first, even before any officer in the battalion. He was born on October 5, 1914, came from Elkins, West Virginia, and like Sink, he was West-Point trained. Each battalion had four companies, and the 3rd were designated HQ, G "George," H "Howell," and I "Item." In training, Bob Wolverton pushed his men to their limits and in doing so carved out a national reputation based on hard work, fitness, and total professionalism.

After being transported by ship across the Atlantic, the 506th PIR arrived in Liverpool on September 15, 1943. The following day the regiment was sent to join the remainder of the 101st Airborne Division (commanded by MajGen Maxwell D. Taylor) who were already stationed in the Kennet valley between Reading (Berkshire) in the east and Ramsbury (Wiltshire) in the west, a distance of about 30 miles. The 101st Divisional HQ was midway between these two points at Greenham Lodge near Newbury. The 506th Regiment established its command post (CP) at Littlecote House, while the 3rd Bn was installed in huts at Camp Ramsbury, a picturesque old village, 15 miles to the north of Swindon.

During the spring of 1941 this rural idyll along the tranquil banks of the river Kennet was brought to an abrupt halt when work started on the construction of Ramsbury Airfield. At about the same time, a camp was built in a field on the northern edge of the village. On September 16, 1943, this camp became 3rd Bn's new home, and remained so for almost exactly 12 months, until September 15, 1944.

Shortly after 0100hrs on June 6, 1944, the 506th PIR dropped behind enemy lines into France alongside the 501st and 502nd PIR, the 377th Parachute Field Artillery Battalion, and other units of the 101st Airborne Division, launching the first phase of Operation *Overlord*, codenamed *Neptune*. The first thrust started on June 5, when some 5,000 ships and 1,000 transport aircraft began making their way across the Channel towards occupied France. The attack was set along 40 miles of coastline between the Vire Estuary in the west and the river Orne to the east. The initial seaborne landing was to be carried out by 21st Army Group, under command of Gen Bernard Montgomery and consisted of six infantry divisions augmented by three airborne divisions, one British (6th), and two American (82nd and 101st under overall command of VII Corps). The eastern beaches, codenamed "Gold," "Juno," and "Sword," came under the control of the British Second Army, led by Gen Sir Miles Dempsey; and the western beaches, codenamed "Utah" and "Omaha," were controlled by the United States First Army under LtGen Omar Bradley.

The parachute landings for the 101st Airborne Division took place behind Utah Beach and were spread across three drop zones (DZ) designated "A," "C," and "D." Col Sink parachuted with 1st and 2nd Bn onto DZ "C," while Bob Wolverton and 3rd Bn were inserted onto DZ "D" with the mission to capture, defend, and hold two wooden bridges spanning the Canal de Carentan near the village of Brévands. These vital crossing points (one pedestrian, one vehicular) had to be held or destroyed to prevent an enemy counterattack.

Throughout most of D-Day, Sink had no idea where his 2nd and 3rd Bn were, as most of the 506th communications equipment had been lost during the jump. Despite sustaining the regiment's highest casualties of the day, 3rd Bn's drop onto DZ "D" was statistically the most successful. Although Wolverton was killed, a company-sized force, led by Capt Charles Shettle, 3rd Bn Operations Officer, managed to capture the bridges and thus establish the 101st Airborne Division's right flank.

By the morning of June 7, although Shettle and his growing force were still unable to communicate with the regiment, they were fairly confident of a successful conclusion to their mission. Ironically it was the continuing lack of communication that sealed the fate of the bridges, because at lunchtime the United States Air Force (USAF) arrived and within a few terrifying moments both bridges were destroyed. With the mission now effectively over, 3rd Bn was replaced by the 327th Glider Infantry Regiment, and withdrawn to the vicinity of St-Côme-du-Mont.

On June 13, the Germans launched a fearsome counterattack and 3rd Bn (temporarily led by Capt Robert Harwick from H Company) rejoined the 506th to defend the nearby town of Carentan in an action that became known as the battle of "Bloody Gully." From an American perspective, the battle was one of the most important and decisive actions of the entire Normandy campaign. The 101st was only expected to be in theater for seven days, but because of numerous difficulties encountered by VII Corps (which also included the US 4th Infantry Division), they remained in the region until the end of June, when Cherbourg was finally captured. The 101st Airborne suffered a staggering 4,670 casualties during the campaign, with 3rd Bn 506th experiencing the highest overall concentration. These original "Toccoa" men would be hard to replace, and the loss of LtCol Wolverton was deeply felt by all of those who had survived. During the second week of July 1944, the 506th PIR were withdrawn from Normandy and returned to the UK to rebuild and restructure in preparation for the next mission.

Market Garden

At short notice, on September 17, 1944, the 101st Airborne Division parachuted into the Netherlands as part of Operation *Market Garden.* The plan was to secure the main highway that passed through the city of Eindhoven – facilitating the advance of Gen Sir Miles Dempsey's Second (British) Army towards Arnhem (which was some 40 miles away to the northeast). Dempsey's troops had been fighting their way across France since the Allied landings in Normandy. By early September, Second Army had reached the Escault Canal in Belgium and due to the acute lack of intermediate seaports and railway lines, Dempsey was now able only to support a single tactical thrust by XXX Corps. Although the German Army put up a strong resistance in Belgium, Montgomery's intelligence reports suggested that they were incapable of resisting another determined advance. Once the German front line had been punctured, Montgomery doubted that the enemy would have enough strength remaining to prevent a breakthrough.

The objective of the 506th PIR was to capture four crucial bridges over the river Dommel in southern Eindhoven. Third battalion, now led by Maj Oliver Horton, spearheaded the advance on September 18, taking heavy casualties along the way at the villages of Vlokhoven and

Woensel. Upon entering Eindhoven (the first Dutch city to be liberated) thousands of people spilled onto the streets to embrace the paratroopers, overjoyed after four dark years of Nazi occupation. A few hours later, when XXX Corps entered the city, the roads were so crowded that their tanks and vehicles were unable to get through. The celebrations were short-lived as Eindhoven was bombed the following evening by the Luftwaffe (German Air Force), causing hundreds of civilian casualties.

With the capture of Eindhoven, the 101st Airborne thought that its mission was over. However, this was only the beginning of a bloody campaign that would see no quarter given by either side. Thousands of heavily armed enemy troops, trapped behind Allied lines, were reorganized into temporary fighting groups and sent on the offensive. Supported by Tiger tanks and self-propelled artillery the German Army began an audacious series of counterattacks along the road to Arnhem that became known as "Hell's Highway." Over the next two weeks, the 506th PIR were constantly called upon to defend the transport hubs north of Eindhoven at Sint Oedenrode, Veghel, and Uden.

By October the regiment were sent further north to take over from the British 214th Infantry Brigade near Arnhem. Surrounded by water, "the Island" was the name given by the Allies to the Betuwe, the area of land northwest of Nijmegen between the Neder Rijn (Lower Rhine) and the river Waal. This would be the scene of a two-month struggle fought against determined German attacks amid heavy rain, flooding, and constant shellfire. The mission in the Netherlands would be one that the men would never forget. Many felt that their lives had been misused and wasted; Normandy had been bad enough, but this time the men from 3rd Bn had really been through hell … this is their amazing true story.

∽ 1 ∽

"Tell everyone I said hello"

Rebuilding the battalion – August 1944

For those members of the 3rd Bn 506th PIR who returned from Normandy in early July physically unscathed, it seemed like they had moved from one life into another. While in France, the 101st Airborne had forged a formidable reputation amongst the Germans, earning itself the nickname "butchers with big pockets." There can be no doubt that the contribution made by the 506th PIR had only served to enhance the division's reputation for brutal efficiency.

"Home" for 3rd Bn was still the village of Ramsbury, which, despite all that the men had just gone through, remained tranquil and somehow unchanged. The only sign that there was still a war on was the sound of transport aircraft coming and going from the airfield (USAAF Station 469) located up on the hill. Situated in rural Wiltshire, Ramsbury was one of many beautiful hamlets occupied by the 101st Airborne Division before, during, and after Operation *Neptune*. Regimental Headquarters (RHQ) remained at nearby Littlecote, which was one of the finest examples of an early 16th-century Tudor manor house in England.

Three weeks after D-Day, Assistant Regimental Adjutant, Capt Max Petroff, who had remained behind in the UK at Littlecote, told 3rd Bn's American Red Cross Director, Miss Helen Briggs, known as "Briggsey," not to ask any questions of the men who had been wounded as they arrived back to Camp Ramsbury from hospital. She did as she was told, until one of the wealthier ladies in the village invited Petroff to dinner.

Afterwards Briggsey discovered that Max had casually announced the deaths of 3rd Bn commander, LtCol Wolverton, and his executive officer (XO – second in command) Maj George Grant. As she recalls: "It burned me up so much that I went to one of the local pubs, the Crown and Anchor, and paid three pounds and ten shillings for six bottles of spirits. As the guys returned, I took them back to my office and gave them a few drinks before pumping them for information. All the boys could talk about was Col Wolverton and his prayer in the marshaling area and the idea of a postwar reunion at the Muelbach Hotel, in Kansas City." Col Wolverton was much loved by the men and had felt compelled to speak candidly to them before boarding the aircraft for France. Every single man in the battalion had been touched in some way by his incredibly poignant and emotive words.

God almighty! In a few short hours we will be in battle with the enemy. We do not join battle afraid. We do not ask favors or indulgence but ask that, if you will, use us as your instrument for the right and an aid in returning peace to the world. We do not know or seek what our fate will be. We only ask this, that if die we must, that we die as men would die, without complaining, without pleading and safe in the feeling that we have done our best for what we believed was right. Oh Lord! Protect our loved ones and be near us in the fire ahead, and with us now as we each pray to you.

Maj Oliver Horton had taken command of the battalion in Normandy on June 19, approximately two weeks after LtCol Wolverton's death. Horton was a southerner from North Carolina, who had previously worked for Col Sink, as his Intelligence Officer (Regt S-2). Horton did not possess the same tactical ability as LtCol Wolverton, but nevertheless he was a more than capable leader. "Major Horton was not one of my favorite commanders and I am certain that I was not one of his either," reflected 1st Lt Joe Doughty, who had taken over command of G Company after the death of Capt Harold Van Antwerp on D-Day.

Once again, Parliament Piece in Ramsbury was utilized as a home away from home for most of 3rd Bn's junior officers. Affectionately known as "Lady W" by the Americans, widow Violet Wyndham owned the imposing manor house built during the reign of Charles I. Mrs Wyndham was only too pleased to welcome back the Americans, along with her 20-year-old son, Francis, who had joined the British Army in the summer of 1943, only to be invalided out with tuberculosis and pleurisy. To pass the time during his convalescence, Francis, an aspiring author, wrote his first novel, *Out of the War*. Although she was twice his age, Violet had a "soft spot" for 24-year-old 1st Lt Derwood Cann from Louisiana, who had recently been transferred from G Company to battalion HQ as Intelligence Officer (S-2). Cann had not made the jump into Normandy due to the fact he was in hospital with yellow fever.

Before Normandy, 2nd Lt Bill Wedeking (Machine-Gun [MG] Ptn) had been sharing a room at Parliament Piece with Lewis Sutfin (81mm Mortars), and communications officer Glenn Barr. "All meals were cooked and prepared in the basement on M-37 gasoline-fuelled field stoves by our amazing catering staff T/5 Eugene Spangler, Pfc Irvin Schumacher, and Dean Baxter," recalls Bill:

As the officers' dining room was located on the ground floor, all meals were brought up via hot food containers and served in "cafeteria-style" portions by the cooks. Although the menu was supplemented with "C," "K," and "D" rations, it always amazed me just how Spangler and [the] boys, as basic KP [kitchen police], were able to provide many appetizing and healthy meals using such simple ingredients. Mrs Wyndham did not eat with us in the mess but I have no doubt that the cooks surreptitiously provided her with meals in her private quarters. All paratroopers were issued one and a half rations per day because our training regime required superior body and muscle strength. It was also a weekly requirement for all airborne troops to "battle march," at least 15 miles with full equipment.

After Normandy, most of the field grade officers were relocated from Parliament Piece to other locations around the village as Bill Wedeking explains:

> When I took over the machine-gun platoon after Bob Machen was killed, I was sent to live with Mr Ron Rushen, at his cottage opposite the Crown and Anchor public house. Ron's son was serving with the British Army in India, so I provided the old boy with coal, tea, soap, sugar, and other food items. Some evenings we would sit by the fireplace, without a care in the world, just listening to music. During that time, I got to know the owners of the Crown and Anchor, Ray and Jessie Young. I gave Jessie my silk escape map of France, which she made into a beautiful pillow cover. Ray was Irish and a gifted poet who gave me this verse, "Time may steal our years away – yes, and steal our memories too, but a memory of the past remains and half our joys renew."

Joe Doughty was also on the move: "Admiral Edmond Hyde Parker and his wife Helen offered their large sumptuous house, Ramsbury Hill, as a billet to myself and 'Andy' Anderson." The Hyde Parkers were a delightful couple who treated Joe and Andy like kings. At 76 years of age, Edmond was no stranger to war, having captained a warship during the infamous battle of Jutland in 1916.

After the capture of Capt John McKnight – taken prisoner at daybreak on D-Day after being misdropped over the village of St-Côme-du-Mont – Lt Fred "Andy" Anderson was now in command of I Company and recalls: "It was a real headache trying [to] look after seven officers and 160 enlisted guys, which was enough to drive a sane person crazy." At the time "Andy" was deeply unhappy, drinking heavily and naively wished that Maj Horton would either promote him, or simply send him back to being a platoon leader. After all the good men who had been lost in Normandy,

Anderson was bitter that some of his friends back home in Charlotte, North Carolina, were now in reserve occupations, or deferred from frontline service. "I was the only one who had little enough sense to want to share an active part in destroying the Axis and I felt that for us the worst of the war was over and from now on everything would be easier."

There were a number of changes to the battalion table of organization. All-round tough guy, 1st Lt Ed Harrell joined G Co as Executive Officer, before taking command of 2 Ptn. The most serious change affected H Co, where, much to everyone's surprise, 1st Lt James "Skunk" Walker (previously Mess Officer) was given command, after Capt Robert Harwick was transfered to the battalion staff as Executive Officer.

First Lieutenant Ivan "Moose" Mehosky (H Co 1Ptn) had suffered continuously in Normandy from a large cyst at the base of his spine. By late August it had become so infected that he could barely walk. So excruciating was the pain that Dr Stanley Morgan (3rd Bn Surgeon), sent "Moose" to a hospital near York to have the enormous pustule lanced. He was still in hospital when the alert came for Holland, so Rudie Bolte took over Mehosky's platoon, nicknamed "the 40 thieves," with replacement 2nd Lt David Forney as his assistant.

Rudolph Bolte was a family man in his early thirties with piercing green eyes. An experienced lawyer, Rudie turned down a comfortable army posting in Washington DC to become a paratrooper. Lt Bolte was amiable, conscientious, and hard working but sometimes came across as an eager-beaver college sophomore type. Originally from Madison, Wisconsin, Rudie had been an accomplished athlete and musician, and a former "Golden Gloves" boxing champion. When he arrived at the road bridge on D-Day, Bolte had been dazed, confused, and totally disorientated. It later transpired that he had narrowly escaped death after a shell from one of the Allied warships supporting the seaborne landings had exploded near him. Soon after completion of the bridge mission, Bolte was diagnosed with concussion and sent to a field hospital. At the time he was also suffering numbness in his hands and feet, possibly exacerbated by a serious head injury sustained as a youth.

Whatever the reasons for his evacuation, it did not sit well with the men from 1 Ptn, who felt that the lieutenant was beginning to show a lack of moral fiber. Before returning to duty (still suffering from a loss of feeling in his fingers and toes) Bolte was promoted to first lieutenant and given temporary command of 1 Ptn. Rudie desperately needed to regain the respect of the men and therefore declined to go to hospital for any further treatment.

First Lieutenant Alexander Andros took over H Co 3 Ptn, from Peter Madden (now assigned to Greenham Lodge as Gen Taylor's UK Control Officer). "It was my good fortune to have S/Sgt Harry Clawson, as my platoon sergeant," recalled Alex. "Harry always wanted to be involved in the forefront of any action." After Normandy, Clawson wrote a letter to his father, reflecting a deep concern for his wife, Melba, and their three children: "Dear Dad, I really don't know why I'm writing this – I guess I'm just a bit worried about my family. I know Melba wouldn't tell me if things were amiss but I think you would. Is she getting along OK? Enough money and such, what about her family are they giving her any trouble? Does she work too much and are the kiddies all right? I guess this is all uncalled for because I know if anything happened you would take care of it."

As the letter progressed, Clawson's rhetoric comfortably slipped into ruthless retribution as he asked his father to deliver a clear message to his brothers and sisters.

> You can tell Delwin that I've got one for him and each member of his family. The same goes for Gerald, Bernard, Frank and Louise, as a matter of fact I have done the same for you, mom, Angeline and Rusty and as soon as I get upfront again, I'll start counting some for my own family – it's the biggest of the Clawson tribe now you know. This is a morbid subject, but I just wanted you to know that I wasn't letting you down. Dad, war is just what you think it is (tough); so keep your sons out of it for as long as you possibly can. Tell everyone hello from me and let mom and Melba know what I have been doing on their

behalf! Oh yes – my unit won a presidential citation, so I now feel like a Christmas tree with all these medals.* Keep things clicking at home and before long you will have to put up with me again, love Harry.

Sgt Bob Martin (H Co 1 Ptn) returned from the 40th General Hospital after breaking his leg during a training jump before Normandy. Lou Vecchi and Don Zahn were both promoted to sergeant on July 7; and Johnny Hahn, John Purdie, Bob Hoffman, Jay Barr, and George Montilio were all made up to corporal.

During the latter part of July, Pfc Raymond Skully from Cleveland, Ohio, was serving with G Co 2 Ptn when he received an unexpected transfer order. "I had just returned from London on furlough with my buddy T/4 Ed Sokolowski," recalls Ray. "It was no secret that I had played the bugle so I was sent to Company HQ to replace Don Ross, who had been captured in Normandy. Although it was upsetting to leave G Co, I was excited to discover that the other aspect of my assignment was to provide close protection for Major Horton. The major treated me well and personally I think he was equal in professionalism to Col Wolverton."

Sergeant T/4 Bill Galbraith never hated the enemy: "I always thought that he was doing the same thing for his country that I was doing for mine." After replacing Joe Gorenc in the S-3 department – Joe was still missing in action at the time – Bill was late returning from Scotland at the end of his post-Normandy leave as Galbraith recalls: "I'd met this wonderful girl, Anna Nertney, who invited me to stay with her family in Shotts on the outskirts of Edinburgh. Anna and I travelled into town every day where I bumped into a sergeant who was a gunner on a B-17 bomber, who promised me a ride back to England at the end of my furlough. Eventually the time came to go home and I went to the airfield as instructed. After stowing all my gear on the plane, which included a statue of St Patrick (that had been a gift from Anna's family)

---

* Clawson won a Silver Star, alongside S/Sgt Fred Bahlau, for his actions at the road bridge near Brevánds, on June 6, 1944.

I waited all day for the pilot to arrive. Eventually he turned up only to inform me that I couldn't fly because there were no extra parachutes. In my rush to leave the airfield and catch the first available train, I left the statue behind on the bomber and always wondered if the crew kept it and if it brought them good luck throughout the rest of the war?". Consequently, Adjutant and Personnel Officer, 1st Lt Alex Bobuck, reduced Galbraith's rate of pay to that of an ordinary private. However, because the planning and operations role carried a high degree of responsibility, Bill was allowed to retain his stripes in an acting capacity.

Hardened by battle, the men had learned a lot about each other, but the new training program was going to be equally tough as anything that had gone before. It was a question of trying to bring each new man up to the same level and experience of the combat veterans, although not necessarily by the book. "We wanted the replacements to fit in and did our best to treat them accordingly," recalls Sgt Ralph Bennett (H Co 3 Ptn). "Normandy taught us a lot about working together and never to underestimate the ability of the enemy."

Pfc Bob Dunning from the 81mm Mortar Ptn became friends with a replacement named Ramirez but their relationship did not get off to a good start: "One night as I was sleeping, Ramirez returned drunk to the billet. I awoke to find him cursing and swearing, holding the zipper firmly closed on my sleeping bag and a knife against my face. After some fast-talking, he finally let go and burst into tears. Some of the other replacements in the platoon such as Pvt Harold "Flash" Baker and Charlie Smith seemed to take everything in their stride and were far better adjusted than guys like Ramirez."

When 2nd Lt John Weisenberger (Asst S-1 [personnel] Officer) from Columbus, Ohio, first arrived, for some reason he had the MG Ptn practising gun drills in the river Kennet. "He seemed a little crazy and we soon figured that one day he would get himself killed," recalls Cpl Bobbie Rommel.

Pvt Leonard Schmidt remembers his first day on the job: "Just before Normandy, I was sent by truck with a bunch of other new guys to Littlecote House. As we were driving up to the gates, RHQ were in the process of leaving for their designated marshaling areas although we didn't know this at the time. I heard later that the reason why we didn't go to Normandy was because there were not enough transport aircraft available. I stayed at Littlecote for several weeks before being posted to Reading, where I joined the G-2 department at Division. I had always been fairly artistic and for that reason they had me working on sand tables and also as a technical illustrator."

Pvt James Melhus from Eau Claire, Wisconsin, was posted to the battalion as a machine-gunner, aged 23. He recalls "After doing my 17-week basic infantry training at Camp Walters in Texas, I volunteered to be a paratrooper. Upon arrival at Fort Benning there were not enough students available so we were held back for a couple of weeks. Soon after qualifying, I was sent to the UK but was disappointed when one of the friends that I had made in jump school, Eugene Krantz, was posted to the 502."

Most of the men in the machine-gun platoon made Melhus feel at home except for Cpl Audrey Lewallen as Jim recalls: "Lewallen was a wiry, part-Native American Indian, from Casper, Wyoming, who seemingly had a raft of issues. The corporal was an antagonistic type with a big mouth who was always picking on junior soldiers like me." Although James Melhus' case was unusual, the green replacements still had to be drilled and instilled with the same *esprit de corps* and taught the lessons learned from Normandy.

Range work and field problems began in earnest, including combat training against armored vehicles. Several daylight parachute exercises took place, with emphasis being placed on efficient assembly drills as Bill Wedeking recalls:

We returned to the Salisbury training area during the run-up to the invasion of Holland. The place was littered with duds and unexploded ordnance. Before Normandy, there was an accident when an old shell exploded, badly injuring several soldiers from another outfit. When I took over the MG Ptn, I instilled in my guys never to touch suspicious objects. I had aquired a lovely P-38 Walther and plenty of ammunition from a German officer near St-Côme-du-Mont. When we were on maneuvers, especially Salisbury Plain, I used the pistol to shoot rabbits that I skinned and ate back in my billet.

First Sergeant Ed Shames (HQ Co) and S/Sgt George Retan (I Co 3 Ptn) received battlefield commissions and went their separate ways. "I was posted to a staff position with 2nd Bn as assistant intelligence officer (S-2) under Capt Lewis Nixon," recalls Ed. "From the word go I did not get on with Nixon who had a serious drinking problem and I never fully understood how he was able to hold his job down."

On August 10, a parade took place on Hungerford Common, led by Gen Dwight Eisenhower. The review was followed by an awards ceremony, where it was announced that the 101st Airborne Division would now be part of the First Allied Airborne Army, under command of US LtGen Lewis Brereton. The "First Triple A" as it was known, was an amalgamation of British, American, and Polish airborne forces and comprised nearly 30,000 men. The new role did not change the overall American table of organization except for the individual rifle companies. At company level, the order of battle was restructured, with the creation of a fourth squad, dedicated to the 60mm mortar teams.

By September the strength of 3rd Bn 506th PIR, totalled around 650 officers and men. Forty percent of the battalion was made up of new personnel direct from the United States, while others came via the parachute school at nearby Chilton Foliat. Capt Jim Morton, who had broken his right foot on the jump into Normandy, was now in command of HQ Co and replacement 1st Lt Robert Pennell, his new executive officer. Jim recalls: "Pennell was a chubby man who did not fit the mould of a typical airborne soldier. However, he was a gifted armorer with a superb working knowledge of guns and ammunition but had no place on the battlefield." Still in pain, Morton was relying heavily on his newly appointed first sergeant, Fred Bahlau, who threw himself into improving Camp Ramsbury's facilities.

The barracks, orderly room, and ordnance shed were all refurbished and a new supply store and mail shack created from scrap timber. Morton was so pleased with Bahlau that during one of the regular Sunday morning company commanders meetings, he told Col Sink that HQ Co had one of the best first sergeants in the regiment. All praise aside, Bahlau had taken over the role under the worst possible conditions and encountered a certain amount of resentment from some of the non-commissioned officers (NCOs), like Bob Webb. Previously, 21-year-old Webb had been battalion supply sergeant. However, due to a gross misunderstanding, Bob had been demoted to private by Capt Morton, despite his more-than-capable record over the previous year. Two months earlier, during the battle of Bloody Gully, Webb was returning from Carentan when he stumbled across Morton – who was XO for G Company at that time – and several members of the communications platoon sheltering in a ditch. Following a direct order given to him by Bob Harwick (who was acting battalion commander at the time), Webb barked at the men "to get up off their butts and move forward to where they were desperately needed as riflemen." Everyone except Jim Morton sheepishly headed off towards the front line. In the heat of the moment, Bob had forgotten that Morton's broken foot prevented him from moving anywhere quickly. Before the captain had a chance to say anything, Webb turned and walked away, muttering the word "asshole" under his breath. Later that same day Morton was given command of HQ Company and almost immediately started to make life difficult for Webb. On August 23, Jim Morton demoted Webb and posted him to the communications platoon, under 1st Lt Glenn Barr.

The more seriously wounded from Normandy were still recovering in medical facilities up and down the country. One of the soldiers returning from a hospital in South Wales had some interesting news for Helen Briggs. "He told me that the place was full of my guys, so I decided to visit Hereford for a couple of days and see for myself." The 3rd Bn men were certainly surprised to see Briggsey, especially Ben Hiner, who had been accidentally shot on June 10 near the town of St-Côme-du-Mont. "Ben showed me three hideous scars where the doctors had patched up his stomach," continued Helen. "The only problem now was when he stood up, because his gut sank inwards on one side and outwards on the other. I jokingly suggested that he could do with one of my two-way stretch girdles. Although we both laughed, Ben figured that somehow it might actually do him some good! Upon my return to Ramsbury, I cut the garters from one of my slightly worn girdles and sent it to him, with a note that he would have to figure the rest out by himself." At the time Hiner was not doing so well and weighed less than 100lbs: "I figured perhaps with the aid of the girdle that I could pass my five-mile fitness test and return to duty. Despite the fact that I had already failed my first five-mile run, I requested a retest and thanks to the girdle, made the required time and passed 'fit for duty.' The powers that be wanted to send me to the 502, which of course I flatly refused – it would be the third battalion or nothing. I still couldn't move around that well and bending down was a problem but eventually I managed to convince the medics to send me back to Ramsbury."

A couple of weeks later during a visit to battalion HQ at Camp Ramsbury, Helen Briggs was surprised to see Hiner in the office. "Ben walked over with a big smile on his face, gently patting his tummy and gave me a big hug." Hiner had another reason to be pleased. Jim Morton had just promoted him to battalion supply sergeant!

Sgt Manny Barrios (I Co) had been recuperating at the 83rd General Hospital, where he had been admitted on June 11, after being evacuated from Normandy.

Several large pieces of shrapnel were embedded between the two tendons at the front of my ankle. By the time I reached hospital, the wound had become so infected that the doctors wanted to amputate the injured leg. After threatening to "kill them all" if the procedure was carried out, my consultant decided to cut away all the dead tissue but performed the minor operation while I was fully conscious!

Screaming in agony, it was all I could do just to cling onto the edge of the operating table.

After being confined to a wheelchair for several weeks, in a desperate attempt to relieve the boredom, I was taught to paint by a British nursing volunteer. I definitely had a flair for this kind of thing and pretty soon was asked to create a mural depicting a naked girl above the bar in the NCOs' club. One of the chaplains took offense and threatened to have the place shut down if I didn't go back and paint a layer of clothing over my masterpiece. Reluctantly I thinned out some red paint and carefully brushed a semi-translucent veil across her buxom breasts and perfectly proportioned behind. Everyone seemed happy with the result, as I was commissioned to work on a more esoteric project, the ceiling and walls of the hospital cinema.

When the division was alerted for the invasion of Holland, they recalled as many people as they could from hospital. By this time, I considered myself well enough to return but my doctor insisted it could only be for "light duties." As I leapt from the tailgate of a moving truck outside Camp Ramsbury, I fell forward on the slope of the road and reopened the wound on my foot. Dr Morgan carefully read my surgeon's note and insisted on seeing the injury. Despite my protests, he took one look at the blood seeping from my ankle and sent me straight back to hospital. I was beside myself with guilt but the damage had been done and there was absolutely nothing I could say or do to change it.

Pfc Ken Johnson (H Co 2 Ptn), had been recovering at a hospital in Southampton for nearly three months. Ken's terrifying experience in Normandy had shaken him to the very core:

After breaking my leg on the jump, I found shelter with two other guys in a crater on the drop zone. I never learned the names of my comrades, except that one was from the 82nd Airborne, some of whom had been misdropped into our area of operations. The other guy, who was unarmed, had a broken arm as well as an impacted back.

Although the soldier was clearly in a great deal of pain, he volunteered to keep watch on the other side of the crater. At first light, I crawled over to see if he wanted a cigarette, only to discover that he was dead, killed by a single bullet in the face. We could do nothing but remain vigilant, and fire at anything that moved. I blamed myself for that poor guy's death and being trapped for nearly 72 hours with his body had a deep and profound effect on me. As the tide of battle shifted, eventually on the third day, the probing attacks stopped and the medics were able to locate and pick us up.

Back in the UK, Johnson considered himself lucky compared with the baby-faced soldier in the hospital bed next to him:

The kid had been badly wounded in the groin and had to have an "A" frame contraption covering his shredded genitals. Before being discharged, I convinced my doctor to change the paperwork to read "crushed" rather than "serious leg fracture." When I got back to battalion my squad leader, Sgt Bill Cumber, turned a blind eye and never made an issue out of it. In my absence Pfc Don Hegenes had taken over the machine gun for first squad. It was a relief to be assigned as a regular rifleman, because I wasn't looking forward to carrying a 30lb machine gun again.

Pvt Joe Marshall (MG Ptn) wrote a short letter from hospital to Sgt Garland "Tex" Collier. Twenty-five-year-old Tex had taken over from George "Doc" Dwyer after the latter had been posted to the jump school at Chilton Foliat.

Hello Collier – Just thinking of you all and wondering how you got by in France? Do you remember where you last saw me? Well I was there for about 40 hours before an aid man could get to me. I will be in this bed for some time and it will be five or six months before I am able to walk again. I know it will be tough for me to stay in hospital for that length of time and I don't know yet if I will be sent back to the 506. I have about £59.00 of loans outstanding and I would really appreciate it if you will get back as much of it as you can and send it to me. Please tell Cpl Riley to return my watch etc. Here is a list of the boys that owe me money I thank you very much for your trouble. I know it is asking a lot for you to do this but Collier I feel you would care to do it for me a friend… Joe.

PS: Give them my hospital address and get the dough! Send it all in a money order, thank you.

Of the dozen or so people who were on Marshall's list, Les Riley and Bob Boem were dead, Tom Bucher was lying paralysed in hospital and Clarence Kelley was a prisoner of war.

Cpl Mario "Hank" DiCarlo (H Co 1Ptn) felt that he still had not proved himself in battle to his friends. "Despite the fact that I had seen what war could do, I just couldn't wait to get back into combat," recalls DiCarlo, who had been shot in the upper right chest on June 6, while scouting along the southern bank of the Canal de Carentan close to the village of Brévands after crossing the road bridge on D-Day. Dr Morgan had recommended that DiCarlo be kept off jump status until further notice. However, Hank surreptiously destroyed the "note" before returning to the company.

Although she did not realize it at the time, Helen Briggs' destiny, along with that of 3rd Bn, was about to drastically change owing to the rapid expansion of Allied ground forces in France.

The ARC needed experienced club directors and I was asked to go to Paris with the promise that I would be returned to 3/506, whenever they settled in Europe. At my farewell party, I was trying hard not to cry, until my GI brother Clark walked in. The guys couldn't understand my reaction because they knew I was still "secretly" dating Bob Harwick. My brother, who I hadn't seen for eight years, had been on his way to Tidworth with a colleague, to pick up supplies and changed his orders to read "as directed." Afterwards Bob Harwick "directed" my brother to take me to London, which conveniently solved all my logistical and travel problems.

During this time the American paratroops were issued a "new-style" olive green regular M43 uniform and high-buckled boots, intended to replace the tan jumpsuits and brown lace-up high-leg leather boots. Bill Galbraith was worried that the buckles on the new footwear might get caught in his rigging lines when parachuting: "Consequently those of us that had any sense continued jumping with the boots that we had worn in Normandy. However, by far the greatest improvement was made to our parachutes that were now fitted with a quick-release attachment."

The T5 parachute packs were modified in England but only, it would seem, for the 101st Airborne Division. The riggers made up several versions, adding the British Quick Release Fastening (QRF), together with extra webbing straps manufactured for the standard British X-Type parachute. The alterations solved most of the previous problems, making the T5 a more comfortable fit and much easier to unfasten after landing.

In mid-August, the Regiment was ordered to prepare for a jump at Rambouillet, 20 miles southwest of Paris. Luckily the operation (codenamed *Transfigure*) was cancelled, as it was later discovered that a panzer division had been waiting in the forest adjoining the intended drop zone. Joe Doughty remembers, "After returning from the marshaling area, Admiral Hyde Parker inquired, 'Was it a rough show, boys?' Andy Anderson and I were quite embarrassed and had to reply as if we had done something worthwhile but couldn't say anything because it was all very 'hush hush.'"

In early September, the 506th was alerted for two further operations in Belgium, the first called *Linnet* at Tournai and another in the vicinity of Liège. However, George Patton's Third Army captured both objectives before the airborne missions could even get off the ground. After Liège, Ed Shames was astounded to discover that Lewis Nixon had abandoned him to organize the S-2 missions and went to see 2nd Bn's commanding officer (CO), LtCol Robert Strayer.

Strayer quite literally threw me out of his office but I was not going to let this go. A couple of days later, I plucked up courage and went to see Colonel Sink at Littlecote. Firstly, I had to convince Sink's personnel officer, Major Salve Matheson who told me "that I should have known better and used the official channels to get a proper hearing." However, he relented and showed me into Sink's office. The colonel sat and listened to my plea. "Sir, I just cannot work with Captain Nixon, he is in my opinion totally unprofessional and I am getting very little support from Colonel Strayer. I'd rather turn in my commission and go back to third battalion than continue to work under these circumstances." Sink was horrified and almost blew his stack before sending me outside to wait in Matheson's office.

A few moments later the boss called me back in. "Shames, you are truly a pain in the behind but I recognize that there may be certain differences of opinion between yourself and Captain Nixon." Luckily Sink still had a reasonable amount of affection for me, which no doubt influenced his subsequent decision. "Shames, before you say anything, there is no way that I'm going to transfer you back to third battalion. In a few weeks, I am planning to redesignate 3 Ptn, E Company as Regimental Patrols Platoon and would like you to head them up. They are a tough bunch but I think you can handle "the mutineers"★ so what do you say?" Of course I was delighted with the offer and in the meantime, Sink assigned me to assist Regimental Operations Officer, Major Clarence Hester, in the S-3.

Before too long Shames would be back in action and working alongside 3rd Bn, but in the Netherlands, not Belgium.

★ So-called because of a controversial incident before Normandy involving a group of senior NCOs after refusing to serve in combat under Captain Herbert Sobel – who at the time was in command of E Company.

2

"Circle of fire"

The German invasion and occupation of the Netherlands

Before World War II, the Dutch government naively supported a neutrality and disarmament policy. Despite regular warnings given by the Dutch military attaché in Berlin, Maj Gijsbertus Sas, the government chose to ignore all threats of German attack. It was not until August 1939, when Germany invaded Poland, that the Netherlands began to mobilize and strengthen its land forces but by then it was too late.

Originally created in 1745 to counter French aggression, the country's main area of defense was known as the "Vooruitgeschoven Stellingen," or the "Grebbe Line," named after the hill feature. Covering a distance of 80 miles, the Grebbe crossed the heart of the Netherlands from the IJsselmeer in the north to Hertogenbosch in the south. Before reaching the province of North Brabant, the Grebbe joined the "Peel Line" and continued south to Roermond on the Belgian border.

In 1939 two smaller defensive lines were dug closer to the frontier with Germany. At one point the Maas–Waal Line, as it became known, extended along the southern bank of the river Waal, close to villages and towns such as Appeltern, Wamel, Beneden-Leeuwen, and Boven-Leeuwen. The purpose of the system was to delay any possible enemy advance – by defending vital road junctions, railway lines, and ferry crossings – long enough to allow Dutch forces to withdraw back to the Grebbe Line.

Dirk van Tintelen, a 21-year-old army reservist, was living and working on his father's dairy farm in Dodewaard on the river Waal when he received his joining instructions for mobilization at a camp at Leersum:

I was a member of a five-man heavy-machine-gun team sent to defend the *dijken* [dikes] along the Maas–Waal Line. Most of us who were in the reserves were driven by a sense of duty and a hatred for the Germans. Due to the lack of motorized and horse-drawn transport we had to put on special harnesses and physically pull our guns like pack mules. There were only a handful of concrete bunkers along this stretch of the line, as the bulk of the defenses were constructed from wood. We dug deep gun pits into the wall of the dijk and settled in to await the German attack.

Our billet was at a nearby farm and selfishly the farmer made it quite clear to us that his apple orchard was out of bounds. One night we thought to hell with it and decided to raid the orchard. The following morning the farmer demanded to see our boss, Lieutenant Reidingf [sic], who, anxious to keep good relations, promised to post a guard. Not to be outdone, I made a couple of small chicken coups and hid them inside an old threshing machine. Before long, I was collecting around twenty eggs a day and cooking them every morning for the lieutenant and our two gun teams.

About a week later the old farmer began to notice that his chickens were not laying their usual quota. Much to our amusement he couldn't figure out what was happening. It was hard for Reidingf to keep a straight face, as the old man blamed the shortfall on the amount of noise he thought we'd been making. Reidingf told him in no uncertain terms to stop being so petty, as we could be at war the next day and fighting for our lives.

As a joke we made a large wooden sign declaring in big letters "*Het Scheutige Boertje* [The Generous Peasant]" and fixed it firmly to a post along the road from his house. The old farmer didn't find this at all amusing and complained to the local police. After talking with us for a while, the officers realized what was going on and instructed that the sign be left exactly where it was. I guess you could say this wasn't a great start to protecting my homeland from the Germans.

In the early 1930s, work had begun to restructure and re-strengthen the entire Grebbe system, but its design was flawed and outdated even before the rebuilding commenced. The German Army was well aware of this fact and noted that the northern bank of the Neder Rijn near Rhenen was weak and vulnerable to attack.

On February 6, 1940, Gen Henri Winkelman took over as supreme commander of Dutch forces after his predecessor General Reijnders was discharged due to personal issues with the government. Winkelman realized how desperate the military situation was, but he did not have enough time to do what he thought was necessary.

Fortuitously some antiaircraft units (AAA) had been recently equipped with the most modern 40mm Bofors guns. This was due to the generosity and foresight of a wealthy businessman, who donated around 45 artillery pieces to the army. Most of these weapons would be used to good effect around the country against the Luftwaffe (some were later transported to England where they played a vital role in Britain's air defenses). Despite this the Dutch Army was lacking in soldiers and incredibly had only a handful of tanks at its disposal.

In the event of an invasion, Winkelman's plan was to stage a tactical withdrawal, westwards from the Grebbe and Peel lines to form a defensive perimeter along the coast, which he called "Vesting-Holland" (Fortress Holland). This perimeter would encompass the Dutch capital, Amsterdam, to the north and The Hague and Rotterdam in the south. In theory this delaying tactic would give French and British forces time to reach the beleaguered Dutch Army and repel any German assault.

At 0355hrs on Friday May 10, 1940, the attack on the Netherlands began when the Germans attempted to break through the main defensive line at several points. Primarily the German plan was to drop airborne troops and capture two main airfields around The Hague, allowing the 22. Luftlande-Infanterie Division (22nd Air Landing Division) to be flown in. The division consisted of nearly 9,000 men whose orders were to attack The Hague, and capture the Dutch royal family. However, Princess Juliana, her husband Prince Bernhard and their children managed to escape by sea to the UK, closely followed by Queen Wilhelmina, her government ministers, and senior military staff.

As the first enemy troops stepped across the Dutch border, the Luftwaffe attacked airfields to the west. Thousands of paratroopers dropped around The Hague, near key airfields at Valkenburg and Ypenburg, and bridges along the main road leading to Rotterdam. The Germans completely underestimated the Dutch AAA defenses and lost nearly 450 transport aircraft on the first day. As a result a large proportion of German ground forces were unable to link up with the airborne troops, who had been devastated by the losses incurred by the Luftwaffe. The Dutchmen on the front lines did a wonderful job, and in many instances took the enemy by surprise, proving that they were no pushover.

Anxious to get into the action, Dirk van Tintelen's machine-gun crew had been moved to a section of the Grebbe Line at Maarsbergen, 20 miles east of Utrecht. "This time it was for real as we watched helplessly as hundreds of German aircraft flew overhead. We sat and waited until the order was given to withdraw towards Rotterdam, where we were to support the marines defending the Maas bridges at Moerdijk. It was imperative for the enemy paratroopers to capture not just Moerdijk but also the bridges at Dordrecht and Rotterdam, to allow their ground forces clear access to The Hague." At 1030hrs on May 14, a German official visited the headquarters of the Dutch Army in Rotterdam, with an ultimatum that read:

To the Town Master, Alderman and the Authorities of the city of Rotterdam. If you do not cease all military operations immediately the German Army will be forced to take effective action against the city and Rotterdam will be destroyed. I implore you to responsibly consider this ultimatum because if you do not then the consequences will be disastrous. I request that you send a Minister immediately who has the necessary power to act. You have two hours to come to a decision. If no word reaches us within that time then you leave me with no choice other than to order the destruction of the city.

That same morning Dirk van Tintelen was ordered to "the White House" in Rotterdam, a high-rise office building with commanding views across the river Maas.

Using an elevator to carry the heavy equipment up to the roof our commander set up our machine gun behind a solid brick wall. At first we were apprehensive about opening fire but that soon changed after we shot down our first aircraft. It wasn't long before the German artillery marked our position and began to return fire, killing one of our crew. The same explosion also damaged the gun but we managed to keep firing until running out of ammunition. With the building now under heavy bombardment, and the lift rendered unserviceable, we were forced to abandon our post and seek shelter in the basement of a nearby warehouse. Not long afterwards, we heard the sound of aircraft and began praying as the bombs started to drop. Moments later the ceiling collapsed as the building received a direct hit and everything went black. Trapped under the rubble our situation seemed bleak but nobody said a word, I guess we figured that this was the end. When the dust settled one of the guys noticed a small bead of light. Realising that this might be our only chance of survival, we dug furiously with our bare hands and managed to escape. Outside, the scene that greeted us was truly horrifying. The city was in flames, dead bodies were lying in the streets and we were speechless at what the Germans had done to innocent civilians.

Another infantry attack came from the north across the low ground from Friesland, and stalled when it reached the heavy fortifications on the IJsselmeer. Again the 40mm AAA guns played a vital role in defending the area at Afsluitdijk. Except for the paratroopers, most of the enemy soldiers from Army Group B never reached "Fortress Holland" or even came close.

The evacuation of "the Island"

By far the largest and most aggressive assault came in the northeast, six miles west of Wageningen, along the Neder Rijn, against the recently rebuilt Grebbe Line. Commanded by Gen Jan Godfried, the Grebbe was defended by 2nd and 4th Army Corps, who put up a fearsome resistance around the Grebbeberg. At nearly 50 meters in elevation, the Grebbeberg is the highest and most densely wooded point in the Veluwe (the area north of the Neder Rijn). The imposing hill was dissected by the main trunk road between Arnhem and Utrecht, and was also close to a vital railway bridge crossing the river at Rhenen.

For several days Godfried's men held out against attacks by hundreds of tanks supported by fanatical SS troops who showed no mercy. Nearly 400 Dutch soldiers were killed in action around the Grebbeberg and nearby Wageningen. After the indiscriminate bombing of Rotterdam, Hitler threatened to do the same to other cities if Dutch forces did not surrender immediately.

Situated northwest of Nijmegen, Betuwe, known by the Americans as "the Island," is bounded by the Neder Rijn and the river Waal. The area measures a maximum of 30 miles wide by eight miles deep and is split in the west by the Amsterdam Rijn Canal. The canal was built at the end of the 19th century and today still connects the port of Amsterdam to the main shipping arteries of the Rijn. Before the German attack on the Grebbe, most of the civilian population on the Island was placed on evacuation alert, while in the Veluwe, larger towns like Wageningen moved 12,400 people in less than two and a half hours.

It was originally planned to transport the people from Opheusden (in the Betuwe) along the Neder Rijn to Krimpen a/d IJssel (Krimpen on the IJssel), but due to the ferocious attacks on Rotterdam, the evacuation only reached the town of Groot Ammers. However, there was a separate plan in place for Dodewaard and the suburb of Hien, where a small fleet of coal barges had been moored in readiness on the river Waal. "The idea was to move the population further south to the islands of Beveland and Walcheren," recalls Dodewaard resident Frits van Schaik. "Everyone was covered in coal dust by the time we reached Tiel, where we spent the night on the barges because the Dutch Army had blocked the river with a pontoon bridge. The next morning the armada was allowed to continue west to Papendrecht (14 miles southeast of Rotterdam) where we anchored for the night. The area had only just been bombed and we were now surrounded by a ring of burning buildings. As the evening progressed the circle of fire grew larger forcing us to move back upriver to Sliedrecht where we were billeted with local families."

In 1940, Clazien Hermse was eight-years-old and lived with her family on a large farm on Groenestraat in Hien. She recalls:

The local church verger, Wim van Schaik, was a member of the *Luchtbeschermingdienst* (LB-Civil Air Defense)and told us that we were to report, along with my younger brother Marinus, to the dockyards at Dodewaard. Rather stupidly we didn't take any food because our neighbors said that they had enough for both families. But after we set sail they selfishly kept all the supplies for themselves. My dad had been mobilized and was stationed at Culemburg, from where by chance he witnessed the armada sailing along the Waal. Of course he had no idea why this was happening or that we were on board. Finally we arrived at Sliedrecht and were sent to a family who owned a large house from where they ran a printing business. The Van de Waards were very welcoming and allowed us to share their bathroom and dinner table and we remained with them until the capitulation.

On May 17, after four futile days of heavy fighting, the Dutch military machine capitulated. Hitler was bewildered by the fact that the Dutch

Army, which was for the most part composed of farmers like Dirk van Tintelen, was capable of inflicting such severe losses among his own highly trained storm troopers.

After the surrender most of the "refugees" from Dodewaard and Hien returned to their homes, as Frits van Schaik, who was 22-years-old at the time, recalls: "Many returned in the same filthy coal boats, but some luckier families like ours went home by lorry. Our house had been ransacked and everything we possessed was gone. The first German troops we encountered tried to tell us that they had taken the Netherlands to prevent the English from invading! We laughed but I think they actually believed it was true." The Dutch Army was decommissioned and the regular soldiers sent to prisoner-of-war camps, while the reservists either went back to work on their farms, or were eventually sent to Germany as forced labor. After forcing Dutch soldiers to sign a combatant register, the Germans pledged to release all prisoners of war as a sign of goodwill. However, the gesture came with one alarming caveat, that if any man wanted to work he had to go to Germany to do so. Unemployment benefit was denied to those who refused, and any worker who had the audacity to return to the Netherlands was automatically denied benefits or a ration card. The German war machine needed food, so Dirk van Tintelen returned to his father's farm in Dodewaard, hopeful that some day in the future his military training would once again be needed.

The German occupation

In the weeks that followed the surrender, the main Dutch political parties tried hard to preserve the ideals and identity of the country without clashing with the Germans. Publicly, Reichskommissar Dr Arthur Seyss-Inquart (appointed on May 20, 1940) encouraged a tolerant attitude on both sides, but he knew it could never last. High-grade civil servants felt justified by continuing to work on under German rule in accordance with a pre-invasion cabinet directive.

The order instructed that in the event of enemy occupation, "it would be in the public interest to carry on the administrative process in the best possible way." The judicial system also continued in the same manner, except for those crimes committed against the occupying forces, which were ruthlessly dealt with by the military regime.

The German Army requisitioned the shipyard at Dodewaard, where Frits van Schaik worked to convert river vessels into troop transporters:

> The bows were removed and fitted with ramps, before the wooden floors were ripped out and replaced with concrete to enable access for tanks and other military vehicles. It was no secret that the barges were intended for use in the proposed invasion of England. All copper, brass, tin, or nickel objects had to be handed over to the authorities. To the average person iron and copper were scarce, but we used large quantities in building the invasion barges and were able to utilize some of these raw materials to repair tools and engines for local farmers, who paid us with produce such as meat and butter.

Civil engineer Anton A. Mussert founded the Dutch Nationaal Socialistische Beweging (NSB or National Socialist Movement) in 1931. The Dutch disliked Mussert even more than they did Adolf Hitler, and many were convinced that members of the NSB had fought against the Dutch national forces in 1940. In reality, anybody who posed a threat to security during this period was either arrested or went into hiding. After the capitulation, Mussert welcomed the occupying German forces as liberators and protectors of the Dutch people. Refusing to simply grant the unpopular Mussert leadership of the Netherlands and Flanders, Hitler instead promised official authority if Mussert could obtain the loyalty of the general population.

During the first few months of the occupation, the NSB recruited 20,000 new members, who for the most part were opportunists looking for better jobs or a higher social status. During his speeches, Mussert worked hard to put a positive spin on the "happier times" he thought lay ahead, but the Dutch remained sceptical and it was not long before a new political organization emerged called the Nederlandse Unie (Dutch Union).

The Dutch Union objected strongly to Nazism and believed that it could create a different brand of right-wing government. The Union's aim was to present an alternative to the NSB by representing the people in a peaceful and more practical way. Hoping that this would be instrumental in spreading pseudo-fascist ideas, Seyss-Inquart allowed the Union to flourish. Most did not take the anti-democratic ideology of the new party seriously but hoped that it would somehow protect the country's national integrity. The Germans banned the Dutch Union in 1941, after realizing that its once-peaceful doctrines were giving way to anti-Nazi resistance.

Food and clothing rationing was soon introduced and the population given a weekly allowance of coupons, which proved woefully inadequate. Many households pooled their vouchers to purchase high-value items such as shoes, and as a direct result the traditional wooden clog came back into popular use. Some families, out of pride and respect, did not wear clogs to church but would often share the only decent pair of shoes they possessed for "Sunday best" by attending different religious services throughout the day.

As the dynamic of authority began to shift, so did the freedom of the people. The Socialist Trade Union (one of the largest unions in the Netherlands) collapsed politically after Nazi infiltration. Many non-commercial organizations came under scrutiny and were banned, like Freemasonry, and youth groups such as the Boy Scouts. Proclamations began to appear in every village and town, on large notice boards printed in German and Dutch, publicizing new laws that often ended with the chilling phrase "failing to conform will be punishable by death."

Before the occupation all bicycles approaching from the right-hand side of a road intersection or crossing had the right of way. The Germans abolished this rule in 1940, so that their tanks and vehicles would not have to constantly stop and give way (bizarrely the rule stood until 2005). No cars were allowed on the roads after 2200hrs. Tyres had to be applied for and petrol was only really available for professional people like doctors or high-ranking civil servants. Public transport soon became scarce and coupons for bicycle tires were issued to those living more than three miles from their place of employment. Curfews were imposed between the hours of midnight and 0400hrs. Although alcohol was free from rationing, cafés and restaurants were forbidden to serve drinks after 1900hrs. The authorities even clamped down on what the population was able to spend and withdrew all coinage marked with images of the royal family. New currency was introduced and as a silent protest many people made necklaces and rings from the old coins bearing the head of the Queen.

A number of controversial bills were passed and one in particular provoked much attention from the younger population. As the war progressed and more Germans were conscripted into the armed forces, many civilians from occupied Europe were forced to work in German factories as "slave labor," and in a totally separate edict to the one issued previously in 1940 to the Dutch Army, the Netherlands was no exception. Although the figure was much lower for women, over 600,000 men were sent to Germany. Every person between 18 and 25 and not in essential employment, was ordered to spend at least one year in the Labor Service (STO). This generally meant agricultural or factory work in Germany for the males and domestic work for the females. However, later in the war many older men were transported to the coast to help build German coastal defenses in areas such as Zeeland.

Franciscus "Frits" Berens was 20-years-old when he was ordered to Germany in the summer of 1942:

I had been working in the sheet metal department of the Lips Ship Company near the city of Tilburg. After ignoring the requests from the Labor Office at Waalwijk, the Grüne Polizei [officially known as Ordungspolizei or "Order Police" – the law enforcement agency of the Third Reich] came to the factory and arrested me along with several other men; we tried to escape but were caught hiding in the changing rooms of a nearby public swimming pool. The Grüne Polizei sent us to Waalwijk, where we were put on a specially chartered train with hundreds of workers bound for Germany. My girlfriend managed to pass me a hastily packed suitcase through the blacked-out windows, containing warm clothes and a loaf of bread, just before the train pulled out.

Later that morning we arrived at Cologne, which happened to be in the middle of an air raid and took cover in a shelter deep beneath the station. Bizarrely, everybody in the shelter was being continuously buffeted by air pressure as the bombs detonated far above. After the raid, I was among those ordered out into the streets to collect corpses. We were provided with bags and soon mine became full of human flesh and severed limbs. As nobody seemed to be checking identity cards, I dumped the bag and tried to escape but all the bridges out of the city had been destroyed. A day or so later, suspicious of my age and dishevelled appearance, the Grüne Polizei picked me up. They didn't like the fact that I had tried to run away and kicked me down the stairwell of a police station before locking me in a filthy cell with ten other men. During the period of incarceration, we were fed on "water soup" and forced to use a 20-liter sauerkraut tin as a latrine.

Two days later, I was sent to the Dynamit A. G. factory in Troisdorf and forced to work eight-hour shifts on a lathe. I slept with around 50 other workers on bunks inside a large potato warehouse, about five minutes away from the main factory. Strangely, outside of working hours we were free to do what we liked, but of course we had no money so where could we go? Homesick and fed up, after about a month, I managed to board a train bound for Kaldenkirchen, from where I intended to sneak back into Holland.

One night in early July, as I was climbing a border fence, a stern voice screamed, "Stop – Halt." As I was trying to bribe the guard with a pouch of tobacco, another came along and took me to a small office, where I sat with four men who had been caught earlier. The following morning we slipped away, when our guard fell asleep, and headed for the border near Venlo. However, we were recaptured and taken back to the same border office and beaten with clubs by German soldiers, who forced us aboard a waiting truck.

Frits was eventually convicted and sentenced to four months in prison for "dereliction of duty" and "attempting to cross the border without authorization." After a brief spell on remand in Dortmund and Krefeld, Berens was sent to a prison at Duisberg where he served his time.

The first few days were spent in solitary confinement being beaten and at one point the sadistic guards forced me to lick food from the floor of my cell. Although the prison was badly damaged several times by the RAF, for me the single worst moment came when two Dutch sailors were brought in after they had escaped from a prison in Holland. The following day all the inmates were paraded in front of a gallows and forced to watch as the sailors were executed. Afterwards, as a warning every tenth inmate was selected and sent to a concentration camp – thankfully I was number seven. I still get deeply upset at the thought of what happened to those two boys, and the inhumane way we were treated.

In 2005, Frits Berens received a token payment from the German Forced Labor Compensation Programme (a human rights organization based in Switzerland) for the physical and mental abuse he endured under the Nazis.

Knowing the right people sometimes meant it was possible to sidestep the forced labor program, which in Frits van Schaik's case was more luck than judgment:

Several of us who worked at the shipyard in Dodewaard were informed by the local labor office that we were going to be sent to Germany for war work. Resigned to the fact, I visited the Town Hall to collect my transportation papers. A friend of mine, Dirk Willemsen, happened to work there and told me to return the following morning. The next day, Dirk handed me a sealed letter and asked that I take it to the director of the labor office. I went to Tiel and after a long wait managed to give the director the envelope. I never did find out what was in Dirk's note but received a letter a couple of days later stating that I was now exempt.

The first organized strikes – orchestrated by communists – occurred on February 17, 1941, when the authorities in Amsterdam tried to requisition some 3,000 sheet-metal workers for work in Germany. The victory was short-lived as the SS were called in and martial law was declared. The situation worsened when the dockworkers joined the strike, as the authorities deported 400 Jewish residents. After control had been restored, the Germans began to crack down on all political parties, meetings, and demonstrations, by replacing many mayors, town councillors, police officers, and even teachers with German-friendly members of the NSB.

Eindhoven

On February 21, 1942, Dr Hub Pulles, a veterinarian, became the NSB mayor of Eindhoven, a large industrial city in the province of North Brabant. Pulles was sworn in at the Van Abbe Museum of Art, an imposing building built in the late 1930s by Henricus "Henry" van Abbe, who had made his fortune from tobacco. High above the museum's main entrance, the Germans had constructed an observation platform to guard against air attack.

By the early 1940s, Greater Eindhoven was made up of a series of *wijken* or suburbs. The northern wijken of Woensel and Vlokhoven merged into Centrum (city centre), with the suburb of Strijp to the west, while Tongelre, Stratum, and Gestel made up the southern part of the city. At the beginning of the 19th century, despite the fact that there were over 40 cigar factories operating in Eindhoven, the area also began to develop as an important electrical manufacturing centre and affectionately became known as "Philipstown."

Founded in 1891 by Gerard Philips, the Philips Corporation originally produced light bulbs. As the company's industrial powerbase began to gather strength, Eindhoven's religious dynamic slowly shifted from Catholic to Protestant in tune with the Philips family's beliefs. Far ahead of its time, the company had its own in-house healthcare and a superb final-salary pension scheme. Philips also operated a regular bus service and provided a chain of general co-operative stores under the banner of Etos (which still exists today), offering discount rates and loyalty cards for all Philips employees. Every day except Sunday, fresh bread, produced at the company bakery in Philips Dorp, was delivered to the Etos outlets. The *dorp* or town was one of several beautifully appointed housing estates around Eindhoven which were provided by the corporation for its workforce. The dorp was perhaps the most well-known due to its imposing brick-pillared entrance.

By the end of the 1930s, Philips were manufacturing enormous quantities of wireless sets, valves, and electric razors.★ Just before the invasion of the Netherlands, the directors fled to the USA and there they set up a new operation – the North American Philips Company. The only member of the family to remain in the country was Frederik "Frits" Philips, whose loyalty and respect towards the people of Eindhoven would later elevate him to saintlike status. After he died in December 2005 a life-size bronze statue was erected on Markt (Market Square) in central Eindhoven.

The writing was already on the wall when in January 1939, together with a number of Jewish welfare groups, Frits set up the Dommelhuis

---

★ To become more profitable, the innovative scientists at the company developed their own version of Bakelite, called Philite. All the tooling and machinery required to service and manufacture the vast range of products was designed and fabricated on site in Eindhoven. Another item developed by the corporation was a small hand-operated dynamo torch called the "Knijpkat," which became highly popular with the Germans.

project. Mr Philips kindly provided the flats (originally built by his company for single employees) as temporary accommodation for around 200 Jewish asylum-seekers, who had previously escaped persecution in Germany. Soon after the occupation, *persoonsbewijzen* (identity cards) were introduced, the Jewish population began to suffer and were banned from streetcars, cinemas, and public parks. Sadly the asylum-seekers who remained at the Dommelhuis (now a private school called Luzac College) were deported. At the outbreak of war many Jewish people lived in what was known as "the writers' area" of the city near Sint (Saint) Joris Church. During the occupation 280 families were deported from the suburbs, to concentration camps such as Auschwitz and Sobibor. Some went into hiding and were subsequently hunted down by overzealous Dutch national socialists. Callous part-time bounty hunters, mainly working at weekends, earned themselves seven and a half guilders for every Jewish person they tracked down.

At the outbreak of war, 113,000 people lived in Eindhoven with 25,000 working in the Philips radio works and the lamp and valve factory at Strijp. Although much of southern Eindhoven was dominated by tall chimneys, the industrial area was instantly recognisable across the city by the Philips Lichttoren (Light Tower). Constructed in 1929, the Lichttoren was part of the smaller lamp and valve factory, and was topped by a huge illuminated Philips sign.

Piet van den Heuvel lived in the suburb of Gestel, and began working at the radio works as a telegram boy in 1936, at the age of 16.

In the early thirties, Philips purchased several large power stations and manufacturing companies. Many of the sites continued to operate under their original names such as The Nederlandsche Seintoestellen Fabriek (NSF) at Hilversum and The Metaaldraadlampenfabriek N.V. Volt factory at Tilburg. Each factory had its own independent power plant for generating electricity, with its own direct, secure telephone service link back to Eindhoven (operated by Philips engineers and not part of the national Postal & Telephone Company network). I believe that during the occupation, Mr Philips shared these service lines with resistance groups across the region and used the subsequent intelligence to guard against factory inspections and searches.

In 1940, 12-year-old Wim Klerkx from Vlokhoven qualified for a place at the prestigious Philips Technical School on Kastanjelaan. Around 750 young people applied for the four-year course but only 125 were successful. "We had to pass a stringent medical, physical, and practical test," remembers Wim. "I was being trained as a lathe operator to make parts for electrical generators. Around one hundred employees between the ages of 18 and 25 were about to be called up to work in Germany but there was a rule that meant any student or apprentice couldn't be deported. Mr Philips was well aware of the rule and requisitioned the ground floor of the school to establish a fictitious 'training scheme.' All the windows were covered with sheets of thick grey paper, protecting the 'new students' from the prying eyes of the authorities."

In May 1941, the Philips workforce turned the 50th anniversary celebrations of the corporation into a patriotic demonstration, singing the national anthem *Wilhelmus* which had been banned by the Germans. One brave but enterprising employee "borrowed" a forklift truck and wired a radio up to the battery.* Adorned in the national colors, the electric vehicle was then driven to De Laak, Frits Philips' childhood home on Nachtegaallaan, accompanied by hundreds of factory workers all dancing along to music blaring from the prohibited radio. More forklifts followed suit and it was not long before the streets were full of people enjoying the party atmosphere. Wim Klerkx was watching the procession from a second-floor window at the Philips

---

* Radios, like the national anthem, had been outlawed. Soon afterwards all radios were confiscated but many people kept sets covertly and listened to the weekly broadcasts by Radio Oranje and the Dutch BBC. If caught it was possible for the authorities to upgrade the charge to spying, which carried a mandatory death penalty.

School and recalls: "A German sentry was passively observing the parade, when a member of the crowd came over and tied a ribbon around the muzzle of his rifle, exclaiming 'go home the war is over!' By the end of the day, the party was well and truly 'over' because the authorities quickly posted notices ordering people back to work the following morning." The German police made many arrests that evening after a series of fights broke out in the Philips-sponsored bars and social clubs with the Weerafdeling or WA (the militant wing of the NSB that had been re-established after the occupation).

In 1942, 20-year-old Noud Stultiens lived with his parents and older brother at 3 Jacob Catslaan, in the district of Stratum – a five-minute walk from the centre of Eindhoven:

> As a chemistry graduate I got a job working for a large textile company Jansen en Mit who owned a dye works in Schijndel and a hosiery mill at Geldrop. By that time raw materials such as wool and cotton were no longer available because imports from Australia, South America and the UK had ceased. Ladies' stockings and tights were fabricated by the company from viscose and for socks they used a mixture of flax, viscose, and lanital, a fiber bizarrely made from skimmed milk. After two years of occupation, everything was rationed but luckily I was able to exchange socks and stockings for black-market goods such as wheat, meat, butter, cheese, and even bicycle tires.

Adriana "Jenny" van Hout (neé Soons) lived in Woensel and reveals what it was like growing up during the occupation: "Most of us kids who lived along Boschdijk [the main trunk road between Best and Eindhoven] went to the Theresia Catholic School. As with so many other teaching establishments, the school was requisitioned and became a German army billet. Subsequently my class was moved several times, firstly to a local pub and then to a timber factory before ending up at the Pastoor Van Ars Church School. Because the school was unable to cater for the extra numbers, we were only allowed to attend class in the morning."

On Sunday afternoons, Jenny's parents, Jacobus (who worked for Philips) and Adolphina, sent Jenny and her older brother Leo to the local library on Fellenoord. However, on Sint Nicolaas Day, Sunday December 6, 1942, Jenny and Leo stubbornly refused to take their books back to the library and stayed at home to play with their new toys.* Around midday, the Royal Air Force attacked Eindhoven for the first time: "As we were arguing, the air raid sirens sounded and the entire family ran down into the cellar. Unaware that this was the first of three raids on the factories at Strijp, many of our neighbors came out into the street after the first wave. Against the advice of my parents, who remained close to the house, I ran to see the factories where most of the damage seemed to be concentrated."

When the second wave of planes appeared, Jenny returned home only to find that her front door had been accidentally locked.

> Standing alone in the street, overwhelmed by the noise of the exploding bombs and antiaircraft fire, I was almost hysterical. Totally oblivious, our elderly neighbor Trine (who suffered from dementia), stepped outside and began shaking the dust from an old cleaning cloth. Beating the duster against the wall she noticed me crying on the doorstep. Trine took one look at my face and scuttled away to find my parents who had been frantic with worry. Sobbing, I threw myself into my mum's arms and promised never to run off like that again. The following afternoon we were horrified to learn that the library had been badly damaged in the raid. My parents were just getting over the shock when an unexploded bomb went off in the ruins causing the entire building to collapse.

---

* Sint Nicolaas Day is far more important than Christmas Day for the younger generation because it is on Sint Nicolaas Day that the Dutch exchange gifts. Sinterklaas (Santa Claus) delivers presents, but according to folklore, his helper Zwarte Piet (Black Pete) would slide down the chimney to take away badly behaved children.

Wim Klerkx was also celebrating Sint Nicolaas Day at home. During the raid, he went outside with his younger brother Jos to wave at the low-flying RAF Mosquito bombers. "Later on we found out that most of the bombs had missed their intended targets and killed over one hundred people in the shopping area of Demer.★ A couple of days later, while walking past the burnt-out ruins of the technical school, I couldn't help but notice that all of the large circular light bulbs hanging from the ceilings had melted into bizarre candle-like shapes. Although regular Philips students like me were found new places in local schools, the bombing also sadly marked the end of Mr Philips' protection scheme."

The Lichttoren was so badly damaged that many of the staff had to be laid off as Piet van den Heuvel recounts: "At the time of the raids, I was working at the lamp and valve factory and my office was in the administration wing situated in the lower part of the tower – below the main test facility. Luckily the works manager from City Hall, Mr Tops, stepped in and offered many of us new employment working for the municipality. I got a job as an accountant and worked at City Hall until September 1944, when I joined the British Army as a sergeant translator."

Many other raids followed and the local population soon got used to being woken up in the dead of night by the sirens and the sound of gunfire from the antiaircraft batteries along Marconilaan. Located close to the Philips Radio Works were three 40mm AAA guns, sited next to the football fields at Woensel. A small group of Russian POWs lived there in crude wooden huts, acting as cooks and cleaners for the German gun crews. The Russians were always hungry as Jenny Soons recalls: "Often on our way to school we would throw sandwiches over the perimeter fence. One night we were awoken by the unusual sound of small-arms fire coming from the gun site but no alarm was given so we stayed in bed. The following morning while walking to school we

---

★ Civilian casualties were almost unavoidable due to the close proximity of the factories to the densely populated areas.

passed by the guns and noticed that the Russians were no longer there. A few days later we found out that there had been a minor uprising and most of the prisoners had escaped and been shot."

Due to shortages of domestic utilities, electricity and gas supplies were rationed and subsequently proved woefully inadequate during the bitterly cold winters of 1942 and 1943. Jenny Soons and her family spent most of their time in the kitchen where it was warmest. "My dad placed our heavy wooden dinner table outside and converted it into a makeshift air-raid shelter using sandbags and a cast-iron sheet," recalls Jenny. "At night every household had to adhere to the 'blackout' and the appearance of any external light was forbidden. However, there were exceptions. For instance street lighting and bicycle lamps were fitted with hoods to diffuse and direct the light source downwards onto the ground. Bizarrely the Germans wrapped the golden statue of 'the holy heart' on top of the spire of Paterskerk church near Tramstraat with a black drape so that it would no longer be visible from the air."

Civil air defense patrols from the Luchtbeschermingdienst (LB) policed the streets after dark to make sure that the regulations were being strictly adhered too. Sometimes after school in the winter when it got dark earlier, Jenny and her friends would play the *Licht Aus* [lights out] game.

> Before the LB arrived we would march around the streets in a group, stamping our feet like soldiers, looking for any houses that were breaking the rules. We would bang on windows and mischievously shout "*Licht Aus, Licht Aus*," forcing our nervous neighbors to scramble around frantically trying to adjust their heavy blackout curtains – much to our childish amusement!
>
> One of my friends told me that there were toads living down the manholes along Oirschotsedijk. But instead of amphibians we found a network of German underground communications cables belonging to the nearby Constant Rebecque Army Barracks [named after Dutch general Jean Victor baron de Constant Rebecque]. The next day

I took my dad's rubber-handled combination pliers and cut some of the wires. Of course there might have been serious consequences if we'd have been caught but although we were just kids the Germans were still our enemy.

Across the street from Jenny's house on Boschdijk was a Ford dealership known locally as the Obam Garage. The building was occupied by the Germans, and behind it was a small barracks.

One of my friends lived next door to the garage so we decided to climb over the fence and explore. At the rear of the premises we found an old wooden storeroom, containing German vehicle spares and military equipment. We helped ourselves to handfuls of 9mm ammunition, a steel helmet and a pair of very smart-looking chrome headlamps. Kids will be kids, and it wasn't long before we had built a camp, smashed up the headlights, thrown all the bullets onto a fire and invented a game that involved being struck on the head with a heavy stick while wearing the German helmet!

Food became scarce and the Philips Corporation opened a number of kitchens, where their staff could receive basic low-quality produce in exchange for ration coupons. Around 50 percent of all vegetable and fruit [produced nationally] was exported to Germany and the remainder split equally between the occupying troops and the Dutch. The food that the company "sold" became known as "Philips grub" and as kids we sang a silly song about the kitchens set to the tune of Lily Marlene…

> *Bij de poort van Philips lag 'n hoopje kak,*
> *We gingen er naar kijken het was de Philiprak,*
> *Alle mensen aten mee,*
> *En moesten weldra naar de plee,*
> *Van hutspot en hachee, van hutspot en hachee, van hutspot en hachee.*
> *[At the gates of Philips there lies a heap of pooh,*

We went to take a look but it was "Philips stew,"
Everybody ate it then had to use the loo,
All from goulash and stew, from goulash and stew, from goulash and stew.]

Another popular rhyme that we used to sing in Dutch was *"Tommy come and throw a bomb, throw it here, throw it there and smash all of Germany, Tommy come and throw a bomb all the way to Berlin."*

In late 1943 Jenny's uncle, Toon Hurkmans, fled from Germany where he had been working as forced labor.

Toon was registered with my grandparents on Jan van Lieshoutstraat. As that was the first place the authorities would look, he came to stay with us on Boschdijk. The penalties for harboring "divers" [people hiding from the authorities] were severe and if discovered my parents and Toon risked being sent to a labor camp or much worse. My parents had to be vigilant because one of our neighbors, Jos van Stratum, was secretary to the NSB Mayor of Eindhoven, Hub Pulles. Although Jos was in his late twenties, he still lived at home with his parents and sister Riet, who was dating a German officer. Van Stratum's father had been a successful cloth merchant before retiring and owned three houses along our street. Bizarrely, at about the same time Uncle Toon came to stay, the Van Stratums began having problems with their domestic electricity supply. When Jos asked if he could come to our house before work to shave, my father had no choice but to say "yes." As Toon was never caught we couldn't work out if Van Stratum was unaware or simply chose to ignore our little secret.★

The Germans requisitioned and collected vehicles, motorcycles, and radios and every household was forced to hand over items made from

---

★ After the liberation many NSB politicians like Van Stratum, were arrested and sent to Camp Vught (an ex-concentration camp) near s-Hertogenbosch (also known as Den Bosch). Dr Pulles was no exception and was sentenced to four years in detention.

copper and tin. Even the bells from local churches were removed and melted down for the Nazi war effort. Jenny remembers walking with her friends past the Antonius Church on the corner of Boschdijk/Fellenoord and seeing the bells on the ground, awaiting collection by the authorities: "One of us had some chalk so we wrote across the bells in large letters, 'HE WHO SHOOTS WITH GOD'S BELLS WILL NEVER WIN THE WAR!'"

Jenny recalls one particular weekend when a Dutch SS man holding a revolver came to the house and spoke to her father:

"Are you Jacobus Petrus Soons? We have reason to believe that you are hiding two fully serviceable motorcycles in a stable at the rear of this property." The soldier knew exactly where he was going and stuck the pistol into the small of my dad's back, frog-marching him through the house into the stable. My mother was out at the time, collecting ration coupons from the local distribution office. Luckily, my baby sisters were too young to understand what was happening.

When the SS man discovered the bikes hidden behind a false wall, my dad knew he was in very serious trouble. Meanwhile, my mother came home and immediately went to see Jos van Stratum, who said he knew nothing about the search but promised to mediate if necessary. A short while later, the Germans collected the motorbikes but no formal charges were ever brought. I can only assume that Jos may have put in a good word to get my father off the hook.

The hunger winter

The situation in the larger cities to the west, such as The Hague, dramatically worsened as the war progressed due to German blockades carried out as punishment for industrial disputes. The most effective was the nationwide rail strike in mid-September 1944. The strike had delayed the Germans bringing in reinforcements from Belgium and the Zeeland pocket in the southwest. The effect was such that the enemy had to bring a large amount of troops in on foot and many of these units marched for several days before reaching the front lines. In order to boost morale, Prince Bernhard and Queen Wilhelmina made regular radio broadcasts from London encouraging "patience and victory" and went on air to proclaim that liberation was now close at hand. The Germans took their revenge through a blockade of The Hague, Rotterdam, and Amsterdam. Many starved to death during this period, which became known across the country as "the hunger winter." Hendrik de Jong was ten-years-old at the time, and recounts his terrible experience living in The Hague:

In 1939, my mother, who was only 39 years old, died from breast cancer. We were devastated and just coming to terms with her death when the Germans invaded. The winter of 1943/44 was one of the hardest in living memory. Although we had ration coupons there was no food in our part of the country, fuel was almost impossible to obtain, and starvation became commonplace.

In August 1944, my dad died of a heart attack and our relatives came together and decided to adopt my sisters. I was sent to an uncle in Rotterdam who was in the NSB, but his wife didn't really want me so I ended up living with a lady who owned a store in the centre of the city. I spent about six months with her until one of my aunts decided to take me in as her own son had been sent to Germany for war work. My auntie had three daughters, one of whom had dated a number of German soldiers and become pregnant. The girls were constantly stealing my food and there was nothing I could do about it. The family sent me to gather wood in Scheveningen, after the population there had been evacuated. We took anything that could be carried from the empty houses, doors, floorboards and staircases … anything that would burn.

Food became so scarce that people broke into grocery stores and stole anything and everything. The Germans arrested many and one man in particular I saw was forced to write "*Ik ben een plunderaar* [I am a looter]" on a board before being shot. They left his body lying in the street for three days. Literally hundreds of people in The Hague died from starvation during the winter. Most of the bodies were taken away in cardboard coffins for burial. I almost died but luckily another relative came to my rescue. My aunt (who was also looking after my sisters) got me into a food kitchen at Loosduinen, which catered specifically for children and I truly believe she saved my life.

Resistance is never futile

In the summer of 1940, a group of ex-Dutch Army officers came together to create the Binnenlandse Strijdkrachten (BS or Domestic Forces). The idea was to recruit and train a covert army that would eventually rise up and fight alongside the Allies. As the occupation progressed, the national press was taken over by the Germans who then forbade any alternative publications that criticized the regime, reported on the royal family, or printed news of the war. Every month the RAF dropped millions of copies of *De Vliegende Hollander* (*The Flying Dutchman*), which were often copied and re-distributed by paramilitary groups like the Knokploegen (KP). Each KP cell was made up of six to ten people and eventually developed into a more cohesive national organization called the Landelijke Knokploegen (LKP or National Paramilitary Group). Expert forgers, KP units also provided "safe houses" for escaped political prisoners, refugees, and Allied airman. Many KP members like Johannes Peerbolte worked under false identities: "I was 18-years-old in 1942 and living in Utrecht. To avoid being conscripted for war work, I moved to The Hague, where my parents lived, and went into hiding before masquerading as a railway engineer called Bob Maas. My sister was also involved with the same KP unit and acted as a money courier for the 'divers' that we were protecting. Although times were tough, we just about managed to get by and the hardship we endured really focused our hatred for the Nazis."

To counter against the crude propaganda peddled by the NSB newspaper *Volk en Vaderland* (*Folk and Fatherland*) early resistance groups across the country prepared, printed, and distributed around 60 different anti-German leaflets that included such titles as *Ons Volk* (*Our People*) and *Het Parool* (*The Password*). Jo Peerbolte's family produced one such publication: "My dad was a typographer for a printing company and owned a small hand-operated desktop printing machine. With the information that was broadcast by Radio Oranje and BBC Netherlands, we started producing an underground newspaper called *Voor God en den Koning* (*For God and the King*). My sister and I regularly distributed around 500 copies by hand to local homes."

More than 700 people were executed during the occupation for being involved in the illegal printing and distribution of anti-Nazi pamphlets or newspapers but this in no way deterred others from taking up arms to physically fight for their freedom.

In early 1944, Jo Peerbolte returned to Utrecht to join his brother Peter in the Binnenlandse Strijdkrachten: "The BS was divided up into many districts and I was working 'district 8' – Utrecht Noord. We were trained in the use of hand grenades and Sten guns and issued dark-blue coveralls with an orange, white, and blue armband to be worn after the liberation. Five tons of supplies were usually dropped at any one time by the RAF – in 24 200kg containers – into open fields at Mijdrechtse polder and transported to a milk factory at Utrecht. All air-dropped weapons were covered in a thick layer of Cosmoline grease to prevent rusting. In total before the invasion we received 41 drops over 15 drop zones."

Others were not quite so lucky as Peerbolte – 30-year-old Henricus "Harry" van Genugten was arrested in September 1943. An active member of the KP, Harry lived and worked as a motor mechanic in the Stratum area of Eindhoven. The group had been responsible for raiding government offices and sabotaging rail networks. After a brief trial Harry was sent to the Kriegswehrmachtsgefängnis (Armed Forces War Prison) in Utrecht to await execution. On September 24, the night before the sentence was carried out – Harry wrote a heartrending letter to his wife Elsje, and son Matthij.

This morning at 7am, the execution verdict was given. Yes dearest, it is sad that I haven't been allowed the opportunity to see you and say goodbye but what can you expect from the Germans? Will you take good care of Matthij and tell him about me? I was so fond of that boy and would dearly have loved to see him grow up. Hold your head high and move on with the loving support from your son, through whom I shall continue to live. Thank you for all the sweet things we have experienced together. We have had a pleasant life although it was all too short. Don't grieve for too long because life goes on but please think of me from time to time.

There are six of us here in the cell, so I am not alone. Three of the men, Gerrit, Jan, and Bennie, are also waiting to be shot. One day the Netherlands will be free so please don't forget the sacrifices we have made. I want to say so much to you but it isn't easy. I am quiet and calm and hope to die as I have lived … the other boys feel the same.

When the insurance money pays out, please put it towards Matthij's education… Give my heartfelt greetings to my brother Louis, and tell him not to forget his little nephew. The same goes for my parents, your mother and father, family, friends and acquaintances … once again thanks for everything my love. Math, when you grow up and become a big boy please bear my name with honor and please be sure to take care of your mother for me. I send you both many kisses and wish you luck in whichever direction life's road may take – from your very loving husband and daddy, Harry.

Despite being tortured Harry revealed nothing. Following his execution everyone who had had any contact with him was brought in for questioning, but all were later released due to lack of evidence. Harry van Genugten's body was never found and he is among the hundreds of civilians murdered by the Nazis in the Netherlands who are still missing.* The Germans regarded all convicted resistance fighters as "terrorists" and buried those executed in unmarked graves, a policy they called *Nacht und Nebel* (Night and Fog).

Other groups were also trying their best to disrupt the Germans, such as Landeljke Organisatie (LO – National Organization) and the long-established Orde Dienst (OD – Order Service, who after the liberation became the Auxiliary Police). Many of these groups were eventually coordinated by the Raad van Verzet (RVV, Council for the Resistance), which became an important national paramilitary organization and a vital link for the Allies. Another group worthy of mention is the part-time Bijzondere Vrijwillige Landstorm (BVL). The BVL were a pro-royalist volunteer force, created in 1918 to protect the country during times of political unrest or revolution.

On September 5, 1944, many of the larger resistance groups combined to become the Nederlandse Binnenlandse Strijdrachten (NBS), or Netherlands Interior Force, under the control of Prince Bernhard. To satisfy international law, the Prince requested official armbands be worn by the resistance displaying the word "Oranje." Bernhard's firm instructions unified the RVV and several other organizations into one group that eventually became known as "The Triangle." The official military wing of the NBS was activated on September 22. Soon after recruiting started, many young men signed up for the newly formed *Stoottroepen* infantry regiment and would fight bravely for the Allies and the Koninklijke Landmacht, the Royal Netherlands Army (RNLA).

---

* Had Van Genugten lived to witness the eventual liberation of Eindhoven it would have indeed been a very special day for him – September 18 was also his birthday.

2 Intelligence Officer, 1st Lt Derwood Cann from Monroe, Louisiana. Derwood was a direct descendant of French national hero General Louis C. A. DeSaix de Veygoux, who was one of Napoleon Bonaparte's most trusted and favorite officers. (Eugene and Vada Montgomery)

3rd Bn, Machine Gun Platoon commander, 1st Lt Bill Wedeking. (Bill Wedeking)

st Lt Fred "Andy" Anderson (right) and his younger brother unk, pictured in 1943 at Quonset Point Naval Air Station, hode Island, shortly before Andy was sent to the UK. The Anderson family)

Just after Normandy Dr Mills held a welcome home party in the garden of Kennet House for 3rd Bn doctor's Stanley Morgan and Barney Ryan. Morgan is pictured here enjoying the sunshine. (Peter Mills)

3rd Bn, Executive Officer Capt Robert Harwick, pictured at camp Ramsbury, 1944. (Mark Bando)

G Co officers: (L to R) 1st Lt Ed Harrell (Executive Officer), 1st Lt Joe Doughty (Commander), and 1st Lt Linton Barling (3 Ptn) on leave in London after Normandy. (Joe Doughty via Mark Bando)

2nd Lt Rudolph Bolte (H Co 1 Ptn) pictured in January 1943 at Davenport, Iowa with wife Erma and two children Karen Lee, aged five and Suzanne aged 18 months. (Merrick and Teri O'Connell)

S/Sgt Harry Clawson (H Co 3rd Ptn), photographed with his wife Melba and their three children (L to R), Ronald, Sharon, and Rodney, pictured in Safford, Arizona 1943. (Aaron Walser)

60mm Mortar Sergeant Ralph Bennett from Michigan, H Company 3rd Ptn. (Ralph Bennett)

Pvt James Melhus, Machine Gun Platoon, pictured in 1944. (Jim Melhus)

Machine gunner Cpl Audrey Lewallen from Casper Wyoming. A Native American, Lewallen could be a little unpredictable at times and, according to Jim Melhus, one of his "favorite" pursuits in Holland was to taunt the junior ranks with a machete. (Bob Webb Jnr)

LtCol Robert Wolverton's successor, Maj Oliver Horton. (Currahee Scrapbook)

1st Sgt Fred Bahlau (HQ Co) sitting on the bridge over the river Kennet near the old water mill at Ramsbury during August 1944. (Fred Bahlau)

Supply Sergeant Bob Webb (HQ Co) strutting his stuff while on leave in Beaumont, Texas, in February 1943. (Bob Webb Jnr)

Sgt Garland "Tex" Collier from Coleman, Texas (still officially listed as missing in action). (Judy Gamble)

August 10, 1944. (L to R) Gen Eisenhower, LtGen Maxwell Taylor, and LtGen Lewis Brereton, photographed during a parade on Hungerford Common to announce the formation of the First Allied Airborne Army. (Currahee Scrapbook)

Mario "Hank" DiCarlo (H Co 1 Ptn), 1943. (Hank DiCarlo)

Members of H Co 2 Ptn pictured at Camp Mackall in 1943. (L to R) Pfc Ken Johnson, Pfc Alex Spurr, Pfc Charles Stenbom, Pfc Lloyd McGee, Pfc Gil Hunteman, and Pfc Frank Malik (front kneeling). Stenbom lost both legs during the shelling at Opheusden on October 5, 1944. (Ken Johnson)

Dirk van Tintelen's heavy machine-gun crew practising drills on Heumensoord ranges before the German invasion of the Netherlands in 1940. (Dirk van Tintelen via Geurt van Rinsum)

The Grebbe Line 1940. Dirk van Tintelen is pictured here standing on the right (next to a boy) taking a break with his colleagues while digging defensive positions at Maarsbergen. (Dirk van Tintelen via Geurt van Rinsum)

The enlistment photograph of Dutch Army reservist Dirk van Tintelen, taken in 1938, at Kraijenhof Barracks, Nijmegen. (Dirk van Tintelen via Geurt van Rinsum)

Dr Hub Pulles (front right without hat) after being sworn in as mayor at the Van Abbe Museum of Art in Eindhoven on February 21, 1942. Pulles became mayor of Eindhoven after all 19 city councillors were replaced by a puppet assembly of National Socialists. (Tom Peeters)

Downtown Boschdijk looking south towards Eindhoven before the German invasion in 1940. (Jenny van Hout)

The Philips factories in Eindhoven were bombed by the RAF on December 6, 1942. (Tom Peeters)

View looking west towards the Philips radio works at Strijp from the German antiaircraft gun site on Marconilaan. The clock tower is out of shot to the right of the picture. (Tom Timmermans)

For *Market Garden*, Capt John Kiley (left) was the battalion Operations Officer (S3) and 1st Lt Jim "Skunk" Walker was the commander of H Co. Kiley was killed by a sniper at Vlokhoven on September 18, 1944. (Bill Galbraith via John Klein)

Chilbolton – the military airfield's original water tower is still in existence along Martins Lane.

German horse-drawn troops fleeing Eindhoven during *Dolle Dinsdag* (Mad Tuesday) on September 5, 1944. (Currahee Scrapbook)

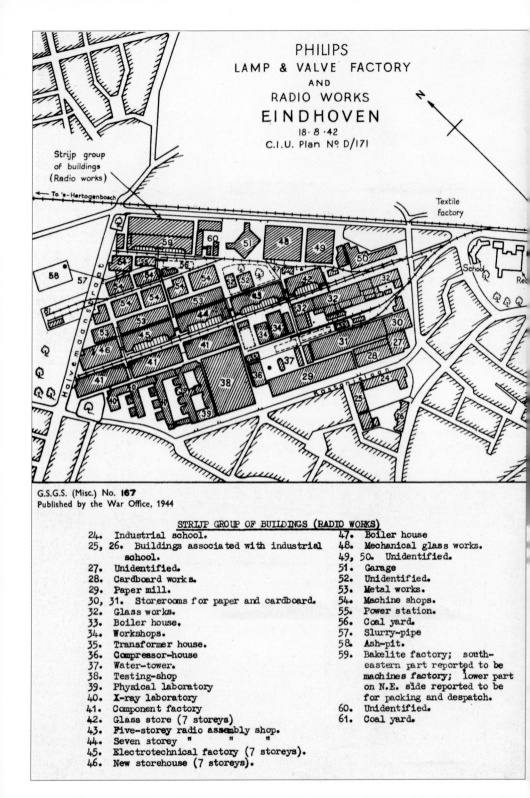

PHILIPS
LAMP & VALVE FACTORY
AND
RADIO WORKS
EINDHOVEN
18· 8 ·42
C.I.U. Plan N? D/171

Strijp group
of buildings
(Radio works)

← To 's-Hertogenbosch

Textile
factory

School

G.S.G.S. (Misc.) No. 167
Published by the War Office, 1944

STRIJP GROUP OF BUILDINGS (RADIO WORKS)

24. Industrial school.
25, 26. Buildings associated with industrial school.
27. Unidentified.
28. Cardboard works.
29. Paper mill.
30, 31. Storerooms for paper and cardboard.
32. Glass works.
33. Boiler house.
34. Workshops.
35. Transformer house.
36. Compressor-house
37. Water-tower.
38. Testing-shop
39. Physical laboratory
40. X-ray laboratory
41. Component factory
42. Glass store (7 storeys)
43. Five-storey radio assembly shop.
44. Seven storey   "   "   "
45. Electrotechnical factory (7 storeys).
46. New storehouse (7 storeys).

47. Boiler house
48. Mechanical glass works.
49, 50. Unidentified.
51. Garage
52. Unidentified.
53. Metal works.
54. Machine shops.
55. Power station.
56. Coal yard.
57. Slurry-pipe
58. Ash-pit.
59. Bakelite factory; south-eastern part reported to be machines factory; lower part on N.E. side reported to be for packing and despatch.
60. Unidentified.
61. Coal yard.

A section of the original 1:5,000 photolithographed map issued to 1st Lt Bill Wedeking (MG Platoon) detailing the layout of the Philips radio works complex at Strijp on the northwest outskirts of Eindhoven. (Bill Wedeking)

Aircraft from the 81st Troop Carrier Squadron, dropping paratroopers from 2/506 onto DZ B at Son. (Tom Peeters)

Bomb damage to the railway station in Eindhoven. In the background can be seen the Philips Lichtoren, or Light Tower, located at the lamp and valve factory at Strijp. (Tom Peeters)

Seen here at USAF Welford in Berkshire, LtGen Taylor (CO 101st Airborne Division) neatly displays modifications to the standard American T5 parachute. The riggers made several versions using the British Quick Release Harness and parts from the X-Type parachute webbing. (Signal Corps)

View from LtGen Brereton's observation plane across DZ B and LZ W. (Signal Corps via Tom Peeters)

eptember 17, 1944. People gathering in Stratum to watch he parachute drop. Today in the square opposite stands one f Eindhoven's few remaining "liberation trees" planted in 946 to commemorate the Allied invasion. (Currahee crapbook)

View looking east towards Son, across drop zone C where paratroopers from the 502nd PIR descended near Brouwerskamp. The plume of smoke in the distance is a C-47 from the 79th Troop Carrier Squadron, flown by 1st Lt Robert Stoddart which crashed on DZ B. (Heemkundekring Son en Breugel)

The air armada turning over Geel in Belgium shortly before lining up for the drop zones. (Chris van Kerckhoven via Ronald Ooms)

TOP: Later waves of tow planes and gliders seen passing over Sint Petrus Church on Kloosterdreef most probably on D+1. (P. Hendrikx)

MIDDLE: One of the Waco gliders that collided over LZ W at Sonniuswijk. (L to R) S/Sgt Joe Crawford (Regimental Headquarters Company, RHQ), Chaplain Tilden McGee, Capt Clovis Tollett (RHQ), and far right wearing goggles, 1st Lt Peter Baronski (RHQ) – note the faces of the men trapped inside wreckage. (Signal Corps via Tom Peeters)

BOTTOM: The 506th Regimental Aid Station preparing to move off the drop zone. Note the smoke from a burning aircraft on right. (Signal Corps via Tom Peeters)

Soldiers from 506th RHQ giving chewing gum to local children on the main track to Sonniuswijk running west across the drop zone. (L to R) Rini Hilgedenaars, Johan and Wim van Nostrum, and their eight-year-old sister Anneke. (Don van den Bogert)

Aerial view of the TB Hospital at Son taken in 1936. The Aloysius Boys School is seen here to the left of the hospital and the Girls School (Divisional Command Post) is bottom right. (Heemkundekring Son en Breugel)

The swing bridge at Son in 1936, photographed from the southern bank of the Wilhelmina Canal. When opened the bridge rotated electronically on a central mechanism and was protected on both sides by a wooden crash barrier seen here in the foreground. (Heemkundekring Son en Breugel)

View looking south towards the bridge at Son, showing the 88mm gun knocked out by D/506 outside the Aloysius Boys School seen here on the right. (Signal Corps via Tom Peeters)

3

"All leave cancelled"

Prepare for action – September 14, 1944

Pfc Darvin Lee (MG Ptn) was engaged to Molly, a physiotherapist living in London. The wedding date had been set for September 27, 1944, but when the alert came for Holland all plans for the big day were hurriedly cancelled. "The operation happened quite suddenly," reflected Sgt Ralph Bennett:

> I had won the battalion's "best soldier" contest and was on furlough in Slough with a buddy when we found out. About the third morning of my furlough, we went into town and it seemed really quiet. Not a soldier in sight. A policeman came over and asked what we were doing. We had started to produce our papers when he said, "I don't want to see those as everyone has been recalled – do you realise that you chaps could be locked up for this?" We didn't know anything about it, so the officer politely escorted us to the railway station and put us on the next train to Reading. From Reading we had no alternative than to hitch-hike the rest of the way back to Ramsbury. Approaching camp we could see the heavily loaded trucks about to depart. We had no time to change and were still in our class "A" uniforms as we clambered aboard.

Luckily for Ralph his friends had thoughtfully packed his barracks bag ("B" bag) and brought along his Thompson submachine gun (TSMG) and a more suitable change of clothing. "I happened to get into the same vehicle as Lt 'Skunk' Walker, who threatened me with a court martial for being late. I don't think that Walker actually parachuted with us but was either flown in by glider or transported by ship along with the kitchens and other less mobile equipment. The Executive Officer, Roy Kessler, took command of the company during the parachute phase until Walker was able to join us later with the rear echelon."

Battle plans

On the late morning of September 14, Col Sink alerted his battalion commanders during an emergency staff meeting at Littlecote House. "We received packets from 'SHAEF' through the British containing a huge amount of material with a rush designation and we knew that this was for real," recalls Ed Shames, who at the time was still working at Regiment with Maj Hester and the S-3 department. "The initial preparations seemed to me to be more or less a joint regimental effort as we worked through the battle plans in the billiard room. When it was time to leave, I was ordered to jump with 2nd Bn as an observer, with no real notion of what I was doing, until I could be assigned to my new platoon."

Fifteen hundred men from 1st and 2nd Bn, along with RHQ, departed later that same afternoon to their designated marshaling areas at Membury. Maj Horton returned to his headquarters in Ramsbury and quietly asked Bob Harwick to gather the battalion staff and the company commanders. A few minutes later, clutching notebooks, the officers strolled casually into battalion HQ with "this must be another show-down inspection" expressions on their faces.

The atmosphere changed when Horton revealed in his heavy Southern drawl, "Gentlemen, I am pleased to announce that the battalion has been alerted for an important mission, somewhere in the Netherlands, and must be prepared to clear this camp by first thing tomorrow morning."

"Everyone in the room was somewhat surprised by the 'good' news and all wondered exactly where we would be going," recalled Derwood Cann (Bn S-2). The battalion was being sent to Chilbolton Airdrome (USAAF Station 404) in Hampshire. Situated four miles southeast of Andover, the airfield straddled an elevated section of the Test Valley, between the villages of Chilbolton and Leckford.

Maj Horton continued slowly and deliberately and explained that the mission was codenamed *Market Garden*. *Market* was the airborne phase and *Garden* would be a ground assault led by the British XXX Corps and Second Army. Derwood Cann recalled the briefing and remembered Horton asking 1st Lt Alex Bobuck (Bn S-1) to supply a roster of every man in the battalion available for the jump. Those soldiers not on jump status were to be sent to a temporary holding area at Littlecote House.

Horton turned his attention to operations officer Capt John Kiley (S-3), requesting that he contact the supply officer Lt King and plan for the battalion to be packed and loaded in trucks no later than 0745hrs the following morning. As Kiley was leaving, Horton asked him for a status report on the crew-served weapons. Cann's section was then asked to move immediately to Chilbolton and establish a briefing room large enough to accommodate at least one platoon. Before departing Cann visited Littlecote for a brief meeting with the Regimental S-2, Capt Bill Leach, in order to collect all the necessary maps, photos, and overlays.

Facing the four company commanders, Oliver Horton continued issuing his orders. "gentlemen, I want all assigned personnel sealed within the camp as quickly as possible. All furloughs and passes are now cancelled, and no one will be leaving this area without special permission. Have your troops pack all their personal property in their 'B' [barracks] bags and clear the huts of equipment. Lt King will contact you later to issue instructions concerning supplies and storage. The men will take nothing except combat clothing, overcoats, and weapons. You will not disclose any of this information, as I'll be briefing the battalion before we leave for the marshaling area." Despite Maj Horton's closing words, the battalion soon realized something important was happening when the first vehicles arrived and began hurtling chaotically around Ramsbury ferrying vital supplies.

Before long, the advance party was ready to depart for Chilbolton. Derwood Cann, Bill Galbraith (S-3), and members of the intelligence section traveled together in two jeeps, towing trailers loaded down with equipment. Cann was deeply concerned about the lack of time his department had to prepare: "Amongst the equipment we carried were several sizable ceiling lamps and reflectors for illuminating maps and overlays. A number of large rectangular plywood boards for mounting documents, plus an aerial photo interpretation kit, several rolls of acetate, technical drawing tools, a heavy black cloth to cover anything that might be deemed sensitive, and a large quantity of fine white sand for the sand tables."

Operations *Linnet* and *Comet*

In the Netherlands, September 5, 1944, became known as *Dolle Dinsdag* (Mad Tuesday), when German troops withdrew across the southern borders desperately trying to escape the Allied advance. The Dutch resistance used this confused state to their advantage and launched several attacks. In one act of sabotage the railway tracks outside Eindhoven's central station were damaged, delaying all train movement for several days. In the ensuing panic the Constant Rebecque Barracks, northwest of Eindhoven, were abandoned and subsequently looted. The barracks were close to the Wielewaal Estate, where Frits Philips had his magnificent mansion, which remained completely untouched by the looters. Rocket-firing Typhoon ground-attack aircraft from the RAF mercilessly strafed German convoys, forcing men and vehicles to find cover under roadside trees. As a future preventative measure many local people took advantage of the chaos and cut back foliage along all potential routes of enemy advance or withdrawal. Noud Stultiens remembers one alarming incident, when a retreating German unit set up a temporary campsite in parkland opposite his house in Eindhoven: "Three drunken soldiers forced their way into our home angrily demanding coffee. Our Dutch Shepherd dog went mad and attacked one of the men, who took out a stick grenade and began to wave it about! One of his colleagues took the grenade away just as my mother entered the room carrying several large cups of coffee (made from tulip bulbs). My mother was blissfully unaware of the struggle that had just taken place and as soon as the Germans sobered up they headed back to their encampment." The Dutch began to think that liberation might not be far away but their hopes were soon dashed when the German High Command regrouped its disorganized forces into a series of *Kampfgruppen* or fighting groups, which numbered around 125,000 men.

On September 1, 1944, the air echelon from the US 442nd Troop Carrier Group (TCG) had taken off from their base at Weston Zoyland in Somerset bound for USAAF Station 469 – Ramsbury in Wiltshire. Commanded by LtCol Charles "Mike" Smith, the 442nd were due to participate in a new Anglo-American operation codenamed *Linnet*, designed to block the German retreat from the French coast.

The *Linnet* mission for the 442nd TCG was scheduled to begin at Ramsbury Airfield on September 3, where gliders from the 101st Airborne Division were waiting to be towed to landing zones near the town of Tournai in Belgium. The order came at short notice and on Monday September 4, the operation was officially cancelled due to the rapidly altering tactical situation between Gen Sir Miles Dempsey's British Second Army, LtGen Omar Bradley's First Army, and LtGen George Patton's Third Army. Equipped with over 90 serviceable C-47 transport aircraft, the 442nd comprised four operational squadrons – 303rd, 304th, 305th, 306th, plus an HQ element. 1st Lt Landon Cozad, a 303rd Squadron pilot, recalls: "The severe weather that followed our arrival at Ramsbury forced many, including myself, to abandon the cold waterlogged tents and sleep aboard our aircraft. As events began to unfold we started to wonder if the planners could actually figure out what they really wanted us to do."

The continual rain was a far cry from Italy and the warm shores of the Mediterranean, where the group had recently been assigned to the 82nd Airborne Division for the invasion of southern France. All members of the 442nd took quiet pride in the fact that they had played a vital role in not one but two invasions on French soil (the latter taking place on August 15, 1944, without the loss of a single aircraft). Five days after arriving at Ramsbury, the 442nd were dispatched to a recently vacated bomber base at Boreham in Essex, where they were given two days to prepare for another assignment.

The following day, September 7, provisional orders for Operation *Comet* were issued primarily on a need-to-know basis, amid much heated discussion and political wrangling between Eisenhower and 21st Army Group Commander, Gen Montgomery.

The 1st Airborne Division and the 1st Polish Parachute Brigade were scheduled for a large-scale parachute and glider assault into the Netherlands. Between late August and September 11, Second Army had advanced 280 miles, from the river Seine in France to the Escault Canal in Belgium. Due to an uncertain supply line, Dempsey had only been able to support and supply a single tactical thrust, by XXX Corps.

Although the German Army had put up a strong resistance in Belgium, Montgomery's intelligence reports suggested that the enemy were incapable of resisting another determined advance. Once the German front line had been punctured, the Allies doubted that they would have enough remaining strength to stop a breakthrough.

A plan was created to capture bridges at Grave, Nijmegen, and Arnhem before linking up with British ground forces from XXX Corps, commanded by LtGen Sir Brian Horrocks. Part of the Second Army, XXX Corps comprised 50th Northern Division, 43rd Infantry Division, 8th Armored Brigade, and the Blues and Royals. However, due to poor weather and a rapidly deteriorating tactical situation around Breda in the south of the Netherlands, Operation *Comet* was postponed for 24 hours.

Immediately after Brussels was liberated, Queen Wilhelmina – who was still in exile in London – sent her son-in-law Prince Bernhard to Belgium, where he assumed overall command of the Dutch Forces of the Interior. The Dutch underground was expected to provide guides and security for any Allied POWs. Now placed on alert, resistance groups were instructed to operate clandestinely until contact could be made with Allied ground forces. The resistance were also ordered to hinder enemy troop movement and sabotage fuel and ammunition dumps.

Operation *Market Garden*

Although XXX Corps decided to postpone Operation *Comet* for a further 48 hours, more time was still required and the following day (September 10) it was decided to push the mission back to Friday September 15. Later the same week, "D-Day" was changed at the eleventh hour to Sunday September 17, and Operation *Comet* transformed and reconstituted into Operation *Market Garden*.

The earlier plan for *Comet* was rapidly modified to include a much larger airborne force of over 30,000 men that would now encompass the US 101st and 82nd Airborne Divisions. LtGen Frederick "Boy" Browning, commander of the British Airborne Corps, was appointed deputy commander of the First Allied Airborne Army, to assist LtGen Brereton in combining all three forces. If all went well, over 16,500 paratroopers and 3,500 glider men would be on the ground in less than one hour and 30 minutes. At this point the only other people in the American camp who were aware of what was happening would have been the divisional commanders (generals Taylor and Gavin) and their immediate subordinates. All British and Polish airborne units were ordered to remain at their departure airfields, while the Americans were mobilized. A total of seven British and 17 American airfields were used to get *Market* operational. The 82nd Airborne Division was marshaled around Nottingham, while the 101st Airborne Division was deployed to airfields throughout the Newbury area such as Chilbolton, Membury, Ramsbury, and Greenham Common.

Montgomery was now more determined than ever to advance north across the big rivers of the Maas, Waal, and Neder Rijn, to form a strong bridgehead around Arnhem, before striking east into the industrial heart of Germany and ultimately Berlin. The main route for XXX Corps was to be Eindhoven, Grave, Nijmegen, and Arnhem. As soon as the drop began (H-Hour), the Guards Armored Division was to lead the advance to Eindhoven, ahead of XXX Corps. Initially the 101st Airborne would be under the command of the Corps until reaching Eindhoven, whereupon the Second Army would assume overall responsibility.

Although it was intended to evacuate the 101st and 82nd within a week, the 101st Airborne Division was to seize bridges along the main axis of advance, ensuring that the British had expedient passage northeast towards Grave and the 82nd Airborne Division's area of operations. In the meantime, XXX Corps was to provide artillery support wherever and whenever the situation permitted.

The Germans were fighting determinedly along the lines of the Albert and Escaut Canals, from Antwerp to Maastricht but they had few reserves. However, the Germans were expected to strengthen the river line through Arnhem and Nijmegen with artillery and flak guns, sited for a dual-purpose role.

Courage and skill

At 1000hrs on Monday September 11, the 442nd TCG received alternative orders and immediately departed Boreham for Chilbolton Airfield. Due to the lightning advance of US armored forces across France, LtGen Patton's Third Army was desperately in need of transport planes to fly supplies and evacuate battle casualties from the front line.

With *Comet* temporarily postponed, the 442nd, along with all other available Troop Carrier Groups, was dispatched to Verdun to assist with Patton's request. Afterwards, the group (now assigned to the 53rd Troop Carrier Wing) returned to Chilbolton at midday on September 16, where the exhausted crews began last-minute preparations for *Market Garden*. Shortly after touchdown, the aircraft were taxied and parked nose to tail, in three rows along the main runway. At 2000hrs, crew briefings began in the Operations Control Room, adjacent to the front entrance of the airfield. Col H. D. Smith, commanding officer of the 53rd Troop Carrier Wing, led each 90-minute briefing.

First to be briefed were the officers from the 305th and 306th Squadrons, commanded by Maj John Crandell, and newly promoted LtCol Royal S. Thompson. The pilots learned that the following morning they would be flying the 3rd Bn battle group to the vicinity of Eindhoven, and then follow up over the next week with glider tows and resupply missions. The 442nd was to be split into two serials: Serial A8, led by LtCol Fred Henry (commanding officer of HQ Squadron); and A10, ably led by "Mike" Smith.

Each serial of 45 aircraft was to deliver approximately one battalion of paratroopers onto one of two separate DZs, designated "A" and "B." The 303rd and 304th Squadrons, commanded by Maj Robert Whittington Jr and Maj Kenneth Glassburn, would be dropping 3rd Bn 501st PIR further north onto DZ "A" near Eerde. The 305th and 306th Squadrons would carry Maj Horton's 3rd Bn, along with one platoon from C/326 Airborne Engineers and 506th Service Company, to DZ "B" near Son.

The drops were to be spaced two minutes apart, with the first scheduled to arrive over DZ "B" around 1312hrs. As the UK was one hour ahead of Europe, owing to double-British Summer Time, at the end of each briefing, all watches were set back one hour to be in harmony with Dutch time (codenamed Zone "A"). Col Smith also delivered a hearty "good luck" message from the commanding officer of IX Troop Carrier Command, MajGen Williams:

This is the knockout blow to an already staggering enemy. The results of this great test of all-important operations are now firmly in your hands. Let's put our comrades down so they can quickly end this damnable war. I am confident in your ability and determination.

That night, around 300 Lancaster and Mosquito bombers from the Royal Air Force attacked enemy airfields across the Netherlands, destroying over 200 aircraft. The following evening diversionary drops of dummy paratroopers were also carried out close to Rotterdam and Utrecht.

The marshaling area, D-2

The 3rd Bn advance party arrived at Chilbolton Airfield on Thursday afternoon. Derwood Cann surveyed the mass of Nissen huts surrounding the tarmacadam runways and selected a large building with a sturdy concrete floor for a briefing room. Bill Galbraith set to work erecting the sand tables in the center of the room and hung the map boards with bright spotlights.

Several hours later, Capt Kiley arrived with further detailed information concerning *Market* and confirmed that the remainder of the battalion would be arriving the next morning. "While the section continued to work on the briefing room," recalls Derwood Cann, "Captain Kiley and I studied the battalion and regimental missions as well as the enemy intelligence reports and it was late into the night before we finished drafting our plans."

Around 1000hrs on September 15, the troops arrived from Ramsbury. Each company was shown to the marshaling area, located on the eastern edge of the airfield along Martins Lane, close to the aircrew briefing rooms, water tower, and main entrance. The battalion was split over several fenced compounds; the largest (now Stonefield Park industrial estate) contained the airfield's mess hall, situated directly opposite Middlebarn farm.

After the battalion had settled in to its hutments and tents (separate from the 501), Maj Horton gathered the S-2 and S-3 together to study the details of the coming operation. Several changes were made to Kiley and Cann's first-draft plans before the final orders were posted in the briefing room. "Overlays were drawn and photographs pasted together," recalled Bill Galbraith. "Rapidly the walls of the briefing area became covered with a plethora of notes and maps and the sand tables transformed into rolling flat countryside studded with green fields, canals, roads, bridges, and small villages."

While these last preparations were being made, Derwood Cann walked around the area contacting the company commanders concerning maps and security measures: "I couldn't help but notice that everyone seemed to have a casual attitude toward the operation and were going about their duties in a most cheerful and determined manner."

The troops were earnestly occupied packing equipment bundles with extra ammunition, K rations, medical supplies, and antitank mines. The place was a hive of activity as machine-gunners assembled belts of ammunition, mortar men uncased round after round of 60mm and 81mm mortar shells, while the rifleman were unboxing grenades and adjusting the pins. A few people were writing last-minute letters to wives, mothers, and sweethearts. Mortar man James Martin (G Co 2 Ptn) had a different opinion about the mood: "There was very little bragging and the atmosphere very subdued. We had 'been there and done that,' so to me there was almost an air of foreboding." Ray Skully had time on his hands and recalls, "Unlike my predecessor, I wasn't involved at all with the S-3 and stayed close to Major Horton."

The battalion ate late in the evening at the large mess hall, which was staffed and operated by area service troops. The enlisted men were relieved not to have KP or any other labor details forced upon them. The food was excellent, with large steaks served and plenty of ice cream for dessert. Operational orders were issued to all company commanders, who, with the briefing room now open, were ready to plan their own small-unit operations. A briefing schedule was prepared for the next day allocating specific time periods for each company. The first briefing was for Oliver Horton, to orientate his senior officers. The second was assigned to the company commanders to prepare their platoon leaders and NCOs. Next, the platoon leaders would inform their own individual units and the last period was geared towards squad leaders and their 12-man teams. Even at this late stage random personnel like Len Schmidt were being reassigned and sent to the airfield. "The night before the jump, I reported to Captain Morton who immediately assigned me to the machine-gun platoon."

At about 0700hrs on September 16, Oliver Horton assembled the officers in the briefing room. There was no loud talking or cheerful greetings but a willingness to absorb every last detail. Maj Horton orientated the group with the high-level plans behind the operation and discussed the Regimental mission, which was to capture Eindhoven and four bridges over the river Dommel by 2000hrs on Sunday September 17. At the time of the invasion, the river Dommel divided into two channels near the basin of the Eindhoven Canal. A pair of bridges dissected the river at Stratumseind, while another two bridges spanned the waterway 300 yards further downstream at de Wal and Elzentbrug, adjacent to the Van Abbe Museum of Art. The bridge at Elzentbrug acted as sluice gate for the local factories and more importantly, as part of the city's flood defenses.

"After the major had finished it was my turn to present the S-2 picture," recalls Derwood Cann.

Using maps and aerial photographs, I pointed out my understanding of the enemy situation before delivering a short report on the battlefield.

The entire area was dissected by deep drainage ditches and canals, sprinkled with patches of dense woodland. The sector straddled one of the principal road routes converging on Nijmegen. A railway ran south to north through Valkenswaard to Eindhoven (Belgisch Lijntje – the Little Belgian Line), with another connecting Veghel and Uden – making the only feasible enemy approaches by either road or rail.

Communications depended on bridges or waterborne transport so all canals and rivers presented a serious obstacle. Concealment and cover would only be available in woods and villages or behind the dikes and ditches. However, the fields of fire opportunities were superb but observation could only be available from elevated places such as church steeples or polders. Gaining possession of all canal and river crossings leading to Groesbeek and Nijmegen would in effect block the enemy route of withdrawal to the east, forcing the German Army further north through a 30-mile-wide "kill zone" between the river Maas and the Zuider Zee. Put like this everything seemed so simple but there was little known about the enemy disposition in the area around Eindhoven. The Regiment was aware of a small number of German Security, Pioneer, and Headquarters troops garrisoned in Eindhoven and a Luftwaffe Officers Candidate School located somewhere in Son.

Ultimately the bulk of German troops encountered by the 506th PIR came from the German Army Parachute School at Den Bosch but no major enemy combat units had been reported in Son or Greater Eindhoven, and they were not expected to be on the drop zone either. After Lt Cann finished his briefing, aerial photographs and several 1:25,000-scale maps including northwest Eindhoven and southwest Oirschot were issued. One of the more specialist maps given to key personnel was a 1:5,000-scale photolithograph plan of the Philips factory at Strijp.

It was now for Capt Kiley to explain the mission plans for the Division and Regiment, which according to Cann were as follows:

Third battalion will spearhead the assault and land on DZ "B" shortly after 1300hrs tomorrow afternoon. The planes will fly over the DZ at 110mph, at an altitude of 600 feet. The red light will come on five minutes before the green and a series of white panels will mark our DZ. Immediately after landing, we will assemble on a red smoke signal and bugle call, reorganize and secure the immediate area. Following us onto the drop zone will be the First battalion, whose job is to capture three bridges over the Wilhelmina Canal at Son. They will be closely followed by Regimental Headquarters Company and 2/506 who will assault Son from the north. When both battalions have completed their primary missions, the entire Regiment will attack to the south, capture the city of Eindhoven, and wait for the British tanks to arrive.

After Kiley's briefing, the officers walked around studying the operational maps, photos, and overlays. Throughout the night, the briefing room bustled with platoon activity but despite this many soldiers went away with only a vague idea of what they would be doing after the drop. More importantly, because so little was known about the Dutch resistance, many were unable to identify or even distinguish between bona fide underground workers and opportunistic time wasters.

The resistance and
the Special Operations Executive

Through Dutch expatriate soldiers exiled in the UK, Special Operations Executive (SOE) was able to put together four specialist teams for *Market Garden*. Known as "Jedburgh" or Jeds, some of these four-man units were augmented by British servicemen. Jedburgh selection was rigorous and continuation training for the successful applicants began in the winter of 1943. Before undergoing individual specialist tuition at Milton Hall in Peterborough, all candidates underwent a three-day parachute course at RAF Ringway near Manchester.

In the two years leading up to *Market Garden*, many of the Dutch operatives had not been deployed due to the success of a German counterintelligence plot codenamed *Nord Pol*. This superbly executed German operation managed to confuse and undermine SOE's clandestine activity in the Netherlands. It was only after the elaborate ruse was discovered, in early 1944, that SOE could once again start rebuilding its confidence in many of the Dutch underground groups. But it was still difficult for the Allies to develop a widespread network with the capability of communicating via radio to the UK.

By the end of March 1944, Special Forces Headquarters (SFHQ) had established radio contact with the RVV. Despite exercising extreme caution, SOE realized that the council was legitimate and was willing to work with SHAEF on the upcoming invasion. Agents were dispatched to the Netherlands, where they confirmed that the RVV was a centrally controlled paramilitary organization, closely aligned to many larger resistance groups. It was hoped that RVV could co-ordinate low-level sabotage missions against principal enemy communication systems, such as railways and roads. It was also thought that the widely represented OD would be capable of maintaining administrative services and civil order after the liberation – at least until the Queen and her government could return from exile. Despite rumors of National Socialist infiltration, the Allies still believed the OD to be a vital and important asset. In the area around Eindhoven, another group, calling themselves Partisanen Actie Nederland (Partisan Action Netherlands or PAN), was also active alongside the LKP. However, Allied intelligence had little or no direct radio communications with PAN or any other groups in Eindhoven, Best, or Son.

When plans arose for *Linnet* and *Comet*, the tightly knit Dutch agents training in the UK were re-formed under the new title of the Dutch Liaison Mission (DLM). Milton Hall determined the composition of each team, often augmenting them with other specialist personnel. The newly organized cells began to orientate themselves by studying maps and intelligence, but, like the men from the 101st, the Dutch Jeds would be frustrated as mission after mission was cancelled. At one point they almost gave up hope of ever being deployed, and started to learn languages such as Chinese, for more reliable missions destined for the Far East.

The Jedburgh teams participating in *Market Garden* would be jumping with the divisional headquarters of their assigned units. SFHQ planned to drop limited supplies of orange armbands to selected RVV units and send team "Clarence" to the 82nd Airborne and "Claude" to the 1st Airborne Division. Team "Edward" had overall responsibility for the mission and was attached to the British Airborne Corps. Two Dutchmen, Lt Abraham "Martien" du Bois and Sgt Fokker, became the nucleus of team "Daniel II" which was to be embedded with the 101st Airborne Division. A British team leader, Maj Robert K. Wilson, was assigned to Daniel II shortly before the invasion along with radio operator Sgt G. W. Mason. Wilson and Mason were both long-standing Jedburgh operatives, but they were unable to speak or understand Dutch.

4

"A parade ground jump"
September 17, 1944

Back at Chilbolton, Sunday religious services, led by 442nd chaplain Robert Tindall, were held at 0730hrs, followed one hour later by a final weather briefing. As expected, the layer of fog covering the airfield had begun to lift and by 0940hrs the crews were out by their aircraft.

Forty-five C-47s were assigned to the battalion battle group for the airlift. Each company was loaded across nine aircraft, with the average planeload comprising 19 paratroopers, along with a jumpmaster. By 0900hrs the battalion had formed into plane groups and a guide allocated to march each group out to their aircraft, where the parachutes and prepacked equipment bundles were waiting. "I got back to the UK four weeks before we invaded Holland," recalls medic T/5 Johnny Gibson. "Coincidentally, I was jumping with the 81mm mortar platoon and was once again part of 1st Lt Lewis 'Pinky' Sutfin's stick. We spent most of our time reflecting on the men who had jumped with us on June 6 – three of whom were killed and four had been captured."

The troopers began to attach the heavy equipment bundles to racks under the aircraft, fit parachutes, and readjust personal equipment. The MG Ptn decided to convert the large canvas bags normally used for spare barrels to carry the A6 light machine gun (LMG) and half a belt of ammunition. "We figured it was the most efficient way to jump, tucked safely across the chest under the reserve," recalls Bob Rommel. While the troops were making final adjustments, jumpmasters like Bill Wedeking and Derwood Cann turned their attention to their aircraft. It was the responsibility of each jumpmaster to check the exterior as well as the interior of the plane. Inside, particular attention was paid to the static line anchor cable and its fixings. To avoid snagging, all handles and other projections (inside and out) were covered with masking tape. Seats and safety belts were also checked for serviceability and all loose equipment on board was either stowed or removed. All aircraft, except lead planes equipped with the more sophisticated SCR 717-C radar, were carrying between four and six bundles of equipment.

At 0945hrs, the men began emplaning and almost 50 minutes later, the first aircraft from serial A10 lifted off. It took exactly five minutes for all 45 aircraft to become airborne (15 seconds short of the existing TCG record that was held by the 442nd).

At 1043hrs, serials A8 and A10 joined around 400 other aircraft flying at 1,500 feet along a pre-designated "southern route" (codenamed *Miami*) towards Ghent. An additional 1,033 aircraft were flying a longer "northern route" (*Tampa*), carrying paratroopers and gliders from the 82nd Airborne and the British Airborne Corps to their targets at Nijmegen and Arnhem. An incredible total of 3,957 Troop Carrier Command aircraft were involved in the operation. The southeastern coast of England became an enormous marshaling area as transport planes flying from 25 airfields merged into two streams, stretching for miles. On the ground, thousands watched for almost 90 minutes as the greatest air armada of all time passed overhead. Many who were leaving churches after Sunday services, returned to say an extra prayer for the men above. The southern formation crossed the Essex coast near Bradwell-on-Sea, before turning southeast across the Thames Estuary, toward North Foreland Point in Kent. Hundreds of ships and barges moored in Kentish ports blew their sirens as the planes headed out to sea towards Belgium.

Looking through the open cargo door of his plane over the North Sea, Derwood Cann marvelled at the number of aircraft. "They were on either side and as far back as the eye could see, giving us all confidence in the absolute might of the 'First Triple A.' Before reaching the Belgian coast, we were joined by our fighter escorts who furnished high and low protective cover. The jumpers in my plane were extremely quiet, and most like me were just staring into space or trying to sleep. About 30 minutes from the drop zone, the pilot accidentally turned on the green light and we leapt to our feet. After realizing it was a mistake everyone nervously returned to their seats but we were all on edge for the remainder of the flight."

Radio silence was maintained except for extreme emergency. As usual each formation was divided into three columns (left, right, and center) with three aircraft in each element known as a "V" and part of a nine-ship flight called a "V of Vs." The journey across Belgium to Ghent was uneventful until the mass of aircraft crossed over the enemy lines near Rothy and antiaircraft fire began bursting through the formation. Over 500 fighter-bombers from the 2nd Tactical Air Force (TAC), comprised for the most part of P-47s, P-51s, and a handful of P-39s, were on hand to support the slow-flying C-47s. Many of the concrete flak towers were neutralized by the fighter pilots, who were flying in groups of six or 12, using rockets and heavy machine guns. Ahead of the 442nd TCG were 850 B-17 Flying Fortresses from the US Eighth Air Force, whose job was to bomb gun positions and other military targets across the region. The timing between the 2nd TAC and the "Mighty Eighth" was superb, and together they destroyed over 165 enemy sites.

No further evasive action could be taken after the C-47s reached the Initial Point (IP) at Geel. Maintaining a vulnerable northeasterly heading, about ten miles away from Son, the formation began to reduce air speed to around 110mph in preparation for the drop. As the red light in each aircraft came on, the jumpmasters shouted the order to "Hook up." The paratroopers clambered out of their seats and began checking parachutes and equipment. It was vital that all individual harness fittings were secure before the snap fastener on the static line was locked onto the steel cable. Only then could the jumpmaster personally check each man's equipment before calling the stick forward into the door. "I stood with Jack McKinstry, either side of Herb Spence to make sure that unlike Normandy – he jumped," recalled Bob Dunning. "There was blood everywhere when Ed Templin was wounded by a bullet. Templin said that it had come up through the floor but none of us believed him and thought he'd actually shot himself in the foot to avoid parachuting!"

The drop zone

Approaching the drop zone, the flak grew in intensity, emanating from antiaircraft positions around Best, Valkenswaard, Eindhoven, and a barge moored along the Wilhelmina Canal near Oirschot. The little black puffs of smoke looked harmless but disgorged a deadly cargo of ragged steel with each burst. "I believe that some of the local antiaircraft fire may also have come from two or maybe even three 88mm guns located at Son," recalls Alex Andros. Jim Martin was told that the southern route was more convoluted to avoid flak: "I don't know where that idea came from because there was a lot of AAA but we were also low enough to get plenty of enemy machine-gun fire as well. In fact we were hit several times and the left engine of our plane burst into flames just before we jumped."

Two hours before the main air assault, Allied planes had attacked and bombed the area around the drop zone at least three times. A group of locals had been forced by the Germans to dig trenches adjacent to DZ B, when the second wave of bombers arrived. During the raid three civilians and two German Red Cross workers were killed, after the ambulance in which they were sheltering was destroyed. Thirty-year-old Berta Roefs lived with her family at Helena Hoeve farm, on the southeastern corner of the drop zone at Sonniuswijk, and recalls her own fateful experiences of that morning:

We had been warned not to attend mass on Sunday September 17, because there was a rumor that the Germans would be visiting local churches to round up the congregations for work parties to dig defenses. We decided to stay at home and look after our "guests," the van Dinthers who along with their six children, had been ordered from their home by the Germans a few days earlier.

While preparing lunch around 11am, we heard planes roaring across the fields from Best and moments later they started strafing and bombing the woodland south of the farm. [Ironically many of these were Spitfires flown by Dutch pilots from the Royal Netherlands Air Force.] Afterwards, my sister Dora told us that one of our neighbors, 17-year-old Kees Coppelmans, had been killed during the attack and his father and sister badly wounded. Dora had gone over with Piet and Cor Wilbers [who had been in hiding at Helena Hoeve farm] to offer assistance. It transpired that the Coppelmans had been trying to retrieve their cattle when the raid started. My sister wrapped Kees' body in a blanket and, helped by Piet and Cor, managed to carry him to the nearest house.

Afterwards the families began to hear a pulsating drone as more planes headed towards Son. Berta's father (Bertus) ordered everyone to the air-raid shelter at the rear of the house.

Minutes later the antiaircraft batteries opened fire as the parachutists began to jump. We sat and waited and it was not long before we heard the sound of footsteps outside. Moments later Piet, who had remained in the house with my dad, came over and handed us chocolate and cigarettes given to him by the Americans who had just landed in the fields directly behind our farm.

Around 2.30pm we plucked up enough courage to leave our haven and were surprised to find a parachute draped over the roof of the shelter. We went across to the barn and saw three injured paratroopers lying on the ground. One was quite badly wounded and we tried to express our feelings but sadly the medics could not understand what we were trying to say. Shortly afterwards, the Americans set up an aid station behind the farm and the following morning more wounded soldiers were brought in. We supplied the orderlies with boiling water to help clean wounds and sterilize instruments. Just like tourists, a lot of people came over from Son to see what was going on. On the morning of the 19th, the wounded (who numbered around 60) were evacuated to the Sanatorium at Son. Entering the barn we noticed two German soldiers among the wounded about to be moved. I'll never forget the way they looked at us with pure hatred in their eyes, as if we had betrayed them in some way.

Later that afternoon more supplies were dropped and one of the planes crashed a few hundred yards from our house and burst into flames. It looked to us like one of the crew who had parachuted from the stricken aircraft was going to land amongst the burning wreckage! We wanted to help but were told it was too dangerous.★

Thirteen-year-old Cam Pas and his older sister had been visiting Acht to collect milk from their grandparents' house on the day that the preliminary air attacks began. Hundreds of B-17 Flying Fortresses bombed the airfield at Welschap. "My mother and father lived about three miles away on the northern outskirts of the city along Boschdijk. Walking home we noticed that main road was devoid of pedestrians." The teenagers had not gone far when they heard the familiar sound of air-raid sirens. Moments later, the German AAA batteries opened fire on the first wave of Allied bombers. The children ran behind a nearby house and huddled in the corner of an empty air-raid shelter. "A low-flying aircraft dropped dozens of fragmentation bombs along the main road, no more than 60 yards from where we were hiding. After the raid we emerged to find the asphalt surface of the road ripped to shreds and tree limbs scattered everywhere. Walking towards Eindhoven,

★ Despite the success of the air drop many gliders and their tow planes were shot down. The aircraft seen crashing by Berta was piloted by 1st Lt Walter Hultgren from the 303rd TCG and had been towing a glider when it was hit by flak. Hultgren and his copilot Harold Horowitz bailed out moments before the flaming C-47 hit the ground, killing the radio operator and crew chief. By September 21, the aid station at Helena Hoeve farm was shut down. Afterwards the barn was used to house around 50 German prisoners, who were later relocated to the football fields at Son.

I started to collect pieces of shrapnel that were still warm." Avoiding racks of unexploded fragmentation bombs as they walked, the "all clear" sounded as Cam and his sister passed the clay pits and the Van Hapert brick factory (where the Philips Nederland National Headquarters are today). "At Barrierweg [the railway crossing in Eindhoven] we met up with my dad who was anxiously cycling along Boschdijk trying to find out where we were. The air-raid siren sounded again, forcing the three of us into the municipal shelter on the corner of Wattstraat as the railway station and gasometers on Nachtegaallaan came under attack."

Circling above the vast air armada was a B-17 Flying Fortress and a Douglas A-20 Havoc (Boston) photo recon aircraft charged with observing and recording the airborne phase for posterity. LtGen Brereton was on board the B-17 excitedly watching the proceedings from the front turret. Before leaving England, Brereton had issued a message to his troops:

> You are taking part in one of the greatest airborne operations in military history. The success of your mission today relies not only on navigation and flying skill and courage of the aircrews but also the courage and speed of the landing force – here rests the difference between a quick decision in the west and a long drawn-out battle. I know I can depend on you.

Shortly before the 3rd Bn's departure from Chilbolton, four pathfinder teams belonging to the 101st Pathfinder Company (P/F) took off from the newly established American P/F HQ at Chalgrove in Oxfordshire. Of the four aircraft involved in the mission, two were destined for DZ "B" at Son. On board the first plane, A/C No: 42-93096, flown by 1st Lt Dobbins, were the 506th PIR P/F group comprising ten men led by 1st Lt Gordon Rothwell, codenamed "Team 4." The second aircraft, flown by 1st Lt Gaudio, was carrying "Team 3" from 502nd PIR, commanded by 1st Lt Gordon DeRamus, whose regiment was scheduled to land ten minutes after the 506th along the northern edge of the vast jump field onto DZ "C." The primary function of DeRamus' team was to identify the 502nd DZ, with yellow marker panels and violet smoke. In addition, if required, they were to provide security, spare personnel, and equipment for Rothwell.

Flying in close formation, the pilots reduced airspeed from 180mph to 85mph as the planes approached the jump field, before successfully delivering the teams within yards of each other onto the ground. Although there was slight enemy resistance, Rothwell was able to set up and activate his five-channel electronic Eureka beacon (coded A to E) and radio magnetic direction finder (MF) within one minute of landing. Officially known as CRN-4, the transmitter (which had only recently been introduced) was interfaced to each aircraft's onboard radio navigation compass. Within four minutes all air panels and visual markers for both DZs were in place. The 3rd Bn serial arrived several minutes later than expected, due to marshaling problems and a slight navigational error over Europe. Both P/F teams remained on the landing field for nearly a week, to direct subsequent glider lifts and resupply missions before their own was finally complete.★

Back in the formation, Derwood Cann was watching from the open cargo door of his plane and could see the red smoke and white identification panels, set up by the 101st Pathfinder Company, stencilled with the letter "B." Ten seconds after crossing the Beatrix Afwatering and Wilhelmina Canals, the red lights in the aircraft switched to green, signalling the start of the drop. Altogether, 2,195 paratroopers from the 506th PIR (including 12 Forward Observers from the 321st Glider Field Artillery Regiment – GFA) were dropped from 131 planes onto DZ "B" along with hundreds of heavy equipment and supply bundles. For the sky soldiers, the vast 400-acre site at Son (three miles long by one and a half miles deep) seemed to reach out to infinity. Being the first to jump, 3rd Bn was assigned to secure the DZ. The drop was

★ It is interesting to note that Rothwell's plane, A/C No: 42-93096, is now on permanent display in the National D-Day Museum at New Orleans.

followed three minutes later by 1/506 and Regimental HQ and then after another three minutes, by 2nd Bn. The entire regiment was expected to be assembled and clear of the drop zone within one hour of landing.

First Sergeant Fred Bahlau and 14 men from HQ Company had been aboard chalk 57, flown by 1st Lt Ken Bain, from Oakland, California. "The jump was fantastic but I ripped my trousers and cut my leg on a wire fence as I landed," recalls Bahlau. "One of my buddies from Michigan, Pvt Bernie Rinne (A Co), was shot in the forehead by a sniper and killed as the first battalion were clearing the field."

At 1333hrs, ten minutes after 2/506 had landed, the 502nd PIR flew in from Greenham Common and Welford to begin their drop onto DZ "C." The three main serials, totalling 144 aircraft, dropped another 2,000 paratroopers, including Gen Taylor, Divisional HQ, and SOE team Daniel II.

Maj Horton was so impressed with the 3rd Bn drop that two weeks later he was compelled to send an official note of thanks to Mike Smith:

Though I write this letter personally, I am expressing the feelings of each man in my battalion, thanking you for the manner in which we were set down. Our men fell in a pattern on the proper DZ, allowing sufficient immediate reorganization that small units were on the offensive before all men were clear of their 'chutes. This situation has never before been attained, not even during maneuvers. We had no men unaccounted for and our jump casualties were extremely light. I fully understand that such situations do not just happen but are the result of your own planning and the excellent training and sense of duty of each member of your command, our sincere thanks to you and your men for a difficult and dangerous job commendably done.

Every aspect of the jump was superior to what the men had experienced in Normandy. Approaching the DZ, Hank DiCarlo's aircraft was hit by flak:

Shortly after we stood up at the red light, a burst of 20mm antiaircraft fire came through the seats and out through the top of the fuselage! I heard someone shout "Good God Almighty," it was a damn close call but thankfully nobody was hit. Second Lieutenant David Forney panicked and jumped moments before the green light came on. By then the rest of us were so worked up that when the light did change to green we emptied the plane in a matter of seconds. I was amazed by the size of the landing area, with almost no trees to speak of and very few obstacles. My head was too far down and snapped backwards when my camouflage-pattern parachute opened. Somehow my aviator kit bag with my TSMG, ammo clips, grenades, and two 60mm mortar rounds tore loose. Later, as I was heading toward the assembly area, I spotted what was left of my kit bag. The grenades and mortar rounds had survived along with my TSMG but the spare magazines had burst open like a jack-in-a-box. I was not happy but we were safely on the ground as the second wave came in.

Despite missing the DZ by several hundred yards, Dave Forney later managed to hook up with his stick, all of whom landed safely. It seemed to Hank DiCarlo that there were virtually no Germans around to oppose the drop. "A Dutch farmer's wife told us there had been a squad at her house on the DZ requisitioning breakfast but they had run away as we began jumping."

Jim Melhus (MG Ptn) jumped with corporals Audrey Lewallen and Nathan Bullock. "Although it was difficult to believe, this was the first time that I'd ever parachuted with a machine gun. To make matters worse the gun was also loaded and made ready with a belt of 50 rounds. The aircraft was undulating so violently on the flight over that I became airsick. Being stuck at the back of the stick, I threw up all over the floor beside the crew compartment. The stench was miserable and the soles of my boots got soaked with vomit. When the green light came on, I slipped in the doorway and because of the weight of the gun, I had to crawl on all fours out the door like a donkey."

3rd Bn 506 PIR overview of Operation *Market Garden*, September 17–November 27, 1944

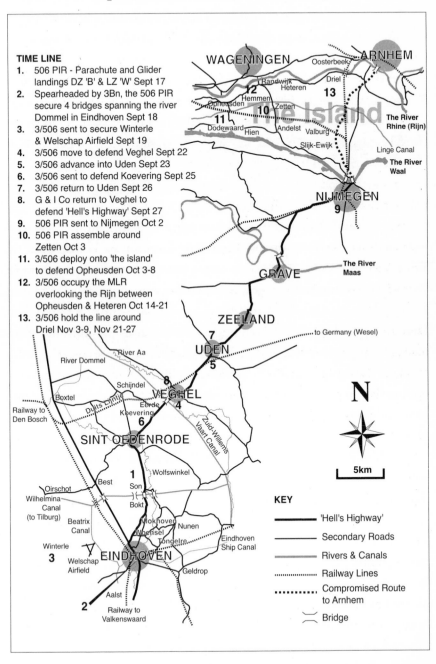

TIME LINE

1. 506 PIR - Parachute and Glider landings DZ 'B' & LZ 'W' Sept 17
2. Spearheaded by 3Bn, the 506 PIR secure 4 bridges spanning the river Dommel in Eindhoven Sept 18
3. 3/506 sent to secure Winterle & Welschap Airfield Sept 19
4. 3/506 move to defend Veghel Sept 22
5. 3/506 advance into Uden Sept 23
6. 3/506 sent to defend Koevering Sept 25
7. 3/506 return to Uden Sept 26
8. G & I Co return to Veghel to defend 'Hell's Highway' Sept 27
9. 506 PIR sent to Nijmegen Oct 2
10. 506 PIR assemble around Zetten Oct 3
11. 3/506 deploy onto 'the island' to defend Opheusden Oct 3-8
12. 3/506 occupy the MLR overlooking the Rijn between Opheusden & Heteren Oct 14-21
13. 3/506 hold the line around Driel Nov 3-9, Nov 21-27

KEY

———	'Hell's Highway'
———	Secondary Roads
———	Rivers & Canals
··········	Railway Lines
·■·■·■·	Compromised Route to Arnhem
⌣	Bridge

Alex Andros had never experienced so much pressure as he stood in the door waiting to jump. "When the green light came on, I leapt out like a lunatic." A piece of shrapnel punctured Bob Webb's canteen, sending water cascading down his legs. "There was little or no wind and much to my surprise I landed standing up. I was tasked with transporting equipment bundles from the drop zone to the bridge at the Wilhelmina Canal. Opposite the jump field was a farm with stables. At first the owner, who must have been in his seventies, refused to let me take any horses. His daughter spoke English and intervened and he agreed, but only on the condition that he accompanied my team to the bridge. In the end the old man supplied us with four horse-drawn wagons that we loaded full of equipment."

Several local farmers drove onto the drop zone in their horse-drawn carts helping to collect the bundles. One farmer in particular stuck in Bill Galbraith's memory because of his beautiful white horse. Bobbie Rommel was almost killed getting out of his parachute when a couple of steel helmets smashed into the ground beside him. "I remember looking up and seeing a C-47 beginning to break up and one of its wings falling to the ground like it was made from tissue paper."

The paratroops immediately began to orientate themselves and hastened to their respective assembly areas. Raymond Skully had an important job to do once he was on the ground: "I went over to Major Horton and proceeded to blow 'assembly' over and over again on my bugle, until the battalion rallied around. About one hour later, a jeep arrived and I jumped in the back, behind the boss and headed for Son." The battalion quickly secured the drop zone by encircling it with riflemen and machine guns. The defense of the DZ was only held for a short period before it was taken over by units of the 502nd PIR. After being relieved, Horton's men reverted to regimental reserve and moved into a holding area a few hundred yards southeast of the drop zone. The reorganization of the regiment was almost completed within 60 minutes, with virtually no enemy resistance except for occasional incoming mortar fire.

Initially, 1st Bn failed to fully reorganize but headed off as soon as they had enough people. Col Sink recovered his jeep and drove over to 2nd Bn's assembly point to inquire why they had not yet moved out. Sink was perplexed to discover that they were waiting for LtCol Robert Strayer to arrive. Thirty minutes later, there was still no sign of Strayer. Eager to get things moving, Sink ordered 1st Lt Fred Heyliger to take command and lead 2/506, plus the remainder of the regiment, to Son.

Although the ground had been recently ploughed, it did not stop Pvt Harold Stedman (I Co 3 Ptn) from injuring himself. "The base plate from the 60mm mortar got forced up into my groin, damaging my spine and hip." Despite having difficulty walking, Stedman refused medical aid and asked his ammunition carrier Pvt Wayman Womack for assistance. Womack, a replacement from Freeport, Texas, ran across to a nearby farm and returned with a wheelbarrow. With Womack at the helm, the old wheelbarrow became Stedman's primary method of transportation for the next three days.

Lt Bob Stroud (H Co 3 Ptn) spotted three German soldiers walking towards him waving white flags. "As I nervously pulled my folding stock carbine from its holster, the gun went off, narrowly missing my foot." Pvt Ralph King (H Co 3 Ptn) recalls, "By the time we got to the assembly area, the second echelon was coming in, some of those guys were being dropped incredibly low and several planes went down in flames."

Ed Shames was in the third wave flown by the 436th TCG: "I didn't realize that our plane had been hit until the guy in front of me was wounded in the buttocks. After that we began to lose altitude and were flying very low when the time came to exit. After landing, drained by all the excitement, I reached for my canteen to take a mouthful of water. In the heat of the moment, I'd completely forgotten that it was full of 'GI Alky' given to me earlier by Dr Jackson Neavles, but that is altogether a whole different story!"

Collection points for ammunition and supplies were located in woods adjacent to a wide track on the southern edge of the drop zone. After arriving, Ralph Bennett saw a couple of officers talking to a group of

Dutch civilians whom he assumed were from the resistance. One of the BS leaders, John van Kooijk, was directed towards Ed Shames. "When I first met 'John the Dutchman,' he was living in Helmond, seven miles away to the east. John was around 32-years-old at the time and was deputy underground chief for the southern part of Holland. As Van Kooijk seemed exceptionally well informed, I decided to leap-frog Strayer [who was still nowhere to be seen] and introduce him to the Regimental Intelligence Officer, Captain Bill Leach." Van Kooijk, along with two Belgian colleagues, was able to report that both bridges along the canal to the east and west of Son had been destroyed by the Germans.

Sacrifices

In total four of the C-47s assigned to the 506th PIR (all from the 436th TCG based at Membury) either crashed or made crash landings on, or near, the drop zone. After dropping his first battalion stick, pilot Lt Glenn Toothman achieved a textbook belly landing before hooking up with members of H Co. For the first time in 22 jumps, Pfc Jim McCann, from H Co 3 Ptn, achieved a dreadful exit. "Subsequently I lost everything, including the barrel of a 60mm mortar, and the only thing I had left to defend myself [with] on landing was my trench knife." McCann ended up sharing a ditch with Toothman, who was armed with a .45 semi-automatic pistol. McCann asked jokingly, "How on earth are you going to fight the war with that thing?" Laughing, Toothman replied incredulously, "Jeeze, get out of here, at least I've got a darn sight more to fight with at this moment than you, private!"

The other three aircraft were carrying soldiers from 506th Regimental HQ. Seconds after successfully delivering his paratroopers on target, 1st Lt Robert Stoddart's aircraft crashed in flames a few hundred yards east of LZ "W" (the glider landing zone overlapping DZ B and C), killing both Stoddart and his crew chief T/Sgt Ivan Thade. This was followed by another C-47, flown by Ross Hanna, which crashed on the edge of the DZ without any fatalities. First

Lieutenant John Gurecki was transporting another stick, which included Maj Clarence Hester (Regt S-3), Capt Gene Brown (CO Regt HQ Co), Capt Logan B. Hull (Asst Regt Surgeon), and Capt Thomas Mulvey, when he got hit. While Gurecki continued to fly the plane, everyone on board including the crew, bailed out just before reaching DZ B. Radio operator Cpl Robert Ritter was tragically killed when his parachute malfunctioned. With great skill and bravery Gurecki managed to pilot his low-flying aircraft over the buildings at the junction of Sonniuswijk–Brouwerskampweg (*weg* means road) before crash-landing near Paulushoef farm. Escaping from the wreckage, Gurecki saw the C-47 catch fire and moments later explode in flames.

Pfc Lawrence Davidson (H Co 3 Ptn) came in backwards and was just getting out of his parachute when he was alerted to the fact that Gurecki's plane was now coming towards him. Davidson had only seconds to get out of the way and felt the full force of the blast as the aircraft exploded. Johnny Gibson crawled behind a water-filled cattle trough in an attempt to protect himself from the intense heat.

The initial glider lift arrived about 25 minutes after the main drop. Around 70 gliders were expected, carrying command, recon, signal, and medical personnel, along with the first batch of jeeps for the regiment. Using the ten guilders that had been issued to him in the marshaling area, Johnny Gibson was attempting to purchase a smart-looking Belgian pistol from a resistance worker, when two gliders from the 437th TCG crashed onto the DZ. "I went over to offer my assistance but the medics and members of RHQ were still trying to cut the soldiers out, who were all from the 501." The pilot of the second glider, Flight Officer Lloyd Shuffelberger (84th Squadron), was blinded after colliding with the rear of FO Thornton Shofield's craft during the final approach. Luckily Shofield was able to stabilize his ship before hitting the ground. Later Johnny Gibson discovered that two of his friends from RHQ, sergeants Phil Campisi and Don Doxted, had been badly injured in a separate glider crash on LZ "W." "Like me, both Don and Phil were into bodybuilding and hand balancing, and before the war

Don was well known for having walked up and down the Empire State Building, in New York City on his hands!"

Communications Sergeant Gordon Yates, H Co, was walking towards the collection point with four other men when they noticed what seemed to be bottles of spirits in one of the farms. "After a quick slug we all decided that it was far too strong even for us," recalls Gordon. "As we were leaving, the owner of the house, Mr Boss, appeared and informed us that it was actually the fuel he used in his lamps! After I got over the initial shock of drinking lamp oil, we fell about laughing and exchanged addresses." When 1st Sgt Gordon Bolles (H Co) hit the road after the jump, he spotted a wounded man near one of the farmhouses and called out for a medic – "milk" sounds almost identical to "medic" in Dutch – "A farmer misunderstood what I was saying and came over and tried to hand me a pitcher full of milk!"

Local boy Wan van Overweld was five-years-old at the time of the invasion and lived at Paulushoef farm on the southeastern corner of the drop zone. "Although we were excited to see the Americans, my older brother Paul had been injured during the earlier air raids. When the first paratroopers reached the farm they spotted our water pump and motioned to my father to drink from the well, fearing it might be poisoned! To prove that the water was uncontaminated, my dad asked me to share a cup with him. As soon as the soldiers were satisfied, they smiled, shook our hands, and proceeded to drink the well completely dry!"

On clearing the jump field, each aircraft banked 180 degrees to the northwest (left), opened its throttles and climbed sharply to 3,000 feet for the journey home. It was at this point that two planes from the 306th Squadron, flown by 1st Lt John Corsetti and 1st Lt Tom Mills, were hit and brought down. Copilot Judson Wright Pittam, 306th, was on board A/C No: 42-93681, piloted by 2nd Lt Tom Ezzell, when he witnessed Corsetti's demise: "Tom and I were in the middle of the serial, when we saw Corsetti's plane hit by flak. We both watched anxiously as John's crew began to bail out. Seconds later the aircraft rolled over and went into a vertical dive before exploding into the ground."

Corsetti's copilot, 2nd Lt Ed Hunter, reveals the last few terrifying moments of their mission: "Climbing to 3,200 feet just north of Bladel, we were hit by multiple bursts of flak that knocked out our elevator controls and damaged the right engine along with the fuel tanks. Shortly afterwards, the engine caught fire and flames appeared from underneath the floor in the center section of the fuselage. The aircraft became uncontrollable and began climbing to a stall. As the rest of us had our 'chutes on, Lt Corsetti gave the order to abandon ship. Navigator 2nd Lt Rene Zumhagen, Crew Chief T/Sgt James Swanson, and Radio Operator S/Sgt John Duffy all immediately jumped through the main cargo door. As I pushed towards the rear of the plane, John was still clipping on his chest rig outside of the navigator's compartment. The plane suddenly stalled, throwing me violently against the tail section. Corsetti was still inside as I grabbed onto the edge of the cargo door and pulled myself out. Small-arms and machine-gun fire peppered all around during my descent."

At around 1330hrs, Hunter found shelter in a nearby drainage ditch, between two fields. Later, under cover of darkness, he attempted to make his way towards friendly forces. After walking across country for about three miles, the airman found himself in the middle of a German supply dump. "I hid in a haystack for a couple of days until Wednesday afternoon, when a Dutch boy arrived and started spreading the wet hay to dry in the sun. Not long afterwards he saw me and although clearly frightened, the lad motioned for me to stay hidden. About an hour later the boy returned with food and a note, written in poor English, explaining that he would come back at 9pm and take me to a more suitable hiding place. The boy appeared at the specified time and gave me a pair of overalls to put on. After being taken to Bladel, I was handed over to the Dutch underground and hidden beneath a woodpile in the rear garden of a house."

On Friday September 22, a British unit arrived and took Hunter to their Company HQ, and the following morning he was reunited with Zumhagen and Duffy and taken to XXX Corps HQ in

Eindhoven. Shortly afterwards the three men were driven to Brussels before being flown back to the UK. After routine interrogation by MI5 at RAF Northolt, the crew returned to the 442nd TCG on September 25. It was later confirmed that 1st Lt Corsetti had been killed in the plane crash and T/Sgt James Swanson captured and sent to a prisoner-of-war camp.

Tom Mills' experience could have been plucked straight from a Hollywood film: "I arrived over the DZ at 1316hrs, flying at an altitude of 610 feet. Just after we dropped our stick [from C/326 Airborne Engineers], the port [left] engine was hit by flak. I feathered the prop and started turning away from the jump field. Twelve minutes later, my crew chief, S/Sgt Jesse Beal, discovered a fire in the cabin. Struggling to maintain altitude, I instructed the crew to abandon ship." As copilot FO John Barber and Jessie Beal were about to jump, the starboard engine was hit:

Barber and Beal leapt out at around 600 feet, but I managed to stop my radio operator, S/Sgt Rollin Bailey, and navigator, 1st Lt Olin Jennings, from jumping. As we were rapidly losing altitude, I told the guys to prepare for a crash landing. The aircraft was now on fire and to make matters worse, as I approached the ground, an abandoned German Jagdpanther tank destroyer was directly in my flight path! Kicking the left rudder as hard as possible, we just missed hitting the tank, but tore off the right wing. Bailey escaped through the back door and in doing so was badly burned about the face and hands. Heading for the companionway, Jennings and I tripped over the cabin fuel valves. As we fell, a sheet of flame spurted up inside the plane towards the rear. We immediately turned around and headed for the escape hatch at the front of the ship. Thirty seconds later, there was a series of explosions and the entire plane went up in flames. Barber and Beal joined us at the scene where a British ambulance took us to a dressing station. Afterwards we were taken to the British GHQ at Gheel.

The entire episode happened to be filmed by a British newsreel cameraman and was shown in movie theaters around the world.

Serial A8 did not escape unscathed: one C-47 piloted by Lt Herbert Schulman was hit two minutes before reaching DZ "A" and burst into flames, but continued on course to drop its paratroopers. Two members of the crew, T/Sgt Ralph Zipf (Crew Chief) and S/Sgt Roger Gullixson (Radio Operator), bailed out before the plane crashed into the Zuid–Willems–Vaart Canal, west of Veghel, instantly killing Schulman and his copilot, 2nd Lt Omar Kempshmidt.

Two aircraft made emergency landings at Ghent, and a third, piloted by the 26-year-old 304th Squadron commander Maj Ken Glassburn, was forced to land in Brussels with an injured paratrooper still on board. This was an improvement on Normandy when, after dropping men from the 82nd Airborne, Glassburn had had to ditch his aircraft in the Channel off Utah beach. Squadron Operations Officer Capt James Brown did not fare any better and made an emergency landing at RAF Manston in Kent with a wounded navigator.

For those preparing the next day's glider mission back at Chilbolton, time passed remarkably quickly. At about 1630hrs the first distant specks began to appear in the gray skies to the east as the C-47s began to return. Although around 40 percent of the aircraft from the 442nd had been damaged, the troop carrier mission was by no means over.

5

"Road to Eindhoven"
September 17–18, 1944

Following on behind Regimental HQ, 3rd Bn moved south along Rooijscheweg toward Son, which was only two miles away. The settlement was dominated by the Noord-Brabantse Sanatorium for Tuberculosis (TB) – known locally as the 'Holy Heart of Jesus' hospital. The impressive four-story building was built in 1914 by the Broeders Alexianen, a Catholic religious order from Belgium, and stood close to the Aloysius Boys School (now the Emilius school) and girls school (now La Sonnerie hotel and restaurant) north of the Wilhelmina Canal. By now the Regiment was fully aware that the crossing points at Houtens in the west and Hooidonk to the east had been destroyed on September 11, and so had focussed its full and undivided attention on the swing-bridge at Son.

The locals were cheering and handing out beer, which was a surreal experience for the 506th, especially 3rd Bn, who were behind the main force when the shooting started. "We couldn't really appreciate what was happening," recalled Bob Dunning. "It sounds a little selfish now but we just wanted to keep moving and weren't happy about having to stay in the water-filled ditches."

Up ahead, at around 1500hrs, 1st Bn were forced into a flanking maneuver around the western side of the town, while 2nd Bn attempted a direct assault on the bridge. The swing-bridge could be electronically rotated through 90 degrees on a central mechanism. When fully open, each side of the iron structure was protected by a wooden pier that acted as a crash barrier to passing boats. After *Dolle Dinsdag*, the tiny garrison at Son (which had its HQ in the church) had been enhanced to about 90 soldiers, including the Luftwaffe officer candidate school.

There were at least two 88mm antiaircraft guns in the village, the primary role of which would have been to protect the canal from air attack. The first was located in fields 200 yards northwest of the main bridge, between the TB hospital and the canal. This 88mm gun seriously delayed 1st Bn's advance, causing several casualties, including one of Ed Shames' best friends, 2nd Lt George Retan (A Co), who was among the first to be killed. Before the invasion, another antiaircraft gun (fully mobile) had been placed in a pre-prepared position in front of the Aloysius Boys School, 300 yards from the bridge. From here the crew had a commanding view along the main road in both directions. After D Company knocked out the "Aloysius" gun with a bazooka, members of 2nd Bn discovered another gun site, along the canal bank to the west, which showed signs of recent occupation. One mile further along the waterway, next to what remained of the bridge at Houtens, was a third 88mm AAA gun which had been withdrawn to Best shortly after the drop.

At around 1620hrs, as both battalions were converging on the Son bridge, most of the German force retreated to the southern bank, under a protective shield of machine-gun fire, before blowing up the objective. Several mines were placed beneath the central turning mechanism which, when detonated, tore the bridge in half. The huge explosion threw debris hundreds of feet into the air and some of the heavy wooden planks even landed on the gun site behind the tuberculosis hospital. Col Sink was beside himself with anger as Bob Dunning remembers: "I'll never forget the look of shock and surprise on the colonel's face as he took the cigarette from his mouth and threw it on the ground, calling the Germans all the cuss words under the sun!"

It took ten minutes to overcome the enemy resistance on the northern bank. "After they blew the bridge we came under heavy fire from across the canal," recalls Ralph Bennett, "which was the battalion's first real head-to-head encounter with the enemy. I was part of a small group, comprising men mainly from 2nd Bn, who swam across to create a defensive firebase in a large orchard, from where we were able to push the Germans back."

Under the supervision of Gen Taylor and Col Sink, the engineers from C/326, assisted by Regt HQ Co, began clearing the twisted remains of the bridge, and depositing them on the southern bank. Wooden planks from the structure were then placed over a couple of rowing boats, to create a gangway, and tethered either side of the central wooden barrier using jump ropes. As the bridge repair work got underway, all three battalions were deployed in defensive positions around the vicinity.

While the temporary crossing was being fashioned the Regiment needed to find a place to get supplies and vehicles safely across the canal. The answer was less than 60 yards away. East of the bridge the waterway widened, allowing ships and barges to turn. At this point the angle of the canal bank became shallower, creating an ideal ramp for vehicular access. In a nearby barn, hidden beneath bales of straw, the forward-thinking Dutch had stockpiled around 200 empty oil drums. Several sturdy rafts were built, each one using 16 barrels fastened to wooden beams and topped with planks.

The repairs were completed by 1730hrs, but 3rd Bn were the last unit across the canal: "We crossed around midnight, guided by jump ropes acting as handrails," recalls Pfc George McMillan (I Co 2 Ptn).

The original idea to take Eindhoven by 2000hrs was now out of the question, and the 506th was forced to spend the night at the nearby hamlet of Bokt. A Company remained behind to protect the canal crossing, while 1st Bn went into reserve. The 2nd Bn and 3rd Bn were placed in defensive positions one mile from Son, astride the road at Bokt, facing south, with 2nd Bn on the left and 3rd Bn to the right (in the vicinity of Esp). James Martin's 2 Ptn, from G Company, was selected to act as divisional security, while the rest of the company continued across the canal with the battalion.

Divisional headquarters was established close to the bridge inside the Girls School at the nunnery, as Jim recalls: "Standing outside the front of the school was a very pretty lady. A couple of our guys were making lewd comments, thinking that she couldn't understand. The young woman said absolutely nothing and didn't even change her expression until one of the officers from division came over. She looked across, smiled at my two friends and responded in absolutely perfect English, clearly comprehending every single word they had said!"

Several groups of enemy prisoners were brought in to divisional HQ for questioning. Such was the chaotic nature of the German defensive operation that some of the prisoners-of-war still had cinema tickets with them for a film that had been shown the previous day in Amsterdam.

Just before 2100hrs, a row of houses close to the main road between Esp and Bokt was commandeered for command posts (CPs). "Major Horton took over one of the buildings from a middle-aged couple who were more than happy to oblige," recalls Ray Skully. Derwood Cann thought that the bivouac area, in open fields south of the CP, was far too hastily organized. "The troops were exhausted and many went to sleep without even 'digging in.' No fire plan was used and few patrols sent forward of the immediate area. Some of our people didn't even know that the password for D+1 was 'Uncle – Sam.'"

The night was cold, misty, and wet, forcing Bill Galbraith to share his gas cape with replacement Pvt David Phillips (S-1). Bill and Dave had known each other since high school and had jumped together from the same plane as Capt Kiley. At around 0130hrs, vivid green tracer fire could be seen arching into the night sky to the west. During the early hours, Pfc Frank Lujan (I Co 3 Ptn) was sent out on a recon with several others. During the patrol they came under fire on a couple of occasions and just before dawn, S/Sgt Frank Rick was killed, quite possibly by friendly fire. Several enormous explosions were heard coming from the city as the enemy blew up an electrical substation along Boschdijk, containing 10,000 liters of oil, and the Deutsche Reichspost (German Postal Service Office) on Dommelstraat.

During the night Maj Horton received orders from Regiment to be prepared to attack Eindhoven early the next morning. The plan was to advance the four miles into the city, with 3rd Bn spearheading the advance. The following morning the first jeeps and horse-drawn carts began to arrive after being ferried across the canal on the makeshift rafts.

Assaulting Eindhoven

At 0600hrs on Monday September 18, 3rd Bn kicked off the regimental assault on Eindhoven. The enemy were already withdrawing from the city to the southwest in an attempt to stem the British advance. Forming an extended line straddling the highway, H and I Co led the assault with G and HQ Co following behind in reserve.

Jim Melhus and Audrey Lewallen decided to test their machine gun and thought that a rabbit scampering around a nearby field would make a convenient target: "We fired a short burst at the unsuspecting animal and in the process managed to scare the heck out of everyone around us!" Bringing up the rear, accompanied by the Dutch, were 2nd Bn, Regt HQ and Regt HQ Co, and, last but not least, 1st Bn. The commander of 1st Bn, Maj LaPrade, had been given temporary responsibility for the regiment.

Everything and anything that was available, from ladies' bicycles to prams, was used by the Americans to transport equipment. Farm carts were enthusiastically driven by local farmers and many self-proclaimed "resistance" workers had been enlisted to carry heavy equipment and ammunition.

Capt John Kiley and 1st Lt Cann gathered their respective departments and started south towards Woensel. The initial advance had been split into four phase lines with the fourth being Vlokhoven, a suburb of Woensel. In 1944, the main road was known as Eindhovenscheweg; outside the city it was fashioned from compacted sand, but from Vlokhoven it was brick-paved with wide sidewalks. "We were spread out along both sides of the road about 15 minutes ahead of the battalion," recalled Bill Galbraith. "I was on the left and Kiley the right; ultimately it was our job to locate any potential enemy threats and maintain cohesion between H and I Company by radio."

As the advance party moved out, the two rifle companies deployed into the potato and beetroot fields on either side of the road. Along the route at regular intervals were air-raid trenches that had been dug for public use, and signs reading '*Nur Nachts Fahren*' (German for 'Drive only at night'). The men also noticed that all the streetlights and many trees by the road had been painted with thick white bands to aid with night vision during the blackout.

At 0730hrs, Kiley's patrol had not gone far when it came under sporadic rifle fire 600 yards north of Vlokhoven. "Although one member of our group was wounded," recalls Cann, "we took cover in a nearby ditch and sent a contact report back to battalion via our SCR300 radio operator – assessing the enemy strength over on our left to be possibly one platoon."

At that moment both assault companies came under fire with H Co 1 Ptn bearing the brunt east of the highway. In contrast to what was happening up front, Jim Melhus and his colleagues from HQ Co were relaxing and drinking cups of fresh milk handed to them by a local farmer. As 1 Ptn worked their way through the fields near Tempel, they came to a tall thick hedge. The barrier was almost impenetrable except for a hole about the width of a man in the center. "First to go through the opening was our lead scout Pvt Charles (Charlie) Kier, who was immediately shot in the chest," recalls Hank DiCarlo. Taking a deep breath DiCarlo flung himself through the gap, narrowly missing Kier, and landed heavily on the other side in a deep drainage ditch. Kier was gasping for air, due to a gaping exit wound in his back. In front of Hank was a large field full of potatoes. "One after another, amid sporadic bursts of enemy machine-gun fire, about a dozen of our guys came diving through the hedge, including aid man Pfc Lloyd Carpenter. Moments later, as Lloyd was patching Charlie up, a couple of medics from the battalion came tumbling into the ditch, carrying a stretcher. After Charlie was secured they began to manhandle him back through the hedge. When one aid man inadvertently stood up we cringed but nothing happened. The enemy gun team allowed the first aid guys to carefully slide Charlie to safety without firing a single shot."

While this was happening, Lt Bolte noticed a small section of exposed wire fence further along the hedgerow, and decided it was an ideal spot to gain entry to the potato field. The NCOs told him it was foolhardy but, perhaps anxious to prove himself, Rudie took no notice. Grabbing hold of the wire with both hands, he bravely swung forward into the field, whereupon a single bullet pierced the front of his helmet, killing him instantly.

Back in the potato field, the men were fighting for their lives as Hank DiCarlo vividly recalls:

Immediately to our front was a building, and directly behind that an open-ended barn and two enormous haystacks. Lieutenant Forney, myself, Pvt James "Sharkey" Tarquini, Pfc Bill Briggs, Pfc Godfrey "Jon" Hanson, and Pfc Glenn Sweigart were attempting to outflank the machine gun when we came under fire from somewhere behind the haystacks. The house was empty but as we moved closer to the barn the shooting intensified. Next to the house was a large pile of bricks. As I darted behind the stack, a ricochet hit me and sliced open the flesh on my collarbone. Lt Forney was in front with Sharkey, when he was shot and collapsed, while the rest of us returned fire. After seeing Forney go down, Sharkey displayed incredible courage and sprinted into the house. Using his rifle as a battering ram, he smashed through a rear window, ran around the side of the building and successfully neutralized the enemy.

Afterwards, Tarquini, who was from Boston, explained to us what had happened. At the back of the house there was a three-foot-high packing crate, pushed against a wall under the window. Holding his M1 across his body, the diminutive Tarquini jumped onto the crate and catapulted through the glass frame. Once outside, he ran into an alleyway where he killed four Germans, who had been shooting at us from behind one of the haystacks – truly amazing. Rough and ready, a superb scout, Sharkey was never officially recognized for his bravery on that day or any other. We always pulled his chain by saying that he was just "too darn ugly" to get a medal.

Second platoon was right behind 1 Ptn when Pfc Charles Deem was killed and squad leader Sgt Bill Cumber was riddled across the chest by machine-gun fire. "As we were waiting for medic Lloyd Carpenter to arrive, Cumber told me 'he was hit bad and having trouble breathing' but although seriously wounded he survived," recalls Ken Johnson.

Meanwhile, anxious to keep up the momentum, 1st Lt Roy Kessler came forward with 1/Sgt Gordon Bolles to where Bolte had been trying to slide under the fence. "We realized that the enemy machine gun had the spot zeroed and I tried to stop Kessler from doing the same thing as Lieutenant Bolte," recalled Bolles. "As he reached out and grabbed the wire, the enemy gun opened up, hitting him in both arms." Kessler returned to duty several months later only to be killed during the Battle of the Bulge.

"Being the assistant for 3 Ptn, the company called me over to take command after Rudie and Dave got hit," recalls Bob Stroud. "When I arrived most of the guys were still pinned down in the ditch but there was another channel running to the right, along which S/Sgt Frank Padisak had managed to crawl. I told Sgt Don Zahn to lay down a base of 60mm mortar fire and before we started to move, organized some additional fire support from a soldier with a Browning Automatic Rifle (BAR). We were just getting ready to attack when someone told me that Padisak had silenced the enemy gun – which was the best news I'd had all day." The bravery of James "Sharkey" Tarquini and Frank "the Slovak" Padisak clearly won the morning but the platoon hated to lose Rudie Bolte and Dave Forney at such an early stage. Forney was so seriously injured that it took him several years to recover from his wounds. Bob Stroud stayed, and capably led 1 Ptn through Holland and the remainder of the war. "Dark-haired and athletic, Lt Stroud was seemingly unflappable," recalled Hank DiCarlo. "He knew the score, and believed strongly in an aggressive patrolling policy."

It seemed to John Kiley that the battalion's advance along Vlokhovenseweg was fragmenting into chaos. Several accidents happened as the soldiers misunderstood what they were being told by the Dutch. In one incident, 26-year-old Adri Luykx was shot dead, despite the fact that he was clearly wearing a white PAN armband. Tragically for Adri, the only officially sanctioned armband at that time was orange, with the word "ORANJE" stencilled on in black letters.

As if to make matters worse, all radio contact had been lost with Maj Horton, whose last known position was with G Company, which was at the rear and still in reserve. "The captain sent me back with a clear message for Major Horton," recalls Bill Galbraith. "Kiley wanted him to order H Company to get the hell back on line or the entire battalion would be flanked! I nodded and ran north along the sidewalk for about 100 yards, where I bumped into my old buddy from I Company, Jim Brown, who was now a radio operator with 2 Ptn. I figured it would be quicker for Jim to make the call, as if Major Horton had personally given him the order. He grinned and got on the net to H Company." Brown had just finished speaking when a bullet smashed into the handset only inches from his face. "It scared the hell out of me," recalls Galbraith, "but Jim seemed completely unshaken as he unslung his rifle, said 'See ya later' and walked away."

By the time Galbraith returned to Kiley, battalion HQ had moved forward to Vlokhoven Girls School and established a CP beside a burnt-out German halftrack. As Kiley and Cann were discussing the situation, a disturbing radio message arrived stating that H Co's 1 Ptn was pinned down, and had taken several serious casualties amongst the officers. Moments later, Maj Horton arrived at the CP and immediately sent Derwood Cann back to H Company for a situation report.

Two hundred yards beyond the halftrack, on the eastern side of the street, was the Catholic Church of Onze Lieve Vrouw van Lourdes

(Our Dear Lady of Lourdes). Built during the 1920s, the neo-gothic-style bell tower overshadowed the surrounding area and was known locally as the Vlokhoven Tower. Galbraith took cover in a ditch close to Kiley, then looked on as the lanky officer walked across the street, and stood obstinately in full view, studying the church and road ahead. Even though the captain's bars on Kiley's helmet had been painted out, he could ill-afford to be reckless, "'Sir,' shouted Galbraith, 'Sir – if you don't get back into cover right now you are going to get your ass shot off by a sniper!'" The boss looked back and replied, "'If I get down, Bill, so will everyone else." Moments later John Kiley was struck in the neck by a single bullet and collapsed, his wound pumping out blood.

Galbraith instinctively placed several rounds from his M1 into the arched openings high up on the northern side of the bell tower. Other soldiers quickly followed suit and Galbraith used the opportunity to check on Kiley, who was dead. "I spotted S/Sgt Jerry Beam (I Co 2 Ptn) sheltering in the front garden of the next terraced house," recalls Bill. He asked Beam if he could join I Company for a short while. "Jerry sympathetically welcomed me and pointed out that Bill Weber and George McMillan had already gone ahead towards Woensel to scout a route. That was good enough for me, so I took off and headed for the church."

The heavy double doors at the base of the church tower were closed as Galbraith recalls: "Turning the handle I pushed like crazy but nothing happened. Losing patience, I fired several times into the latch with my pistol before trying to barge the wooden doorway with my shoulder. As the door flexed against its hinges, I was thrown backwards into the street, landing unceremoniously on my butt. It was only years later, I learned that the doors opened outwards and were not even locked at the time!"

About a dozen soldiers approached the church as Galbraith headed off along the street to look for his friends. Moments later, Father Eduardus Odemaere emerged, followed by a small number of civilians who had been sheltering inside. When the priest was asked about the sniper, he told the Americans that the tower had been unoccupied. However, the civilians had seen a German soldier running across the open fields directly behind the church. It soon became apparent that the fatal shot had been fired from the shrubbery on the northern side of the tower.

D-Day in Vlokhoven

On the afternoon of September 17, several trucks carrying German soldiers had arrived in Vlokhoven from the direction of Son. The vehicles stopped near the windmill on Anna Mariaweg to unload the wounded into a nearby house. Not long afterwards a couple of halftracks, each towing an 88mm gun, clattered into the large open square. The Germans demanded assistance to manipulate the two guns into position but the locals hid in their homes to avoid confrontation.

On the western side of the square, across the road from Vlokhoven Girls School, a group of very young-looking soldiers were sitting on the sidewalk. Wrapped in blankets, the youths were seen to be shivering as their colleagues pushed the artillery pieces into place. The two fearsome guns, one antiaircraft and the other antitank, had most probably arrived during *Dolle Dinsdag* and may have belonged to Flak-Brigade 18, part of Kampfgruppe Köppel. One of the cannons was positioned at the southwestern end of the square's central reservation, while the other 88 was placed in the slip road, diagonally behind the first gun.

As it became dark the Germans evacuated the area, sending the civilians to a large barn at Toonders farm, in Anna Mariaweg. The guns fired over the tops of the houses towards Son for nearly two hours before being withdrawn. Wim Klerkx was evacuated along with his family, who lived in one of the terraced houses on the square. He recalls, "As the guns were firing the sound reminded me of a bed sheet being ripped in half. Bizarrely all the windows in our row remained intact, while other houses further along the street had theirs blown in, leaving the curtains fluttering in the breeze."

3rd Bn 506th line of advance into Eindhoven, September 18, 1944

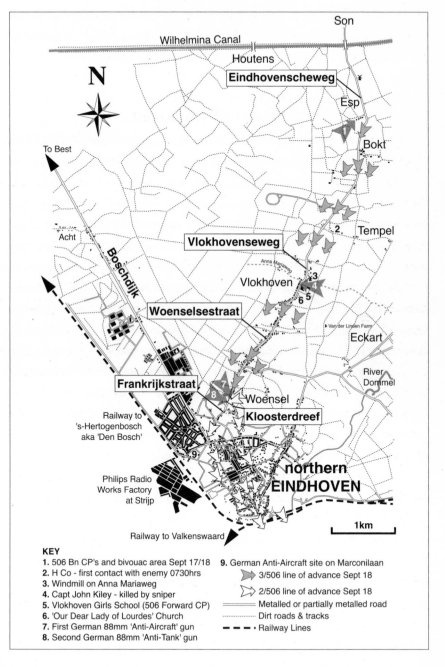

KEY

1. 506 Bn CP's and bivouac area Sept 17/18
2. H Co - first contact with enemy 0730hrs
3. Windmill on Anna Mariaweg
4. Capt John Kiley - killed by sniper
5. Vlokhoven Girls School (506 Forward CP)
6. 'Our Dear Lady of Lourdes' Church
7. First German 88mm 'Anti-Aircraft' gun
8. Second German 88mm 'Anti-Tank' gun

9. German Anti-Aircraft site on Marconilaan
   3/506 line of advance Sept 18
   2/506 line of advance Sept 18
   Metalled or partially metalled road
   Dirt roads & tracks
   Railway Lines

When the 88mm guns were being withdrawn, one of the halftracks broke down on waste ground adjacent to the school and its gun had to be hitched to a horse and towed away. When the cannon reached Woenselsestraat, 11-year-old Albert Roxs was watching: "A group of German soldiers had commandeered a large carthorse but seemed unable to harness the animal correctly. After unsuccessfully trying to cajole the beast into moving any further, the soldiers gave up and reluctantly manhandled the gun along the street."

Directly after the guns were moved, the Klerkx family returned to their home. About 20 minutes later, two German soldiers arrived on bicycles and dropped thermite charges into the abandoned halftrack, which erupted in a shower of brilliant light. After the intense fire had burned itself out, Jos Klerkx, who was 12-years-old at the time, recalled: "An eerie silence settled over the community and we went to bed wondering just what the next day would bring. The following morning my father took me, along with my older brother Wim and our two sisters, to a special holy mass at the church. During the service we began to hear small-arms fire coming from the street. Luckily the building had a back door, which allowed most of the congregation to escape."

Because the Klerkx family lived on the other side of the square, they had no choice but to remain with Father Odemaere and an altar boy. "We could hear bullets striking the outside walls and when one of the windows shattered, the priest ushered us through the sacristy and into the cellar of his house," recalled Jos.

When the shooting stopped, he went outside and quickly returned excitedly shouting, "The Tommies are here, the Tommies are here," not realizing that they were Americans. Elated we emerged from the cellar and began shaking hands with the soldiers who were moving into town along both sides of the street. We ran across the road to see if mum was OK. She had been watching everything from the house and for a moment thought that the Americans were actually German reinforcements!

In the meantime the entire neighborhood came out to welcome the liberators. My mother brewed cups of Ersatz tea and made sure that it was served in our very best china. There were still pockets of enemy resistance and every time the shooting started we were sent inside. The Americans generously handed out packets of cigarettes and my dad shared his first "Lucky Strike" with me but halfway through I felt sick and had to stop. One soldier offered us sweets and was amused to discover that we couldn't pronounce the words "chewing gum." By now all of the kids were looking for souvenirs such as American flag armbands and chocolate. As one guy gave me a handful of cartridges, he joked, "Young man these are a souvenir for Hitler." Another paratrooper gave me a jump knife, but my mother forced me to give it back. Mum placed a chair outside our house and Captain Robert Harwick came over and sat down. I asked him about the insignia on his collar and he unclipped one of the silver bars and gave it to me. All these years later I still have them, a treasured souvenir from an amazing day.

The euphoria of liberation

After four years, four months, and one day of German occupation, the Dutch could barely contain themselves. It was Bob Harwick's first experience of a true Dutch "freedom" welcome as he recalls: "Fruit, flowers, sandwiches of dark bread, kisses in abundance, waving Dutch flags or bits of orange cloth, and such crowds that it became almost impossible to conduct our advance with safety. People were running trying to touch us, yelling happily at the top of their lungs. Apples, peaches, water, milk, juice, and trays of foaming Heineken 'Bier' were all given to us. It was clear that the Dutch hated the Germans but their love for America seemed beyond our comprehension. The Germans we had met so far didn't have the same spirit as those we'd encountered two months previously in Normandy."

When things began to calm down, Jos Klerkx recovered an axe from the incinerated halftrack as a souvenir. By midday Col Chase (Regt

XO) had established a forward CP inside the Girls School and young Klerkx went over to see what was going on. Walking past a pile of captured German rifles and equipment, Jos bumped into 28-year-old Dutch Liaison Officer Lt Martien du Bois (although he did not realize it at the time). Du Bois explained to Klerkx that his family came from a town called Voorne Putten, and asked if he knew how the war was going there: "It was too far away for me to really know anything about, so I went home to ask my parents. While I had been at the CP my mother had noticed a couple of enemy soldiers entering the air-raid shelter (*schuilkelder*) at the back of our house and sent me back to tell the Dutch lieutenant. I returned with a couple of Americans, one of whom bravely went into the refuge, but it was empty. As a precaution the other shelters in the neighborhood were inspected. Tragically two civilians were badly injured when a grenade was thrown into a shelter on Anna Mariaweg."

Now and then US medical jeeps rigged with stretchers passed through Vlokhoven carrying the wounded towards Son. During the clean-up operation around the village, 3rd Bn captured about 50 Germans, some of whom were wearing civilian clothes. Despite the fact that Capt Kiley's body was still lying in the road covered by a blanket, the celebratory mood continued throughout the day. Around 1300hrs, a group of PAN members arrived at the CP towing a trailer piled with bloodsoaked German corpses and offloaded them into an open area behind the school. As the day wore on more enemy corpses were brought to the school and placed under a large tarpaulin out the back. That evening, wrapped in a groundsheet, John Kiley's body was taken to the school and carefully placed on the ground a short distance away from the other corpses. As the sun was setting, Jos Klerkx visited the outdoor mortuary. "Although I felt a deep sadness for Captain Kiley, I also remember thinking that the Germans were also someone's loved ones and perhaps forced into a war they neither wanted nor believed in."

The Van der Linden farm was situated 300 yards southeast of the church in Stoutheuvelstraat. Jo van der Linden was 16-years-old at the time of the liberation, and wanted to know more about what was happening:

> After the drop we got out our wireless set which had been hidden in a wardrobe and tuned into Radio Oranje. Amongst other things the public information broadcast told us to stay away from all windows and to make use of the bilingual phrasebooks carried by the Allied soldiers.
>
> We milked the cows early and as usual placed the churns by the side of the road but nobody from the milk factory arrived to collect them. After breakfast, I went to our barn with my dad and my brother, where we could see clearly for about a mile beyond the windmill, across open fields towards Tempelstraat.
>
> After hearing sporadic bursts of gunfire in the distance, we opened the barn doors so that the Americans would see it was empty. Over to our left behind the church we saw a couple of German soldiers running alongside a hedge just as a barrage of artillery shells exploded nearby. In the distance we noticed American troops patrolling across the open fields from the direction of Tempel. My father thought it would be safer to stay at the barn and wait for the soldiers to come to us. As soon as the paratroopers were close enough we called out to them that we were Dutch and after the soldiers cleared the barn we offered them all fresh milk. The commander pulled out his phrasebook and by pointing to the relevant words, we were able to indicate where we had seen the two German soldiers earlier.
>
> After handing my father some chocolate and a packet of cigarettes, the Americans moved south towards Nieuwedijk and Woensel. They left behind a camera and a pair of binoculars and my mother told me not to bring them into the house because she thought the Germans might return and punish us. Later around 9.30am a second group of paratroopers [probably RHQ] arrived at the farm. The man in charge asked if he could requisition my father's horse and cart. Out of concern for his property, dad requested to go with the Americans but they politely refused.

Two soldiers appeared outside Albert Roxs' house at 43 Woenselsestraat. One of the men spoke to Albert's mother in Dutch and explained that his name was du Bois, and he had been assigned to the 101st Airborne Division with the DLM. The task of the DLM was to advise Gen Taylor on resistance capabilities, support divisional operations, and co-ordinate the actions of local resistance groups. In case of emergency, the team had been issued with 5,000 guilders (a substantial sum at the time given that the average weekly wage was around 40 guilders). Unfortunately the transmitter that would have provided "Daniel's" vital radio link to London had been lost on the drop. Albert's parents invited the men inside and explained about the 88mm guns and also that a small number of Germans had been billeted in the Boys School further along the street.

The battle rages on

Earlier, at around 0800hrs that morning, G Company had been pulled out of reserve and ordered to sweep beyond the right flank of I Company, who had just lost Pvt Victor Deluca. During the engagement, replacement officer 1st Lt Fred Gibbs was killed and Pvt Isaac Brownlow badly wounded in the knee. Derwood Cann believed that the company should have made a wider sweep in order to hit the enemy harder on its extreme left flank. This movement he felt would have relieved pressure on Andy Anderson and enabled I Co to resume their advance.

One hour later, at around 0900hrs, the leading elements of both rifle companies, along with elements of Regt HQ, were pinned down by machine-gun fire as they struck the German main line of resistance a few yards into Woenselsestraat. One of the first casualties of the firefight was Capt Gene Brown (commander of Regt HQ Co), who was wounded in the shoulder and had to be evacuated on a farm cart.

It was not long before 3rd Bn encountered the two 88mm cannons that had been moved from Vlokhoven. The first, a Flak 18 standard antiaircraft version developed by Krupp in 1932, was located on the eastern side of the street outside the Firma AA Notten grocery store, between Tonnaerstraat and Kloosterdreef.★ The AA gun was capable of throwing 15 21¼lb projectiles up to a height of 35,000 feet in one minute.

The second gun – a static Flak 18 AT variant with armored shield – was located 150 yards behind the first, in an open area between two houses opposite Kloosterdreef, on the western side of the street. Under normal circumstances the AT gun (which could penetrate four inches of steel plate at 2,200 yards) would have been dug in up to the level of its armored shield. However, both guns were boldly sited, firing on a flat trajectory along the two streets.

Pfc John Agnew from Regt HQ Co got mixed up with Bill Weber and George McMillan as they were trying to find a way of outflanking the first mobile gun in Woenselsestraat. "Agnew had been wounded in the foot by another machine gun firing from a nearby basement window," recalled McMillan. "We helped him into an empty building where our company medic, Bill Kidder, was able to administer first aid."

McMillan and Weber ran down a side street into an empty house. "The door was unlocked so we went upstairs but were unable to see the '88' or any other enemy movement," recalled McMillan. "Returning to the street we fired three white phosphorous grenades over the rooftops into the vicinity of the guns, hoping to get lucky."

Almost all the houses and shops along Woenselsestraat had front doors that opened onto the sidewalk. Fred Bahlau was inside another house providing fire support. "I couldn't believe it when a lady came up to put a first aid dressing on my leg and then proceeded to repair my trousers that had been ripped on the drop!"

Harassment from the enemy machine guns forced many to seek shelter in the recessed doorways along Woenselsestraat. A light machine

---

★ Throughout the area, the family business of Firma operated a chain of 19 independent stores outside of the Philips Cooperative controlled areas. The shop at 441 Woenselsestraat was easily recognizable by the large exterior sign advertising the German detergent brand Persil.

gun from I Co's 3 Ptn began to return fire, as the first shell screamed in from the 88mm gun further along the street. Around 0845hrs, Jim Melhus was about to run forward, to see what was going on. "Cpl Lewallen stopped me and said that there would be a couple more to follow. Before I had a chance to go any further, sure enough two more shells exploded ahead of our position."

Still in search of his comrades, Bill Galbraith took cover in the entrance of the nearest house. "A shell from the first '88' struck the building across the street scattering debris everywhere. Pvt Earl Copperstone (I Co 2 Ptn) was nearby and idiotically announced 'that was pretty close wasn't it'? 'Close, close … it sure as hell was' I shouted in disbelief as he took off toward the rear!" Seconds later, another high-velocity projectile hit the same building but this time the explosion sent Galbraith tumbling into the street. The force of the blast crushed Bill's left leg, shredding everything below the knee. Fearful of the enemy machine-gun fire, Galbraith tried desperately to drag himself back to safety when a third shell impacted close by: "I was hit in the shoulder by shrapnel, which completely paralysed my right arm. Ploughing through broken glass and debris, I painstakingly pushed myself backward along the sidewalk with one hand, and managed to get into the doorway of the next house."

The owner of the property grabbed Galbraith by his equipment straps and hauled him inside. "Bill Kidder came rushing through the open door closely followed by Jim Brown and Joe Madona," recalled Bill. "Kidder injected me with morphine and as he was bandaging my leg, commented that 'my war was now over.' I thanked the Dutch guy, whose name was Peter Klompmaker, for rescuing me. As Jim and Joe Madona left the house, I handed my cherished Colt .45 (that I had taken from 1st Lt Kenneth Christianson at Bloody Gully) to Joe and wished them both luck."

Ray Skully was wounded during the same shelling, while traveling with Maj Horton in his jeep. "I was hit in the upper left side of my chest by shrapnel. The major stopped the vehicle and helped me to the ground. Fighting for breath, I could hear a rasping sound coming from a small hole. After staggering across the street, somebody placed me on a bed in a nearby house. A chaplain arrived to give me last rites and I remember asking sarcastically, 'Just how bad do you think this is?' Not long afterwards a medic turned up and sealed the sucking chest wound with a field dressing."

The 88mm guns were soon outflanked and silenced by patrols from D and F Company, led by Maj Charles Shettle (now 2nd Bn XO). Earlier, while Ed Shames and John van Kooijk were interrogating a group of German prisoners near Kloosterdreef, Van Kooijk had been approached by Shettle and local man Henk Staals, looking for advice on the best way to access the guns. It was decided that Staals and another local man, Piet Pulles, would guide two squads in an assault. Robert Modracec, an enlisted man from D Company, died on his way into the attack after tripping on a curb outside the Café Monopole, and causing one of his grenades to detonate.

Before being overrun, the breach of the gun outside the grocery store was spiked by the crew using a stick grenade. After capture, the barrel of the "88" was swung through 180 degrees, away from the direction of advance. The crew of the second gun, at Kloosterdreef, fled west into the cornfields but, with help from the locals, they were safely rounded up. While all this was going on, 2nd Bn made a wide sweep around the obstacles to the east and smashed through the German right flank into the city, putting an end to any further organized resistance.

As soon as it was safe, Galbraith and Skully were evacuated by jeep to the hospital at Son, where the previous evening the 326th Medical Company had established a medical facility. Five spacious tents had been erected in the gardens behind the main hospital next to an enormous red cross laid out on the ground, supposedly to protect the patients and staff from air attack.

Bill Galbraith was initially placed in one of the tents. "When bullets started coming through the canvas roof, I thought I was never going to get out of the country alive. German prisoners carried the wounded into the sanitarium and slid us underneath the beds for safety. I couldn't believe my eyes when Pete Klompmaker turned up. Pete had braved his way through a German counterattack and crossed the canal to see if I was OK. 'Do you think you could fetch me a drink of milk?' I asked. 'Sure' he replied smiling, 'Don't go away.' The intrepid Dutchman soon returned with a large glass of fresh warm milk, which at that moment seemed to me to be the very best thing I'd ever tasted."

Later the same day a visiting clergyman asked Galbraith about his religion. "I told him that I was Catholic and he wandered off saying that he had something for me. The priest returned with a rosary and as he placed the wooden beads around my neck, I made a promise (which I have kept to this day) never to lose them."

A short while later Galbraith was transferred to a British field hospital in Belgium.

> I was being transported with six other casualties when the British ambulance in which we were travelling drove into what we thought was a huge firefight. The ambulance stopped suddenly and the driver got out. I'll never forget this but the guy opened up the back doors and said casually, "Relax lads don't worry, we're just waiting for an ammunition truck to explode!"
>
> After the British ammo truck blew up, we were able to reach our destination. I was reassessed and sent to Brussels to have my leg plastered before being returned to the UK. In England the doctors removed the cast and put me in traction. One night I woke up to find maggots crawling all over my injured leg. I couldn't move and cried out for help. One of the nurses who came to my aid told me that this sort of thing was quite common! After that they operated on my shoulder, which miraculously returned full movement to my right arm.

Several weeks later in November, Galbraith found himself on the US Army Hospital Ship *Larkspur* bound for Charleston, South Carolina. Only recently converted, the steamer *Larkspur* had the capacity to transport and care for nearly 600 patients. Built in 1901, the former cargo ship had originally been an auxiliary vessel in the Imperial German Navy. "At times during the painfully slow ten-day crossing the weather was rough," recalls Bill.

On one particular night, storm water came crashing through an open porthole and washed me out of my bunk onto the guy below. The next night during further bad weather, I accidentally tipped my piss pot on the same guy, who needless to say was not at all impressed with me.

After the ship docked in Charleston, the medics fitted a new cast before transporting me to Hammond General Hospital in Modesto, California. My folks came to visit just before Christmas. It was quite a journey for my mom who traveled over 300 miles by train from Long Beach. In January 1945, I was moved to Dibble General Hospital at Menlo Park and then to McCormack in Pasadena, which was much closer to home. Amongst other things, McCormack specialized in orthopaedic surgery and after a lengthy period of rehabilitation I was discharged in June 1947. Ironically the financial impact of being busted from technical sergeant (T/4) to private first class before Holland cost me nearly $2,000 in back pay. However, on a brighter note, Anna Nertney, whom I had met on leave in Scotland after Normandy, wrote me the whole time and eventually I plucked up courage and proposed. The following Christmas in 1948, Anna came to the States and one week later we were married.

Cam Pas and his family lived at 247 Boschdijk in Woensel:

On the morning of September 18, as my mother and I were visiting a local bakery [on De Ruyterstraat] a wounded German soldier came over and asked if we knew where the English were. Pointing towards the center of the city, my mum sent the man on his way. Earlier, around 11am, we saw a British scout car coming from Eindhoven driving across Boschdijk. When we returned home, four resistance men arrived in the street wearing blue overalls, black helmets, and orange brassards. Two of the men took cover in a nearby doorway next to the Obam Garage, while the others hid across the road on the corner of De Ruyterstraat.

We had just heard that several enemy soldiers had been wounded, while manning the two 88mm guns at Kloosterdreef and Woenselsestraat. A local businessman, Mr Erkamps, volunteered to transport one of the wounded crewmen on his bakfiet cargo bicycle to the Binnenziekenhuis Hospital in Eindhoven.* As Mr Erkamps was riding down the street, a German motorcycle and sidecar approached from behind. We fled around the back of our house when the PAN guys opened fire on the motorbike. As the rider accelerated, the soldier sitting in the sidecar flipped a grenade towards the two men firing from the doorway. Erkamps wasn't quick enough and the blast from the grenade severely injured his left leg (which was later amputated). As we waited on the pavement for the Red Cross to arrive, my mum ignored the wounded German (who was still lying on the bakfiet) and gave Mr Erkamps a pillow and blanket.

Meanwhile 2nd Bn was moving around 3rd Bn's left flank into Eindhoven. The link-up with the British seemed imminent when, at 1230hrs, after a brief radio conversation with XXX Corps, Col Sink and BrigGen Gerald Higgins (Asst 101st Divisional Commander) rendezvoused with a recon patrol from the Household Cavalry at a small crossroads northwest of Vlokhoven. In reality the main body of XXX Corps were still several hours away from their official rally point at the Sint Joris Church in southern Eindhoven.

A friend of John van Kooijk volunteered to guide Col Strayer – who had now caught up with his battalion – through the city to the bridges over the Dommel. As Strayer made his way into Eindhoven,

---

* The bakfiet was a type of industrial tricycle with two wheels at the front supporting a 6ft-long high-sided wooden box on a frame.

2nd Bn came under accurate fire from snipers hiding high up in the Oude Toren church tower near Kerkstraat.

Shortly after the two 88mm guns at Woensel were silenced, Van Kooijk happened to mention the telephone service network operated by the Philips Corporation to Ed Shames: "John asked if we knew anything about the telephone lines, which of course we didn't. I was amazed to learn the Germans were also unaware of the network and that the southern command had been exchanging sensitive information via the system for the last couple of years. I didn't waste any time and took 'John the Dutchman' straight to Col Sink. The colonel was keen to exploit the opportunity and immediately attached the two of us to Bill Leach (Regt S-2) and Bob Moon (Regt Commo) as kind of 'unofficial' liaison officers for the regiment."

Earlier that Sunday morning Jenny Soon's mother, Adolphina, had cycled to Vlokhoven to collect fresh milk for Jenny's younger sisters Gerry and Nelly. Before reaching the village, Adolphina was stopped at a German roadblock along Woenselsestraat and told to go home. Across the street from Jenny's house on Boschdijk was the Obam Garage:

We had seen a group of very young Germans peering out from behind the windows. After the resistance shootout which resulted in Mr Erkamps being injured they looked worried and were clearly uncertain of what to do. My dad quietly motioned for them to back away from the windows and remain inside. I think he didn't want to see these boys hurt unnecessarily and felt it might be better to hand them over to the Americans rather than the PAN men who were still in position at the corner of the street. A short while later the Americans came in from Frankrijkstraat and walked past our house. Once it was safe, my dad told the paratroopers about the Germans hiding above the garage, who surrendered without a single shot needing to be fired.

As the day wore on scores of ammunition trucks began to arrive along Boschdijk. The vehicles, which were most probably from the American

QM Truck Company, had come from the center of Eindhoven and were now congesting both lanes of the highway outside Jenny's house. "Most of the drivers were African-American, which caused quite a panic among us kids who thought they were some sort of incarnation of Black Pete!"

Jenny climbed up onto a truck and stared into the face of the driver. Plucking up courage, she rubbed her finger across the man's forearm expecting it to be covered with soot. Shaking her head in disbelief, the soldier grinned and returned the gesture. As Jenny touched the man's hair, he brushed his hands through her long curls and burst into fits of laughter! "After making friends with the African-Americans we stayed outside all day long, shaking hands with every single soldier who passed by. It was an unforgettable afternoon but one of the things that struck me was just how quiet the soles of the American boots were compared to the German hobnailed variety."

～ 6 ～

"A city in chains"

The liberation of Eindhoven – September 18, 1944

Moving through the Philips Wijk, one of the subsidized housing estates along Boschdijk, H Co's 1 Ptn came under fire and Hank DiCarlo witnessed another facet of Sharkey Tarquini's combat awareness:

> Several of us were on one side of the street and Tarquini on the other. The standard procedure when clearing houses was to roll a grenade into a room, then rush in firing immediately after it had exploded. The Germans would sandbag the corner furthest from the door of each defended room. As the grenade was delivered the "bad guys" were expected to dive behind the sandbags, and come up firing as soon as the grenade went off. This procedure somewhat dampened our enthusiasm for rushing through any door and it took us most of the morning to clear our designated buildings. As we walked out into the sunlight, there was Sharkey sitting in a doorway, on the other side of the street, casually smoking a cigarette. Unlike the rest of us he only had one grenade but that didn't bother him in the slightest. Sharkey proceeded to throw his grenade into every room without pulling the pin. When the occupants ducked into the sandbagged area, he simply walked in and shot the inexperienced enemy where they lay … absolutely brilliant and he still had his damn grenade.

Pfc Godfrey "Jon" Hanson was shot in the stomach while house-clearing in the same area and died the following day as Hank DiCarlo recalls: "Jon was such a lovely dependable and sensitive person, who wrote the most amazing poetry, all of us were devastated by his death, especially his best friend Glenn Sweigart."

It suddenly dawned on Ralph Bennett that the Germans were using a nearby church as an observation post (OP): "Using my field glasses, I could see movement from one steeple in particular. After notifying Lt Andros, word came back that we were forbidden to fire on any of the churches with anything other than small arms."

Outside the Catholic seminary on Tongelresestraat, members of PAN were busy shaving the heads of women who had fraternized with the Germans. Fred Bahlau noticed the angry mob jeering at the group of frightened women, nicknamed *moffenmeiden* by the Dutch. "I saw this one pretty girl having her head shaved and thought it was a bullshit thing for these people to do."

More civilians joined forces as the 506th moved deeper into the city. Some were wearing resistance armbands, while others just wanted to be involved in the fight. Many were destined to become scouts, but others offered their services as translators. At the time, very few Dutch spoke English, the exception being teachers, or those who, like 23-year-old Noud Stultiens, had studied the language: "It was about 1pm when I spotted a paratrooper relaxing at the corner of Bilderdijklaan and Stratumseind. Approaching the American, I said in my best textbook English, 'Good afternoon sir and welcome to Eindhoven.'"

The soldier leapt up and rushed Stultiens away to meet Bill Leach: "After a brief interview, I was given a job as an interpreter and my first task was to find a place that had a room and table large enough for the captain to spread out his maps. As my parents' house was not suitable, my friend Mitsy Vosters kindly got her mum and dad to let us use their spacious front room at 109 Stratumseind. My job was then to translate and interpret information coming in from the locals regarding enemy snipers, troop movements, and locations. These were then plotted and relayed via radio to the rifle companies."

Capturing buildings intact such as post offices and telephone exchanges was vitally important, although some, like the Deutsche Reichspost, had already been destroyed. In many instances the Dutch actually hindered combat operations by reporting exaggerated information. Later that afternoon, the intelligence team packed up and headed for the center of town, taking Stultiens with them. "I was issued a 'walkie-talkie' and given the call sign K-4 or Kidnap-4. As the afternoon progressed there were numerous occasions when I was asked to speak directly to a civilian who had been put on the other end of the line. My unforgettable day with the 506th ended around 8pm, after the British Second Army arrived in the city."

Another young man, Leonardus "Leo" Jeucken, lived at Stratum on Leostraat and joined 3rd Bn HQ Company as what the Americans had begun to call an "irregular." The Jeuckens had emigrated to the USA but returned to Eindhoven before the outbreak of World War II. Leo was just 17-years-old, and joined without the knowledge of his parents.

As Harry Clawson and Alex Andros entered the city, they took it in turns running back and forth across Boschdijk, attempting to flush out snipers. "Civilians were emerging from cellars wanting to shake our hands and it was difficult to make them stay down," recalls Andros. Ralph King (one of Andros' men) fired his first shot in anger when Cpl George Montilio ordered him to shoot at a suspicious figure silhouetted behind a nearby window.

After being sent ahead, 2nd Bn was having difficulty communicating but by 1215hrs they managed to get a radio message through to Col Sink, stating that they were now in control of the Dommel bridges.

By 1400hrs enemy resistance in Eindhoven began to collapse. As the crowds gathered, a group of heavily armed PAN men, dressed in characteristic blue boilersuits, brought in five Luftwaffe prisoners and handed them over to a patrol from 2nd Bn. The captives were forced to lay face down on the road at Elzentbrug while their equipment and personal belongings were searched. The prisoners were then marched around the corner to a newly established POW cage at Don Bosco School.

The 2nd Bn were sent to guard the eastern sector of the harbor near the gasworks at Nachtegaallaan, where the Germans had dumped a vehicle in the canal. The largest of the four gas tanks was a local landmark, easily recognizable due to its eye-catching wraparound sign advertising Persil. The remainder of the regiment moved into town following the disused tramlines, establishing their own defensive sectors to southwest.

Jan van Hout was nearly 15-years-old and lived on Leeuwenstraat in the Philips Wijk at Tivoli, southeast of Eindhoven. "Earlier that day, I'd been walking with five friends along a footpath near the woods surrounding Tivoli, when a British jeep fitted for radio (FFR) stopped and an NCO jumped out." The boys were amused to see that the sergeant was using a large-scale map of Eindhoven dated 1926, which did not show Tivoli because the town had been annexed from Geldrop three years later in 1929.

The youths told the British soldier about a German antiaircraft battery 200 yards southeast of De Burg in Stratum. The soldier immediately got on the radio and called for five rounds of high explosive (HE) to be fired onto the site. Later, unbeknown to their parents, the boys headed for the AB Theater as Jan fondly remembers:

Walking along Stratumsdijk we stopped by one of the public air-raid shelters, next to the municipal swimming baths, where we saw our first American soldier. The paratrooper was nonchalantly sitting on top of the shelter cleaning the barrel of his machine gun and excitedly we climbed up to say hello.

Moments later a German lorry with a guard sitting on the front fender came speeding down the road from the south, ahead of the British spearhead... We ran for cover as the paratrooper sprang into action and fired several long bursts into the vehicle as it reached the junction opposite the theater. When the firing stopped we clambered

This photograph, taken well after the construction of the Bailey bridge, clearly shows the access ramp (foreground) along the canal bank used by the 506th PIR to float vehicles and equipment across on the morning of September 18. (Foundation member September 1944 Collection)

Pvt Wilbur Shanklin from RHQ Commo Ptn on a Cushman scooter at the beginning of the regimental assault into Eindhoven. (John Reeder via D-Day Paratroopers Historical Center, St-Côme-du-Mont)

Pvt James "Sharkey" Tarquini (H Co 1 Ptn). This picture was taken in Austria, during a party on June 6, 1945 to celebrate Col Wolverton and his D-Day "one year later" reunion request. (L to R) Bob Hoffman, Bob Vann, "Sharkey," and Lou Vecchi. (Hank DiCarlo)

1st Lt John Reeder's Communications Platoon relaxing with their SCR-694/BC-1306 radio and a GN-58 hand generator in the walled play area behind Vlokhoven Girls School. (L to R) unknown, T/5 Louis Tuttle, T/5 Charles Bolt (not wearing headphones), S/Sgt Richard Roderick, Pvt Wilbur Shanklin (possibly), and unknown. (John Reeder via D-Day Paratroopers Historical Center, St-Côme-du-Mont)

RHQ Commo Ptn digs in on the play area at Vlokhoven Girls School. The bodies of German soldiers were stored behind the shelter (left). The concrete walls have long gone but in 2011 the three-story school building still remains. (John Reeder via Tom Peeters)

Modern view from the base of the church tower across Vlokhoven Square to where John Kiley was killed (the railings and tree in foreground are post-war). Originally on September 17, the two 88mm guns would have been sited on extreme left of the photo.

Now out of action, the first 88mm gun along Woenselsestraat, seen here outside the Firma AA Notten grocery store. The gun crew sabotaged the breach before surrendering – note the rings around the barrel marking 17 previous kills. (Tom Peeters)

ABOVE: A slightly blurred but nevertheless amazing photograph of the second 88mm AT gun positioned along Woenselsestraat, opposite the T-junction with Kloosterdreef after it too was neutralized. (J.J.M Van Kruijsdijk via Tom Peeters)

RIGHT: Captured crewmen, one of whom is wounded, being marched past the gun on Kloosterdreef. (Tom Peeters)

Damage to a house in Kloosterdreef caused by 88mm AT gun in nearby Woenselsestraat. Elements of D and F Co probably used the upper floors of the building to pour direct fire onto the crew during the final stages of the assault. (Tom Peeters)

The first gun was towed away and dumped on nearby waste ground in Hamsterstraat. Local children used the abandoned artillery piece as an adventure playground, until its pilfered remains were broken up after the war. (Piet van Heeswijk via Tom Peeters)

...ented facility belonging to 326th Airborne Medical Company where Bill Galbraith and Ray Skully were both evacuated. Advance ...lements of the 326th operating from the DZ at Helena Hoeve occupied the sanatorium during the afternoon of September 17. ...Heemkundekring Son en Breugel)

Bill Galbraith (far right) recuperating at Hammond General Hospital in 1945. Muscle and tissue were harvested from Bill's legs and back to rebuild his damaged body. (L to R) Bill Colbrook (I Co – wounded at Bastogne), his fiancé Lucy, her sister Jean, and Bill Galbraith. (Bill Galbraith via John Klein)

This photo is believed by the author to be T/4 Alcide Leveille from RHQ Commo Ptn, posing with local man Mr Kluijtmans in front of his house on Frankrijkstraat. Note leather wrist compass hanging from Leveille's left shoulder. (John Reeder via Tom Timmermans)

Photograph of 3/506 taken by teenager Piet van Heeswijk while visiting his fiancé Rieky Janssen, who lived with her family at 82 Frankrijkstraat. (Piet van Heeswijk via Tom Peeters)

is scout car from the Household Cavalry was the first British vehicle to arrive in Vlokhoven around 1300hrs on September 18. is same vehicle later went on to make contact with H/502 at Best. (John Reeder via D-Day Paratroopers Historical Center, -Côme-du-Mont)

J6th PIR commander, Col Robert Sink salutes Gen Taylor as he departs the forward CP at Vlokhoven. Taylor visited the Girls :hool at 1335hrs to advise Sink about relocating to the former German HQ in Eindhoven. (John Reeder via D-Day Paratroopers istorical Center, St-Côme-du-Mont)

Troops from the 506th PIR moving along Frankrijkstraat on their way into Eindhoven. (Tom Timmermans)

Local farmers from Son helping the 506th PIR move supplies and equipment into Eindhoven. (Piet van Heeswijk via Tom Peeters)

Rieky Janssen smiling at the camera hands a peach to a passing soldier from 3/506. (Piet van Heeswijk via Tom Peeters)

A soldier from 3rd Bn, probably from the MG Ptn, advancing along Boschdijk carrying an A-6 machine gun. (Tini van der Voort via Tom Peeters)

The crowds begin to gather as members of 3/506 reach the Texaco Groot Tourisme Service Station at the junction between Boschdijk and Marconilaan. (J. J. M. van Kruijsdijk via Tom Peeters)

Paratroopers from the 506th PIR searching German prisoners near the Philips Company electricity sub station on Lijmbeekstraat just off Boschdijk. (Tom Timmermans)

As German influence collapsed many unofficial "resistance workers" took to the streets such as this group outside the Van Abbe Museum of Art. (Hendrik Beens)

pt William "Bill" Leach, Regimental Intelligence Officer
2). (Currahee Scrapbook)

17-year-old Leonardus "Leo" Jeucken joined 3rd Bn as an irregular and fought with HQ Company up until his death at Opheusden on October 5, 1944. (Bernard Florissen – Opheusden)

/506 gathering in Eindhoven while waiting to be deployed. (Hendrik Beens)

TOP: Troops from 2nd Bn searching POWs at Elzentbrug. Mainly Luftwaffe personnel captured at Hagekampweg-Zuid by the local resistance. Nowadays the bridge is near the finish for the annual Eindhoven Marathon. (Tom Timmermans)

MIDDLE: More prisoners are brought in by the 506th PIR accompanied by Dutch police officers. (Currahee Scrapbook)

BOTTOM: German POWs waiting to be processed outside Don Bosco School (now called De Trinoom) along Bilderdijklaan, not far from the Art Museum. (Tom Timmermans)

TOP: This picture of a 3rd Bn trooper posing with locals at Stratumseind, close to St Catharina Church was taken shortly after the 506th arrived in Eindhoven. A few hours later, when the British arrived, the streets were packed with people. (Tom Peeters)

MIDDLE: Mail clerk, Cpl Richard Stockhouse (left) from Indiana and Assistant S1 2nd Lt John Weisenberger both seem to be enjoying the moment. (Hendrik Beens)

BOTTOM: 24-year-old Cpl Harry Buxton and Sgt Norman Capels are pictured with 22-year-old Francisca Janssen and her sister. Francisca (right). (Hendrik Beens, Tom Peeters, Tom Timmermans, and Jell Jansen)

LEFT: Cpl Nathan Bullock from the Machine Gun Ptn, seen here on the raised lawn outside the Van Abbe Museum of A▮ admiring a pair of souvenir clogs. Bullock is also sporting a lapel broach, which like the shoes was most probably a gif▮ from a member of the local population. (Tom Timmermans▮

ABOVE: A modern view of Den Elzent, which became the command post for Col Sink and Maj Oliver Horton, 3/506, from late afternoon of September 18 to 21.

The Catholic Community Centre on de Wal, became the command post for Regimental HQ Company on September 18. (John Reeder via D-Day Paratroopers Historical Center, St-Côme-du-Mont)

ABOVE: US troops moving through the Demer area which was destroyed during the bombing by the RAF on December 6, 1942. Note the twin towers of the St Catharina Church at Stratumseind in the background. (Tom Peeters)

LEFT: 3rd Bn Executive Officer Capt Robert Harwick (left), Maj Oliver Horton (3Bn commander), and possibly Sgt Donald Embody (HQ Co) touring the Demer area. Note the peach in Harwick's left hand and the .38 Smith & Wesson revolver on Horton's belt. (Tom Timmermans)

Post-war aerial view of Sint Joris College. (Eindhoven Regional Historical Center)

British vehicles trying to enter the city begin to back up along "P.Czn. Hooftlaan." Note the main gate to Den Elzent (506 regimental command post) on far right of picture. (John Reeder via D-Day Paratroopers Historical Center, St-Côme-du-Mont)

back onto the roof of the shelter and watched with anticipation as the smoldering truck began to catch fire. As nobody got out we realized that the German occupants had all been killed. Moments later, a US Military Policeman stepped onto the junction and began to direct the military traffic towards Boschdijk and Son as if nothing had happened.

The 3rd Bn took over the bridges at de Wal and Van Abbe (Elzentbrug) while 1st Bn (who were now in reserve) were handed temporary control of the bridges at Stratumseind. Maj Horton and Col Sink occupied Den Elzent, an imposing property diagonally across the street from the art museum. The large three-story townhouse had previously been the German *Wehrmachtkommandantur* (military headquarters). When Sink arrived at 1740hrs, he received a warm welcome from the town's officials. The colonel then called a battalion commanders' meeting, to begin drawing up defensive plans for the area.

The regiment began to make its home in the wealthy suburbs of Elzent and Villa Park. Regimental HQ Co established a base at the Katholiek Leven ("Catholic Life," the Catholic Community Center and Social Club), on de Wal (where the council offices now stand adjacent to City Hall). Before the liberation, the Katholiek Leven was used as the central bureau for Eindhoven's Luchtbeschermingdienst.

Bobbie Rommel could not believe the reaction from the population: "Scores of people surrounded us, asking if they could help carry the machine guns. Upon reaching the Van Abbe, I instructed my team to set up our gun on one of the traffic islands opposite the museum, amidst the beautifully manicured flowerbeds." The MG Ptn were treated like celebrities as they relaxed on the sloping lawns in front of the museum. Teenage boys and girls moved among the soldiers, asking for autographs and souvenirs. "Afterwards we took up positions further south along the riverbank, where we established a defensive perimeter. My guys had been lucky as we didn't sustain a single casualty on the move into Eindhoven," reflects Bill Wedeking. Executive Officer

Bob Harwick recalls: "We did our best to keep everyone in line but formations were almost impossible, as our soldiers were quite literally dragged away into homes and local bars." By early evening each company had been assigned a sector within the battalion area. Maj Horton and Capt Harwick even found time to tour the bombed-out shopping area at Demer and were greeted by an adoring public.

During the afternoon, 1st Lt Ed Harrell and 2 Ptn were sent back to Eindhoven from Son, and joined the rest of G Company, who were already bivouacked at Sint Joris College (Saint George High School) close to Elzent. The empty college had previously been used by the Germans as a collection centre after *Dolle Dinsdag*. The three rifle companies dug in for the night around the college: "We set up our 60mm mortar on a nearby playing field," recalls Ralph Bennett. Gene Johnson remembers: "Even after we'd dug in, the civilians still kept arriving to say hello and shake our hands." This did not last long because at 1830hrs, after spending a wet night near Valkenswaard, the main body of British armor arrived in Eindhoven. A single column of over 10,000 vehicles and 1,000 tanks met with an overwhelming welcome as the civilians blocked the streets in excitement.

The support begins to arrive

At 1530hrs on D+1, over 400 gliders landed on the LZ at Son, bringing with them 3/327 Glider Infantry Regiment (GIR), an engineer battalion, elements of 377 Parachute Field Artillery Battalion, and the remainder of the medical and signals personnel. Glider pilot 1st Lt Lloyd West from the 442nd TCG, was flying a CG4A Waco as part of Serial A-41:

We took off from Chilbolton, at 1158hrs on September 18. The flight to Son was smooth with good visibility. However, when we arrived over the landing zone at 1514hrs, there was another group trying to land, which confused our final approach. Luckily we could see smoke signals on the ground indicating wind direction, but despite this it was still a struggle to land with our unusually heavy loads. Afterwards, we helped unload our gliders before proceeding to a nearby bivouac area designated for pilots, and signed in for the night. We didn't realize at the time how hard it would be to get transport to the rear. On September 21, we got permission from a British tank officer who took our group out on some of his supply trucks, but they were only going as far as Hasselt in Belgium. From here, we split into smaller teams and worked our way back to Brussels, where we were able to catch flights back to the UK. Our journey was further complicated by the fact that for some reason we were not issued maps and currency for the countries we might be expected to travel through.

Still wearing the girdle given to him by Briggsey, Ben Hiner came in on one of the 22 gliders carrying the 506th vehicle echelon. Before joining the army, Ben had received six months' rudimentary flight training and therefore was able to act as a copilot for the mission. After a rather hairy landing, S/Sgt Hiner helped capture a group of enemy soldiers who were ransacking a glider that had landed the day before. Hiner was sent to the Sint Josef Milk Factory, situated on the banks of the Dommel between de Wal and Paradijslaan.★ The milk factory was situated in the industrial part of town surrounded by several tobacco companies (such as Karel 1 Sigaren, and Mignot en de Block) and a large clothing factory that generated its own power supply. For the next few days the factory became the main collection and distribution point for the 506th PIR's equipment and supplies.

The Medical Detachment (Med Det) occupied an office at the milk plant and soon discovered a vegetable garden at the rear of the building close to the river: "We made a lovely stew that lasted us for a couple of days while we waited for further orders," recalls John Gibson. During

---

★ Built in 1928, at its height the milk plant processed 7,049,276 liters of milk per annum. It closed in 1947.

this period Gibson also found time to practice his hand-balancing tricks with T/4 Dave Marcus (Regt S-3 and runner up in the 1942 "Mr America" contest) on the lawn outside battalion headquarters at Den Elzent. With the mission now "complete" the 506th was expected to secure the flanks of XXX Corps and Second Army as they made their way towards Son. When the British reached Bokt, at 2100hrs, the Royal Engineers immediately set to work constructing a Bailey bridge across the Wilhelmina Canal.

∽ 7 ∽

"The burning sky"

The bombing of Eindhoven – September 19, 1944

The 3rd Bn spent the morning of September 19 improving its defensive positions, patrolling, reorganizing, and cleaning equipment. At 0815hrs, Col Sink and Maj Clarence Hester (Regt S-3) visited the areas held by the regiment and were pleased by what they found. A steady stream of Allied vehicles was now moving northward bringing a range of bridging equipment, cranes, and bulldozers, some of which were destined for Welschap to help rebuild the airfield. Shortly after the main highway was captured by the 506th PIR, it was marked using a club sign but a week later, due to lack of momentum from XXX Corps and Second Army, two more routes were opened through Tilburg (heart) and Helmond (diamond).

Capt Leach was doing his best to disseminate the information coming in from the resistance regarding enemy troop movements. As a result he asked Ed Shames and John van Kooijk for assistance as Ed recalls: "One of John's friends was a local doctor from Veghel, who volunteered to drive us around in his sumptuous black Opel Kapitan, which was originally intended for use by Colonel Sink." Despite these intelligence issues, Eindhoven was still in a celebratory mood but all that changed during the afternoon.

Orange bunting around the city suddenly vanished when forward elements of the German 107th Armored Brigade, led by Maj Freiherr von Maltzahn, were seen in the vicinity of Nederwetten, two miles east of Woensel. Supported by a ferocious armory of Mark V Panther tanks and self-propelled guns, the brigade had recently been rerouted by train from Aachen. Von Maltzahn had orders to capture Sint Oedenrode and cut the Allied supply route to Grave. Unbeknown to the Americans, the immediate threat was not aimed at Eindhoven but the newly built Bailey bridge at Son.

While searching for alternative routes into the city, a recon unit from the 107th Armored Brigade, comprising five half-tracked vehicles, discovered that the bridge over the Dommel near Soeterbeek was a potential crossing point. Courageously, 50-year-old local groundsman, Wilhelmus Hikspoors, took full advantage of the situation, approaching the German recon commander and convincing him that continuing would be pointless, as the bridge could never support the weight of a main battle tank. Hikspoors' cunning and subterfuge paid off as the German commander, not wanting to take unnecessary risks, carefully turned his vehicles around and drove away. Meanwhile, the British, using the railway system at Vaartbroek, managed to transport some of their armor to temporarily counter the enemy threat on the northeastern edge of Eindhoven.

A squadron of tanks from 15/19 Hussars and a recon troop from the Blues and Royals was attached to the 506th PIR. Another squadron from the Hussars went to assist the 502nd, who were still battling the Germans at Best and Sint Oedenrode. A/506 (less one platoon) was attached to the Hussars, forming a mobile task force to patrol the surrounding countryside.

After receiving fresh orders to widen the regiment's defenses, 3rd Bn was sent to the small town of Winterle, six miles west of Eindhoven. At the same time 2nd Bn moved east through the suburb of Tongelre to protect Nuenen and Helmond from Von Maltzahn's brigade.

Hank DiCarlo and his friends were standing around talking in the grounds of Sint Joris College when Pfc Luther Myers ambled over to see what was going on: "We told him that the battalion was now on a 'warning order' for a rapid movement to Winterle," recalls DiCarlo. "Myers told us that he needed to find a latrine before we left and Harry

Clawson pointed towards an old outhouse about 30 yards away." As the men were resuming their conversation, the door of the outhouse flew open and Myers launched himself, pants around ankles, onto the ground. "A split second later, the toilet exploded," recalled Hank. It would seem that as Luther Myers sat down he unwittingly dislodged the pin from a hand grenade hanging from one of his equipment straps and luckily survived to tell the tale.

Around dusk, 3rd Bn marched out of the city along Grote Berg passing the Police HQ, with G Co in front, followed by I Co, HQ Co, and H Co. No forward patrols were sent to Winterle and Derwood Cann was not alone in thinking that a recon should have been made of all the possible approach routes. It was beginning to get dark as the column moved due west through the industrial area at Strijp, over the Beatrix Afwaterings Canal and into the rough open heathland towards the railway and Winterle. As Teddy Dziepak (I Co 1 Ptn) remembered:

> Shortly after leaving the city we came under mortar fire and were maybe 150 yards away from an isolated pocket of enemy troops when they started to withdraw... I got one guy in my sights, squeezed the trigger and he went down. As we pushed forward, I saw that the man who I'd just killed was an officer, and took his Luger pistol as a souvenir. During the same action, my lieutenant was hit in the leg and rapidly began to lose blood. Dressing the wound, I yelled to Pvt Martin Dodge, who was closest, to find a medic. He chose to go the wrong way along a hedgerow, inadvertently exposing himself, and was killed.

Two miles from Winterle, the lead scouts ran into a group of civilians who reported that the Germans had recently pulled out. At 1915hrs, as Maj Horton was deploying his reconnaissance patrols, the battalion was instructed to return to Eindhoven via the airfield. Within minutes of setting off for Welschap, the order was suspended when the unthinkable happened, as Bob Harwick recalled: "The movement was a complete success so far as the enemy withdrawal was concerned. As it was getting dark we heard planes flying overhead and were totally shocked to see lines of parachute flares appearing over Eindhoven. The markers grew brighter and brighter until the whole city was covered in a yellow light that hung suspended like some kind of giant chandelier."

That evening in Eindhoven the streets were jammed with civilians all trying to express their deep gratitude to each and every Allied soldier, as Cam Pas recalled: "We wrote all kinds of good wishes and slogans on the vehicles like, 'Away with the bloody Krauts' and 'Long live Orange.' I handed out peaches (from our own garden) and in return received chocolate, cigarettes, and biscuits." During the celebrations, Frans Kortie climbed up onto a tank with a couple of his friends: "At one point, I became worried that somebody was going to get run over. In my best English, I asked the tank commander to stop but he couldn't understand because he was actually Scottish!" Frans worked for the recently reinstated city council and was asked by his new boss, Mr van Elk, to act as an interpreter for the 506th PIR:

> The regiment needed a point of contact within the council who could speak English, and Van Elk volunteered me for the job. When I arrived at City Hall (which was located in Stratum at that time) the Luftwaffe had already started dropping flares. Many mistook the bright orange lights as fireworks, celebrating the liberation. When the bombs began to fall there was mass panic as everybody ran for the public shelters across the city. A smartly dressed British officer came down into my refuge and demanded in no uncertain terms that he wanted to speak with the mayor. After a brief introduction the officer said that he was the representative for the Dutch military authority in the UK. I was surprised by his aggressive tone and politely replied that "there was nothing we could do right at that moment, due to the fact that there was a bloody air raid going on."

The first flares appeared overhead at about 2030hrs, followed a few minutes later by the bombers. Before long the southern part of the city was in flames, telephone lines were down, and the mains water pressure had failed. Streets close to Col Sink's CP at Den Elzent – such as Bilderdijklaan, Hertogostraat, and Keizersgracht – were badly hit. Eindhoven's Air Defense Platoons were completely overwhelmed when buildings began to collapse, burying dozens of people in the rubble. The AB Theater and part of the municipal gasworks were totally destroyed. Over the next 20 minutes two more raids struck Stratumseind and Vestdijk, annihilating the Van Piere bookshop, damaging St Catharina Church, and blocking vital roads.

A British ammunition truck exploded and set fire to a number of dwellings in Hertogstraat, including the headquarters of the renowned marching band Apollo's Lust. It was virtually impossible to evacuate the residents of the affected areas, even though Sint Joris College had been converted into an emergency reception centre. Even the spirit of Eindhoven, Frits Philips' boyhood home, De Laak on Nachtegaallaan, was damaged by fire. The worst tragedy occurred at the entrance to one of the public shelters on the northern edge of the city at Biesterweg, where almost 50 people were killed.

A large crowd looking for missing relatives began to gather at City Hall. Frans Kortie was the only person from the council who turned up, and he did his utmost to assist the worried families. In total 227 civilians were killed during the bombing, and 800 were wounded. Three men from Regimental HQ were also killed, including Sgt Bill Myers, who three weeks earlier had led the honor guard during the ceremony for the missing at Littlecote House. A Jewish family, the De Wits, who had been in hiding for several years, had been storing their belongings at a friend's house on Potgeiterstraat, which was also destroyed in the bombing.

Before the raid, Woenselsestraat, on the northeastern edge of the city, was clogged with tanks, artillery, armored cars, trucks, and jeeps as Jos Klerkx recalled:

> Later in the afternoon, we were told to evacuate as a large group of
> enemy tanks from the 107th Armored Brigade had been sighted near

the village of Nuenen [four miles northeast of Woensel] heading in our direction. Not knowing if, or when, we would be coming back, we put on as many layers of clothing as possible. The authorities instructed the neighborhood to move on foot to the center of the city, but it was getting dark by the time we left Woensel.

We had just reached the Boys School when the first aircraft came over from the east. As the bombs began to fall, my family took cover behind a nearby stone building. Mother started praying out loud and we all quickly followed suit. A German aircraft strafed the street and the British opened fire with everything they had; the noise was incredible as the enemy pressed home their attack.

One plane crashed nearby sending pieces of flaming wreckage hurtling over our heads. After the raid, we were told that the German armor supposedly approaching Nuenen were no longer a threat, so my parents decided it was time for us to go home. The road was full of debris from damaged buildings but despite this Vlokhoven remained totally untouched. The next day a newspaper boy arrived selling copies of *Eindhovens Dagblad* [*Eindhoven Daily News*] and I vividly remember that the pages were edged with a black border as a mark of respect to the victims of the raid.

Along Boschdijk, Jenny van Hout was taking part in a street party when she heard the sound of the approaching aircraft. "My brother guessed correctly that they were German because of the high-pitched engine noise and everybody started shouting, 'Orange fire, orange fire' and the party came to an abrupt end. My father quickly collected Mr and Mrs Faber, who lived opposite at number 249, as we fled around the corner to a shelter below the bakery in De Ruyterstraat. Luckily none of the ammunition trucks parked along the street were hit, because the consequences would have been utterly devastating."

Before first light the following morning, 3rd Bn returned to Eindhoven, while G Co remained behind at the airfield. Bob Harwick soon began to realize how fortunate the battalion had been: "Moving through streets strewn with glass and burning embers, several people timidly inquired if we were German. With daylight we found that the damage wasn't as great as we'd first imagined but so many people had been killed and injured." It was a sobering thought for all concerned, that despite the earlier carnival atmosphere, the Germans were still a force to be reckoned with as Jim McCann recalled: "When we came back to Eindhoven, the people believed that we'd received inside information about the raid. It was only after the Dutch underground, who had been with us all along, explained the situation, that good feeling and friendship returned."

The 3rd Bn reoccupied its original positions at Sint Joris College and were placed on standby in regimental reserve. Medic T/5 Mainard "Cliff" Clifton became the last person from the unit to die during the liberation of Eindhoven. John Gibson remembers: "I think Cliff was shot in the kidneys on September 19, and died the following day." During the night 1/506 (less A Co) was sent to Son, to assist 1/327 GIR, along with a company from 326 Airborne Engineers, to defend the Bailey bridge. This was well timed because shortly after dawn on September 20, the German 107th Panzer Brigade launched another attack against the crossing.

LtGen Brereton and Gen Taylor met with Col Sink, at Den Elzent, to discuss the worsening situation. As a result A Company were sent to Nederwetten, and two companies from 2nd Bn were recalled to Nuenen, along with elements of 15/19 Hussars.

Another British unit, the 44th Armored Regiment, was also attached to the 101st and sent to Helmond in a further attempt to destroy the enemy tanks. The 2nd Bn established a CP at Tongelre, on the eastern edge of Eindhoven, from where two roads led directly to Nuenen and Geldrop. It was obvious that the Germans might attempt a breakthrough towards their forces fighting at Best, therefore the regiment was keen to gather more intelligence about what was happening east of the city.

A friend of John van Kooijk – Mr Van Lierop – who lived along the Nuenen road, volunteered to supply information to the 506th. Early on the morning of September 20, acting on information provided by Van Lierop, Ed Shames and "John the Dutchman" visited Nuenen, where John's family were living. The two men were unable to reach the center of town because the German Panzer Brigade was closing in from Eckart. Standing behind a tank (most likely from the 44th Armored Regt), Shames and Van Kooijk were surprised by the lack of aggression shown by the British, who did not fire on the enemy although they were clearly within range. Afterwards, Shames and Van Kooijk were driven to Schijndel but were forced to withdraw at Sint Oedenrode due to the continued heavy fighting around Best. The various task forces were unsuccessful in stopping the enemy, and as darkness fell, the troops returned to Eindhoven to protect the city.

After the 506th finally departed from Eindhoven, the Royal Artillery established a number of heavy gun positions along Boschdijk, and the Scots Guards set up a field hospital, HQ, and kitchens at the Theresia Catholic School on Barrierweg. The dead were buried in a makeshift cemetery next door to the school and the graves were later cared for by the Dutch. Many British servicemen were billeted with local families like Jenny Soon's, who befriended two men, John Lambert, a Royal Engineer from London, and airman Len Mills from Liverpool. Len's detachment was now occupying the Obam Garage across the street, which had been slightly damaged during the recent bombing. Ten-year-old schoolgirl Jo van Dongen (neé Van der Water) also lived on Boschdijk: "The day after the big raid we had several Englishmen living in our home. One guy, a cook from the Royal Army Service Corps, procured extra food for my family and was quite a bit older than Trooper Jeffries, from the 15/19 Hussars. On September 20, before leaving in the morning, Jeffries hung his rosary beads over my mother's fireplace and said that they would protect us from harm. Later that afternoon we learned that the poor fellow had been killed at Best." Several days later, Jan van Hout and his school chums decided to follow a convoy of vehicles along Boschdijk, hoping to get a closer view of the fighting at Best. When the boys arrived at the Wilhelmina Canal, Scottish troops from the 15th Infantry Division would not let them pass, as Jan cheekily recalls. "We told the 'Tommies' that we lived on the northern side of the canal and had to get home as our mums and dads would be worried sick, so they let us through! We spent the rest of the afternoon 'sightseeing' and when it was time to return, told the soldiers the same story and they let us back across the bridge." It is interesting to note that despite successful operations elsewhere in the region, Best was not liberated until October 24, 1944.

The new "guests" introduced their hosts to the music of Glenn Miller, Bing Crosby, and Vera Lynn. Joop van Ginderen's mother took in laundry from the hospital at Theresia Catholic School to earn a little extra money. "Things started to return to normal. Despite the occasional food parcel from the British, life didn't get much easier but at least the people of Eindhoven were now free."

When the Allied battle lines were drawn along the corridor to Arnhem, nearly 300,000 German troops were trapped in the Netherlands. At their disposal was an almost unlimited supply of tanks, self-propelled guns, and 88s.

8

"No time to bleed"
Hell's Highway –
September 21–October 1, 1944

By September 21 the German 107th Armored Brigade had joined forces with two other fighting groups and turned away from Son to focus its attention further north, launching a series of ferocious attacks along the "supply corridor" transport hubs of Sint Oedenrode, Veghel, and Uden. The town of Veghel stood equidistant between Sint Oedenrode and Uden. Veghel was crucial due to its position on the road networks, railway system, and its close proximity to the Zuid–Willems–Vaart Canal. Due to the constant German attacks the 40-mile stretch of road between Eindhoven and Arnhem became almost impossible to keep open. The fighting became so fierce along the route that the 101st Airborne Division named the road "Hell's Highway."

Fortunately, the 101st now had a limited number of rocket-firing RAF Typhoons at its disposal, but there were still other operational issues as Hank DiCarlo recalls:

The British Army could be quite inflexible, but sometimes they were prepared to take ad lib orders and go off-road to support our infantry. However, we soon discovered that once provoked they proved to be a worthy ally. I wasn't alone in believing that we owned the highway, because when the Germans managed to interrupt the flow of traffic, we promptly attacked and restored order. I remember the first time we went into Veghel, the Germans were shelling the town and we were running from doorway to doorway. As we reached the town square, I could hardly believe my eyes: amidst all the shelling were British tanks, jeeps, and trucks all parked up as the troops stopped for a tea break. The other amazing thing about the British was how they could subsist and fight, considering the food they were issued. We were allotted the same 24-hour ration packs during our stint in Holland. I mean our K rations were bad enough, but compared to bully beef and rock-hard biscuits, packed in tins dated 1918, the US stuff was haute cuisine. I didn't smoke but I am reliably informed that smoking the British Woodbine cigarettes [also called coffin nails] was like inhaling wet hay.

At 0930hrs on September 20, Gen Brereton established his HQ in the 506th CP at Den Elzent, and before heading to Brussels for a conference, he met with Gen Taylor and Col Sink. After the meeting, Regimental Liason Officer Capt Dick Meason was asked to form a patrol (supported by a squad from I Co) and go to Best to discuss the possible surrender of the German garrison. Under a flag of truce, with Dental Officer Capt Sammy "Shifty" Feiler acting as translator, the patrol visited the German commander at the Bata shoe factory south of the Wilhelmina Canal, but the commander vowed never to capitulate.

The previous afternoon, Daniel II had received intelligence reports from a KP group east of Veghel, that a sizable enemy force was planning an attack 22 miles north of Eindhoven, at Uden. There were unanswered questions regarding the enemy disposition on the western flank of the regiment. Col Sink thought it might be possible for the Germans to launch an assault from the industrial town of Tilburg. Previous aerial reconnaissance had shown that the Germans were using the city as a depot for operations in the northeast.

Ed Shames and John van Kooijk were elected to go to Tilburg and assess the situation, using the Philips telephone lines at the de Volt factory. The doctor from Veghel had a colleague who lived two miles east of the city in the village of Oisterwijk, and who agreed to look after the team. Oisterwijk was situated close to the main railway line, where sizable ammunition and medical supply depots were located.

From Eindhoven, the doctor drove Shames and Van Kooijk to Nuenen, where Van Kooijk was able to briefly meet up with his family. "Afterwards we traveled towards Best, before diverting to Uden as part of the regimental recon for a meeting with a local resistance group," recalls Ed Shames. "The doctor dropped us off in the Opel on the outskirts of town, where we rendezvoused with Milo [head of the southern command local resistance] and a couple of his men who decided to drive us to the village of Zeeland, situated three miles northeast of Uden." When the men arrived, John went into the local unisex hairdressers on Kerkstraat 50, and asked the barber if he knew anything about the whereabouts of the enemy.

The owner of the salon, Martien van Ganzewinkel, told John that the Germans had gone and, as far as he knew, Ed was the first American paratrooper to enter the town. "I just couldn't resist the temptation and there and then decided to have a shave and a haircut, while John waited outside in the car with Milo." The lieutenant was shocked to learn that one of the 32-year-old barber's seven siblings, Piet, lived in the same town – Portsmouth, Virginia – as his older sister, Anna.★

During the late evening of September 21, Ed Shames, Van Kooijk, and Milo arrived at the spacious home of 56-year-old Dr Frans De Sain and his family in Oisterwijk. Milo's vehicle was parked out of sight in the doctor's garage, situated behind the large outer wall surrounding the house. "A couple of guys from the local resistance group were already waiting and quickly ushered us upstairs into the attic towards the back of the house," recalls Shames.

★ Piet was a Catholic priest who had settled in the United States in 1931. Martien dashed off and came back with a letter he had written to Piet in April 1940 which he had been unable to send because of the German invasion. Shames agreed to redirect it to his sister via the army postal system. Although Piet had moved, Anna managed to track him down and pass on the letter. Piet then replied using Shames' APO address in Holland. Martien died in January 1978, six months before his brother Piet. Today in 2011, Martien's granddaughters, Peggy and Leslie, run the business from the same location at Kerkstraat 50, although the original building was redeveloped in the 1950s.

De Sain ran a medical practise from consulting rooms on the ground floor. As a representative of the local Red Cross, the doctor had volunteered to work with the German medical services and a surgeon from the nearby evacuation hospital was billeted in the house. This did nothing to deter Frans from covertly treating wounded airmen and anyone else needing his help. Allied aviators were hidden in an adjacent attic, belonging to the Friars of Sint Hermanus, connected by a small hole through which supplies could be passed. Shames explained: "We didn't hear or see anything of the Kraut doctor but the resistance told us that this was the nearest and safest place to Tilburg. The following morning we were given a set of overalls, similar to those worn by the local textile workers. The thought of being shot as a spy was terrifying but as we seemed to blend in easily with everyone else going to work, I managed to calm down a little by the time we reached Tilburg, which had the largest textile, leather tanning, and shoe manufacturing factories in the country."

The seven-man team walked along Oisterwijksebaan, a wide path that ran close to the railway from the edge of Oisterwijk to the swing bridge over the Wilhelmina Canal, which was almost identical to that blown up at Son. After crossing the bridge, the team headed for the southern district of Broekhoven and the Metaaldraadlampenfabriek N. V. Volt factory on Nieuwe Goirleseweg (now Voltstraat).

Once safely inside the powerplant, Ed waited as the Dutch dispersed throughout the city to gather intelligence. "Once the surveillance phase was complete," reflects Ed, "I collated and verified the information before the resistance boys patched me through via the service line to G2 in Eindhoven. I told the divisional intelligence people that the situation was negative as to any enemy troop or vehicle concentrations in the area. Afterwards we were ordered back to regiment and got out of Oisterwijk as quickly as possible."

The following day, September 23, Shames and Van Kooijk reported to Capt Leach at his CP located in a farmhouse at Eerde. Almost immediately Leach sent them into Veghel with 1st Lt Russell Hall (HQ

2/506), to hunt for snipers. Shames' luck nearly ran out when Hall was shot in the forehead and killed. Because of the developing enemy situation along the highway, Col Sink extended Shames' time with John van Kooijk as he recalls: "Owing to the higher risks we were now facing, I could no longer accept responsibility for the doctor, who kindly agreed to let me requisition his car. John and I used the vehicle for the next couple of weeks and found it perfect for gathering intelligence and troubleshooting."

In the meantime, 3rd Bn had been moving northeast towards Uden, behind an advance party from 2nd Bn that was being led by Col Charlie Chase. In the early hours of September 22, 3rd Bn was closing on Sint Oedenrode, where Gen Taylor had established his new CP at Kastel Henkenshagen. At 0300hrs, after marching ten miles, the battalion went into reserve as back-up for the 502nd and spent what was left of a cold and wet night in a wooded area on the outskirts of the town. "Shortly after arriving we were ordered back to Veghel where the Germans had blocked the road," recalls Alex Andros. Around 40 tanks from 107th Armored Brigade, supported by SS Kampfgruppe Frunsberg, were attempting to seize the town and destroy the bridges over the Zuid–Willems–Vaart Canal and river Aa. Back in Uden, Col Chase was cut off and stranded until the following afternoon.

The 3rd Bn arrived in the centre of Veghel on foot at around midday, and were immediately sent to an assembly area near the church. It was not long before they were deployed and took part in the confused fight raging through the town as Alex Andros recalls:

We arrived at Veghel the following morning and my 3 Ptn were instructed to attack along the road. We ended up facing south, on the right-hand side of the road, where the Germans had a machine-gun position with superb fields of fire. Because of the low ground we could only move forward through deep drainage ditches. It took us all day to get to a point where we could actually do some good. I was deeply concerned by the accurate grazing fire especially after several bullets ripped through the top of my musette bag!

During a flanking attack later in the afternoon, Sgt Richards and 2nd Lt Willie Miller were ahead of me, about 50 yards from the enemy positions. Moving forward, I just reached Richards as he shouted "To hell with this, we just can't take any more, let's get up and go." The entire squad charged ahead only to find that Germans had pulled out, leaving two young paratroopers behind manning a machine gun. These two kids had kept us at arm's length all that time. After pulling back we were too damn tired to dig foxholes so we used the ditches for cover. It rained all night and the following morning, I woke to find that I'd been sleeping the sleep of the dead in about five inches of water.

Intermittent poor weather over the next three days severely hampered effective air support. Because of the information provided by the KP, the division, sustained by British armor, was able to block several important German tank assaults along the four-mile length of the highway, except for Uden, where Col Chase and his small force still remained isolated. The situation was so critical that the commander of XXX Corps, Sir Brian Horrocks, turned some of his artillery units around to assist. The next morning, September 22, Sint Oedenrode was attacked by an organized enemy force from the west; however, the assault reached no further than the outskirts of town. Although the fighting around Veghel was fierce, the battalion was amused to see an assortment of orange flags being raised and lowered as the battle ebbed and flowed.

The 3rd Bn were in semi-reserve on the afternoon of September 22 when the enemy launched another set of attacks against Veghel. This time the thrust came from the north and was directed against the main railway bridge over the Zuid–Willems–Vaart Canal, which was being held at the time by elements of 2/501.

Earlier that morning, Col Sink relocated his CP to the Mariaschool in Uden and the Regimental Aid Station to a community centre nearby. The doctors from the 506th PIR were not the only medical teams working in the vicinity. Attached to the 101st Airborne Division were A Co from the 50th Field Hospital, who had recently established a facility in Veghel, at an old granary as their company commander, 2nd Lt Robert Radman, recalls:

> Although dozens of major operations were performed here we were unable to evacuate the wounded. A convoy of British tanks had begun to attract enemy artillery fire, after gathering near the aid station while waiting for the road to reopen. It was clear we couldn't stay here any longer, so my boss contacted divisional HQ and got permission for us to relocate to a Catholic convent closer to the centre of town. The sisters at the convent were most helpful and provided hot food, mattresses, blankets, and bed linen for the patients. Despite the large red cross placed on the roof, it wasn't long before we were targeted. The following evening, the convent was hit by two enemy mortar rounds and three of our wounded, including a German, were killed. On the 24th, one of our patients, a German officer, informed us that the convent's tower had previously been used by the enemy as an observation post, and it was likely that they thought we might be doing the same He suggested that we take him under a white flag to advise his countrymen of their violation. Before a decision could be made we were hit again and the German officer was wounded for a second time. Five nuns were also killed when another shell went straight through the door of the chapel and exploded in the basement.

A lucky break in the weather that day meant that the division was able to co-ordinate air strikes on a large enemy force gathering east of Veghel. Elements of 2nd Bn were sharing a defensive area astride the highway and came under almost immediate attack by enemy infantry, supported by tanks.

At 1400hrs, D Co, led by Charles Shettle and assisted by guns from the Royal Artillery, attacked another force moving in from the northwest, and took many prisoners. H Company was asked to furnish security for the railroad bridge over the canal while G Company deployed into a defensive position to the southeast. "1st Lt Doughty had us dig foxholes in an orchard bordering the road," recalls Jim Martin (G Co 2 Ptn).

I'd just finished digging mine with Joseph Eagon, when Sgt Oscar Saxvik came across and told us that we'd have to move further back and dig new positions. Saxvik wanted Sgt Harold Brucker and Cpl Charles Rogers to use the holes we had just dug because they had all the communications gear and needed to be close to Lieutenant Doughty. Although we were all good friends, I threw a fit about having to dig more holes but it did no good. After finishing the second set of trenches, we came under a heavy barrage that lasted about 20 minutes. Afterwards, Sgt Saxvik returned to our position and said, "I hope you sons of bitches are satisfied – Brucker and Rogers have just taken a direct hit and are both dead!"

John Gibson was acting as medic for G Company at the time. "After the barrage, I was asked to go and check for survivors. The bodies were a mess and 'Jiggs' Rogers' was only recognizable by his distinctive dark moustache. Shortly after this incident, I was first on scene to help a guy from F/506, Pfc Roy 'Dutch' Zerbe, whose entire lower jaw had been blown away. The wound was shocking and seemed untreatable but he survived and had over 40 operations to rebuild his face." A few days later, Jimmy Martin's war was abruptly halted after his ankle was shattered by enemy shellfire and he was evacuated to the UK.

Charged with holding Veghel at all costs, the Divisional Artillery Commander, Gen McAuliffe, threw together a task force comprising the 506th PIR and several other American units, plus a squadron from the 44th Royal Tank Regiment. In the meantime, to relieve pressure, 1/501 pushed several miles to the west and occupied the town of Schijndel, capturing nearly 400 prisoners, while the rest of the outfit moved into positions around Eerde to protect Veghel from the west.

H Co's 2 Ptn and 2st Lt Clark Heggeness and became deeply involved in the fighting around Veghel on what became known as "Black Friday." "September 22, 1944, was one of the proudest days in my military career," recalls Clark. "My platoon earned a Regimental Citation for its defense of the line near the railroad bridge over the canal west of the town." The 2 Ptn had been designated by RHQ to defend a smaller bridge at Dorshout where the single track Duits Lijntje (Little German Line) spans the river Aa, about one mile north of the highway. The Little German Line dates back to 1878 when, as part of a high-speed passenger system, it carried rich and famous clients between London, Berlin, and St Petersburg. In 1925, the Noord Brabantsch–Duitsche Spoorweg Maatschappij (North Brabant–German Railroad Company) ceased all passenger services to concentrate on transporting livestock, chemicals, and munitions from its main hub at Boxtel to Wesel in Germany.★

"That morning I had about 20 men at my disposal as we quietly moved into position around the bridge," recalls Heggeness. A machine-gun team, led by Cpl Charles Ritzler from D/501, had been left behind to guard the obstacle after the rest of his company had been ordered to defend the corridor northeast of Veghel. Heggeness was surprised when Ritzler remembered him from his training days back in the States with the 501.

The SS 107th Armored Brigade had broken through after crossing a bridge over the river Aa at Eerpe, which had previously been rigged for demolition but failed to detonate. This unexpected opportunity allowed the enemy tanks and infantry to infiltrate towards the Zuid–Willems–Vaart Canal close to the northwestern edge of Veghel.

It seemed obvious to Clark that the bridge they were now defending might be used to either support an attack on the highway, or

---

★ After the war the railway fell into decline and the last section between Boxtel and Veghel closed in 2004. Today in 2011, the wetlands that surround the old bridge abound with wildlife making Dorshout an area of outstanding natural beauty.

recapture the main crossing over the canal – which was only 1,500 yards away to the southwest. The depleted platoon established positions about 100 yards east of the river Aa, on a gentle slope rising behind a small treeline.

With the bridge now on Heggeness' right flank, the position held commanding views northwest across the river and railway embankment into the open fields beyond. On the other side of the river, in front of the American positions, was a large open field, dissected by a tree-lined path that led south towards Dorshout farm. Clark described:

> I noticed the higher ground would control possession and allow us direct effective rifle and bazooka fire. A tank attack on the main bridge could only come from the open pasture to the west, forcing the enemy to advance across our front at a range of about 300 yards. Our field of fire was bounded on both sides by woodland, making tank maneuver difficult. I requisitioned the machine-gun crew from the 501 and split our small force into two groups, assigning a bazooka team to each section. As expected, during the afternoon we heard the sound of heavy armor approaching from the woods. Two tanks soon came into view heading our way, supported by around 250 infantry, and began firing wildly at the bridge.

Along the northern side of the embankment was a 15-feet wide drainage ditch, with unusually steep banks (angled at 45 degrees) about nine feet deep and full of water which the tanks stood little chance of crossing. However, the enemy force seemed unaware that only 400 yards along the line to the west it would have been possible for the tanks to cross. Perhaps the Germans had overlooked the opportunity, while trying to avoid what they wrongly assumed to be an American stronghold at the Coenen and Schoenmakers fertilizer factory, located no more than a mile away to the west along the Zuid-Willems-Vaart Canal.

About 50 enemy soldiers clambered over the embankment on the western side of the Aa, and moved cautiously into the open ground behind Dorshout farm. Heggeness instructed his men to hold fire until the advance force was perfectly bracketed into a killing zone. Clark took careful aim and gently squeezed the trigger of his M1A1 carbine, signalling the men to commence firing. All hell broke loose and eventually, after several further attempts, the German infantry abandoned their assault.

At this point Heggeness led one section of 2 Ptn over the bridge. Keeping at a safe distance, they followed the retreating enemy soldiers from behind the embankment. Moving due west, Heggeness and his men came to a small farmhouse about 400 yards away from the bridge where they saw a British tank approaching from a sparsely wooded area. Thinking the Sherman was attacking the enemy flank, the paratroopers waved their orange recognition panels. Much to everyone's surprise, the infantry accompanying the tank opened fire, killing T/5 Tony Yodis. "Realizing that the Sherman had been captured, we took cover behind the house as the crew turned their attention towards us and fired a couple of rounds," recalls Clark. "Blanketing the area with smoke bombs, we began throwing grenades and were relieved when the tank finally withdrew into the woods."

Shortly afterwards the platoon captured 43 enemy soldiers in an area adjacent to the farm. After the prisoners were disarmed, they were placed under guard in the cellar of the farmhouse. Searching the Germans, Heggeness and his men were surprised to find that they were carrying French currency, indicating that they had arrived recently from France.

Ken Johnson recalls his experience of the action at Dorshout:

A group of German infantry came over the railway embankment in close order, completely unaware that we were there. We were watching from our positions overlooking the river. It was a nervewracking business as the enemy began to fan out, and were no more than 50 yards away when the lieutenant gave the order to fire. We slaughtered the German troops who were completely exposed with nowhere to run. When the Krauts got over the initial shock, they began to return

H Co 2 Ptn unit action, Dorshout bridge, September 22, 1944

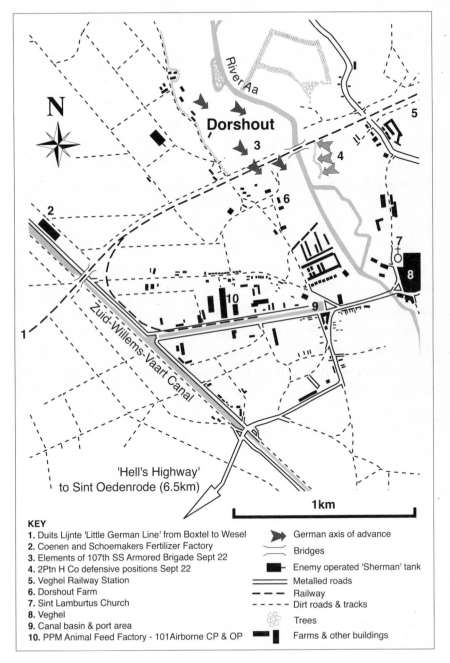

N

River Aa

Dorshout

'Hell's Highway'
to Sint Oedenrode (6.5km)

1km

KEY
1. Duits Lijnte 'Little German Line' from Boxtel to Wesel
2. Coenen and Schoemakers Fertilizer Factory
3. Elements of 107th SS Armored Brigade Sept 22
4. 2Ptn H Co defensive positions Sept 22
5. Veghel Railway Station
6. Dorshout Farm
7. Sint Lamburtus Church
8. Veghel
9. Canal basin & port area
10. PPM Animal Feed Factory - 101Airborne CP & OP

German axis of advance
Bridges
Enemy operated 'Sherman' tank
Metalled roads
Railway
Dirt roads & tracks
Trees
Farms & other buildings

fire, but soon realized the situation was hopeless and surrendered. I remained behind with my group as the others followed the enemy as they retreated onto the northern side of the embankment.

"The battle was really won by the enlisted guys who maintained discipline and didn't panic in the face of the enemy," concluded Clark. Afterwards 2 Ptn counted 52 dead and 25 wounded enemy soldiers. If they had not prevailed, the German force would have almost certainly crossed the canal and retaken the bridge on the highway near Leest.

Before the attack, 3 Ptn had been holding a railroad crossing opposite the station in Veghel. SO Phillips found a small hand-cart in a nearby barn and decided it would make a good ammunition carrier. "The following morning we took off the cover and were pleasantly surprised to find the cart stacked full of bread, which went down well with the guys." Shortly afterwards, the platoon was ordered to support Heggeness but when they arrived the battle was over. Harry Clawson, Alex Andros, and his runner Elmer Swanson crossed over the narrow bridge to reconnoiter the area. Clawson, an avid souvenir-hunter, carefully checked the enemy corpses for personal items such as medals and badges before crossing over the embankment to search the nearby farmhouses.

Flesh against steel

Veghel was heavily shelled during the late afternoon and early evening of September 22, as 327th GIR arrived to take up defensive positions either side of the main bridge. Maj Horton's men went into reserve and began preparing for the following day, but it was short-lived as Harold Stedman (I Co 3 Ptn) recalls:

We got so used to seeing British and German tanks burning that it became commonplace. Across the road from our bivouac area was a Tiger tank that had us well and truly pinned down. Several of our bazooka teams moved up on my left flank and fired a couple of rockets into the tracks and managed to set it on fire. Finally we got some artillery support and the enemy was forced to withdraw. There were 11 inches of steel plate at the front of a Tiger, and the only option with a bazooka was to get up close and aim at the tracks. If the operator didn't hit the target square on, the carbide steel rod inside the projectile wouldn't detonate and penetrate the armor. The order came down the line to attack, and we crossed the road to where a panzer officer was lying dead beside the burning tank. I couldn't stop to check the body because we were receiving so much small-arms fire.

Pfc Walter Lukasavage (I Co 3 Ptn), was horrifically wounded when another tank opened fire as he was taking aim with his bazooka. "Luke was hit in the face and neck before he had a chance to fire," continues Stedman. "For a moment, I thought that he wasn't going to make it, as his head was a mess with blood pouring everywhere. I had a T-shirt that Jim Brown's sister had sent me a week or two before the invasion. Taking the clean white shirt, I stuffed it into the gaping hole in Luke's jaw before dragging him down a ditch to our medic, Bill Kidder.★ After Luke was evacuated, one of our guys came up behind me, and boy had he ever hit the jackpot! The dead Kraut officer that I'd passed earlier had been loaded with money, a solid gold pocket-watch, a diamond ring, and a beautiful ivory-handled SS dagger."

With 2nd Bn holding the highway northeast of Veghel, 3rd Bn was sent to cover their left flank. Soon after dawn on September 23, the Germans launched several small-scale attacks against defensive positions to the southeast and throughout the day enemy artillery rained down onto Veghel.

Bob Webb found himself sheltering from the shelling in the basement of a house with a smartly dressed man in his early 30s, who was cuddling a little girl.

★ Lukasavage spent the next two years recuperating in England, El Paso, Texas, and O'Reilly General Hospital, Springfield, Missouri, from where he was finally discharged in 1946.

I offered the child, who was about six years old, a D-bar and reassured her terrified father that everything was going to be OK. The guy wanted to show me something, and on the dusty floor was a leather case from which he produced a beautiful antique violin. It dawned on me that except for his daughter, the violin was probably the most precious thing he had left, which started me thinking about the true cost of war.

The risk of further collateral damage meant that we could no longer rely on close air support. Often when the Germans cut the road we would have to be resupplied by air. During these missions the German AAA would be used to good effect but more often than not their attacks against the highway were never properly consolidated.

Later in the afternoon, both 2nd and 3rd Bn pushed north about 2,000 yards towards Uden, to link up with a forward patrol from the Guards Armored Division. The British were unable to sweep any further south, and both battalions were redirected to Heuvel – a small village one mile southeast of Veghel – and established a defensive line facing east.

Over the next 48 hours, the enemy was able to deploy a much larger force comprising Fallschirmjager-Regiments 2 and 6, Infanterie-Regiment 1034, and Sicherung-Regiment 16 (Security Regiment 16), launching a series of probing attacks against the 501st, in an attempt to breach the highway around Koevering. D/502 and H/502 were sent into the settlement to intercept a small enemy force of two tanks and about 40 infantrymen. Although the Germans were denied Koevering, the 502nd could not prevent the highway from being cut a few hundred yards northwest of the village. At the same time, Jedburgh team Daniel II moved north to Veghel with Gen Taylor, and established contact with OD and the local KP. During this period over 400 German prisoners, who had been previously captured by 1/501 at Schijndel, were being contained at a factory building in the town. Due to a lack of available troops, Daniel II's leader, Maj Wilson, was ordered to co-ordinate with the Veghel KP to supply guards for the prisoners.

The 506th were moved to Uden, along with 321st GFA and Battery "B," 81st Antitank Bn, where 3rd Bn was tasked with defending an open area northwest of the town overlooking the Leigraaf Canal. Elements of the machine-gun platoon dug in on a small farm near the settlement of Bitswijk, near to the old maternity hospital on Vijfhuizerweg (Five House Road). Bill Wedeking positioned his three available guns with interlocking arcs, facing north towards the expected German threat. By late afternoon on September 24, enemy tanks, vehicles, and artillery were spotted moving southeast towards Koevering.

During the night Pfc Frank Cress, I Company, was killed by concussion from an enemy shell. The following morning before dawn, the regiment was sent back to Veghel, where the road had been severed near Sint Oedenrode as Bob Rommel recalls:

It was raining heavily as we dug our foxholes around the assembly area. In an attempt to stay dry we covered ourselves in a thick layer of straw. The next day, a German soldier nonchalantly strolled over to our position and surrendered. Compared to us (who looked like a bunch of raggedy asses) his uniform and mess kit were clean as a whistle. We accepted his surrender and then I ordered my guys to roll him on the ground until he was covered from head to toe in a thick layer of mud.

During a fluctuation in our front line, the battalion executive officer, 1st Lt Bob Pennell, was left behind in his foxhole, probably after falling asleep. We found his crumpled body at first light with two gunshot wounds to the head. Afterwards the unit moved out along a road passed dozens of burned-out trucks. One of the guys spotted a dead German wearing a gold wedding ring and cut off the man's swollen finger to obtain it. Despite all that had happened over the last few days, I could never bring myself to be so barbaric.

Bob Dunning, an 81mm mortar man, was nearly killed during the first battle of Veghel and recalls: "We were surrounded in a culvert by German paratroopers when one of them attacked us with a machine pistol. A 9mm bullet entered my left knee and traveled along the femur before lodging in the ball joint of my hip. After being evacuated to the aid station near the church, my section leader, Sgt Joe Hunter arrived, shaking uncontrollably and demanding to be evacuated! Hunter was a rank-conscious bully who in my opinion 'faked out.'" The German medic attending to Dunning also agreed that Hunter's behaviour was disgraceful. "The Kraut orderly was confused as to where exactly I was wounded," recalls Dunning, "Pointing to the injury, I noticed a long piece of stringy flesh poking out from my left leg. The guy took out my pocketknife, cut the skin away and gave me a shot of morphine before wishing me luck! Ultimately the bullet was too difficult for the doctors to remove and after several months in the hospital, I discharged myself and returned to the unit."

That night near Koevering, two miles southwest of Veghel, the enemy strengthened its stranglehold on Hell's Highway with more men, tanks (including captured British Shermans), and self-propelled guns. Around 1130hrs on September 25, 3rd Bn was sent into action.

Leading south down the highway, accompanied by half a squadron of tanks from 44th Royal Tank Regiment, 3rd Bn moved towards Koevering, followed by 1st Bn on their right flank. As 3rd Bn moved into the village, the leading elements came under well-directed artillery, tank and small-arms fire. I Company maneuvered around the enemy front line to the right, as the men from H Co 1 Ptn pushed forward hugging the ditches. Heavy bursts of machine-gun fire were coming from a large red brick farmhouse called Van Genugten farm, located alongside the main road, several hundred yards ahead. The platoon split into two assault groups. The first continued forward, while the second team, led by S/Sgt Frank Padisak, attempted to encircle the building from the west.

Padisak's team left the highway opposite a neatly planted orchard, and proceeded along an unpaved road called Heikampenweg, which was partially lined by a row of tall poplar trees. The team headed due west for nearly 400 yards, until reaching a minor intersection with

Wolvensteeg. West of the junction, on the northern side of the track, was another house, unoccupied at the time. One mile away to the southwest (right) the patrol could clearly see the Knoptoren church steeple at Sint Oedenrode. Approaching the junction, the men came under a hail of bullets from Van Genugten farm. Hank DiCarlo picks up the story: "Returning fire, we moved down a ditch on the left side of the track trying to get closer to the red brick house, which was only 300 yards away across an open field. Cpl John Purdie was in the lead, closely followed by Pfc Lloyd Carpenter, Cpl Johnny Hahn, and me. Just ahead, the ditch turned left through 90 degrees, onto Wolvensteeg towards the main highway. Purdie and Carpenter made the turn and Hahn had just reached it, when a tank came out from behind the house. We watched the Sherman, marked with British identification panels, as it slowly moved towards us along Wolvensteeg."

A few moments earlier along the highway, Ken Johnson, Tom Fitzmaurice, and another soldier from 2 Ptn had noticed the same Sherman from their position by the highway: "The tank, flying a black flag inset with a white skull and crossbones, trundled past and stopped about ten yards away," recalls Johnson. "We were hiding in a ditch and thought for a moment that the crew had seen us. We nearly had a fit when the hatch opened and a German got out to take a leak!"

On the edge of the field, Hank DiCarlo and his friends were suspicious of the Sherman and displayed their orange flags to show that they were friendly:

> The tank turned and opened fire with its machine guns before backing off a little. By that time, Purdie and Carpenter had reached the corner of the ditch and turned left towards the tank. The tank jockey knew he couldn't hit the ditch, so he began firing high explosive into the trunks of the trees behind us. Hahn was just about to crawl around the corner when the first shell slammed in. One round struck a tree close to Johnny, just as he was trying to disperse some of our guys away from the line of fire. The blast hurled me out

of the ditch and onto the gravel road. With no better place to go, I immediately jumped back in and crawled up to Johnny to check if he was OK. When he didn't answer, I turned him over and he was dead, most likely killed by concussion, as there were no visible wounds on his body. Crawling around the corner of the ditch, I discovered that both Purdie and Carpenter had been hit by shrapnel and were beyond help and could never have known what hit them. At this point [1720hrs] a wide slow sweeping attack came in across our front from 2nd Bn who had been pulled out of reserve.

The attack on the German right flank, supported by British tanks, dislodged the troops occupying Van Genugten farm, and caused the renegade tank to withdraw. Elements of the British 50th Division, assisted by heavy tank support, began to advance from the direction of Sint Oedenrode along the highway with the 501st and the 502nd PIR. By nightfall, the enemy had been cleared from all but a very small area to the south and despite one or two further attempts, Hell's Highway was never cut again.

"Don Zahn was lucky when he challenged the Sherman before it withdrew with only a TSMG and a couple of grenades," recalls DiCarlo.

If 2nd Bn hadn't chosen that exact moment to launch their counterattack, he may well have joined the list of fatal casualties we suffered that day. These men were not only my comrades, but they were my closest friends and I couldn't make any sense out of what had just happened. Some losses hit you harder than others but three at once was next to unbearable. That night it poured with rain as we held the line facing west. In the darkness the day's events replayed themselves over and over in my mind and I cried like a baby. Sometimes, I envied Don Zahn, who was one of the coolest guys under fire. All of us in the platoon agreed that when he received his battlefield commission and went to C Company, he earned it the old-fashioned way, by constantly putting his life on the line for his friends.

H Co 1 Ptn unit action, Koevering, September 25, 1944

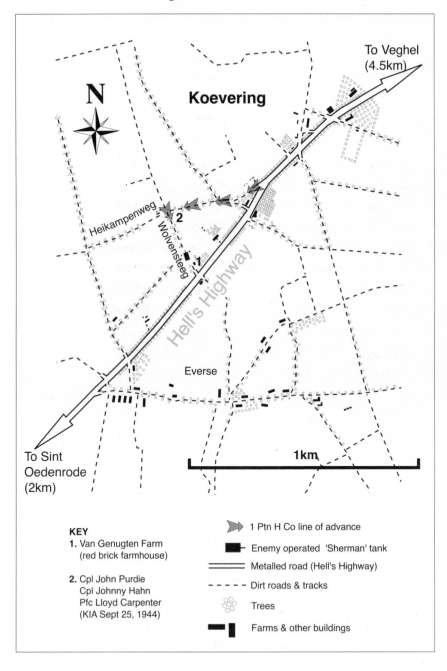

To Veghel
(4.5km)

N

Koevering

Heikampenweg

Wolvensteeg

2

1

Hell's Highway

Everse

To Sint
Oedenrode
(2km)

1km

KEY
1. Van Genugten Farm
(red brick farmhouse)

2. Cpl John Purdie
Cpl Johnny Hahn
Pfc Lloyd Carpenter
(KIA Sept 25, 1944)

1 Ptn H Co line of advance

Enemy operated 'Sherman' tank

Metalled road (Hell's Highway)

Dirt roads & tracks

Trees

Farms & other buildings

The casualties from Koevering were recovered the following morning and buried with full military honors in the Divisional cemetery near Son. Before John Hahn's body was removed, Don Zahn took a silver St Christopher medallion from around his friend's neck as a keepsake. Bob Harwick saw fit to award Hahn a posthumous Silver Star for his selfless act of gallantry under fire. Four other members of H Company also died during this period – Cpl Jay Barr, Pfc John Hattenback, Pfc Trino Mendez, and Pvt Melvin Morse. Fred Bahlau helped to recover the dead:

> We collected the bodies of Hahn, Purdie, and Carpenter and placed them together with Cpl Jay Barr and Lt Pennell who had also died the day before. Jay's stomach had been torn wide open by German tank fire. I wanted to spend a moment alone with Jay and the other boys and sent my assistant, S/Sgt Billy Byrnes, ahead to a battalion meeting being held in a nearby ditch. Placing my hand on each man's forehead, I said a little prayer as a kind of blessing. A few moments later a rifle shot came from the direction of the meeting. There was a heck of a commotion and I ran over to see what had happened – unbelievably, Billy Byrnes had just been shot in the chest and killed.
>
> During the meeting, Andy Anderson, the commander of I Company, had inadvertently kicked over a loaded carbine. Anderson was devastated, but it had happened and there was nothing anyone could do about it. This one event really hit me hard, as it so easily could have been me. Along with another guy, I carried Billy's body down this little dirt road, where I sat quietly with him for an hour or so, holding his hand and saying my goodbyes. He was such a fantastic friend and it all seemed such a damn waste.

Pvt Jim Mock (HQ Co), a 21-year-old from Meadow View, Virginia, was also killed on September 25. Mock's body was not discovered until the end of October, when farmer Harry Vermeulen returned to his farm near Eerde, and noticed an American helmet on top of a grave in a field about 300 yards north of the Sint Oedenrode/Veghel road. As the civilian population had been evacuated during the fighting, it would seem that the Germans had buried Pvt Mock's body.

By September 25, Daniel II's mission with the 101st came to an end when the team was ordered to Brussels for a meeting with Prince Bernhard. By this time the KP were making every effort to co-operate with the Americans, and were now focused on suppressing discipline issues within the Dutch irregular forces. Before returning to the UK, Maj Wilson and Lt du Bois gave the Prince a personal report on their activities. Daniel II's mission was not an overwhelming success, the inability to communicate with SFHQ and the fact that only two members of the team spoke Dutch were both serious setbacks, and unlike the other teams they did not have time to co-ordinate fully with resistance forces.

On September 26, after the two main battles at Veghel were over, the 506th PIR resumed its attack at Koevering, and by 0900hrs had driven the enemy north of Hell's Highway and connected with the 501st. Two days earlier, the 506th seaborne echelon, comprising 90 officers and men, had arrived at Veghel, bringing with it much-needed transport. As part of a supply convoy from 506th Service Company led by Capt George Barton, 22 of the vehicles were forced off the highway and captured by the enemy. The drivers were rounded up and ordered to shelter in a roadside ditch as German artillery began destroying vehicles further ahead. At one point Barton and his men were left unattended as their guards were called away to help with the ongoing enemy attack. At this point Barton grasped the opportunity and led his troops back to the trucks and drove away to safety. As a result most of the vehicles were saved and the men awarded a commendation for their cool-headed bravery under fire. Ralph King from H Company was hit during the same barrage: "I had shrapnel lodged in my rifle and the right sleeve of my jacket was torn. That night as we withdrew and were digging in, I noticed that my wrist was badly swollen and covered in blood. I was sent to the aid station for treatment and along the way was constantly challenged by the new arrivals. On several occasions, I heard safety catches being clicked off before I'd even had a chance to utter the password. The medics tried unsuccessfully to remove a small piece of shrapnel from between the bones on my hand. The operation made matters worse and after a day or so they decided to evacuate me to a field hospital."

British forces continued to attack towards the north, slowly squeezing out the 506th and the 502nd. The assault was followed by several RAF bombing raids against enemy forces situated in woodland either side of the canal, two miles northwest of Veghel. At 1300hrs, 3rd Bn returned to their original positions at Uden, while the rest of the division remained on the highway.

The next day, September 27, "G and I Company were sent back to Veghel," recalls Joe Doughty:

As we were moving parallel with the highway we became pinned down by machine guns firing along a secondary road. At the time, I had two British tanks following the company and I went back to ask them to advance and take out the gun positions. They moved forward in tandem and the lead tank arrived very close to the machine gun that was holding us up. As the tank turned onto the secondary road, a self-propelled 88mm gun, hidden from our view, opened fire, disabling the tank and killing two of the crew. During the firefight that followed, as the second tank withdrew, my wonderful runner, Pfc Alex Rapino, who had been with me since the States, was killed. After taking casualties all day, I'd had enough and got on the battalion net, telling Andy Anderson, who was on my right flank, "If you lay down a base of fire, I'll knock out the machine guns." Before we could take the conversation any further, Major Horton got on the phone and said, "Lieutenant Doughty – get off the damn net; you're giving away vital information to the enemy!" We couldn't believe Horton's crass stupidity and as a consequence my company suffered even more casualties.

Cpl Harry Buxton (G Company) and Pvt John Kincaid (HQ Company) lost their lives in the sporadic fighting that continued throughout the day. Although over the last ten days the division had taken 3,511 prisoners, the enemy were by no means beaten. The battle of Hell's Highway for the 506th PIR ended quietly at Uden, with the men believing that their job in the Netherlands was well and truly finished. But at the beginning of October, the 101st was both surprised and disappointed to learn that it would not be going to a rest camp in France. The announcement stated that they would now be moving forward to "the Island," near Arnhem, 30 miles to the north – taking it over from the British XII Corps.

Ultimately, Gen Taylor regarded the assistance given to the 101st Airborne Division by the Dutch underground as crucial in the liberation of Eindhoven, Son, Sint Oedenrode, and Veghel:

> Without this the fighting would have been costly in men and time. It was in the field of intelligence that these sturdy patriots did their greatest work. They brought us timely information of all German movements so that at no point was the 101st ever surprised by a hostile attack. The loyal support rendered to our troops created a feeling of friendship that will always remain fresh in the memory of our soldiers. Particularly those smaller detachments that came down in enemy-held territory. Our soldiers owed a debt of gratitude to the Dutch underground for their safety and well being during the hazardous days while awaiting the arrival of friendly units.

Before the regiment moved out, Bob Harwick found time to visit the temporary cemetery opposite the drop zone at Wolfswinkel. Harwick wanted to pay his last respects to the men, especially Johnny Hahn, whose white wooden cross was adorned with a bouquet of geraniums simply inscribed "From Mother, Father & Family."

❧ 9 ❧

"Life and death on the Island"
Surviving the nightmare

In 1944, the civilian population of the Betuwe, "the Island," numbered around 40,000 people and many of the towns and villages – such as Kesteren, Opheusden, Zetten, and Valburg – were made up of deeply religious farming communities, while others, like Echteld, Randwijk, Dodewaard, Heteren, and Driel, depended on shipbuilding, tobacco, and jam-making industries. Brick manufacture was another important employer, with at least a dozen factories situated along the Rijn (to the north) and the Waal (to the south). Dissected by three main railway networks and the Linge Canal, which comprised two channels during the war, the Island had superb transportation links to Arnhem and Nijmegen in the east and also the larger industrial cities to the west. These transport networks were heavily policed by the NSB, and the Quisling militia, who were easily recognizable in their brown uniforms.

One power-hungry NSB activist from Hemmen, Johan den Dunne, became synonymous among the local populace for being corrupt. Den Dunne, who was 23-years-old, was instrumental in establishing checkpoints around the island at railway and coach stations, looking for what he deemed to be "contraband" goods. On average, black-market supplies were usually sold in the more urban areas where one could expect to pay at least five times the normal price. Items such as sugar were highly sought after, and one kilo could cost as much as 25 guilders (nearly two weeks' salary for some agricultural workers).

Incredibly the town of Zetten was out of bounds to all German troops. There were around 16 educational facilities and homes in

❧ 166 ❧

Zetten, all belonging to the Heldring Stichting (Foundation), a church-funded charity for underprivileged girls aged 12 to 18, originally established in 1848 by local Protestant priest Father Otto Heldring. Soon after the invasion in 1940, Heldring's great-grandson Otto, also a priest, managed to convince the Germans that if their troops were allowed to fraternize with the older girls they could be exposed to all manner of sexually transmitted diseases. Of course this was completely untrue but owing to the fact that several homes were dedicated to underage mothers, the German military authority believed the trick. From 1940 onwards, signs were placed on roads leading into the village stating, *"BETRETEN DES ORTES FÜR ANGEHÖRIGE DER DEUTSCHEN WEHRMACHT VERBOTEN"* (Entering this place for members of the German Army is forbidden). Even so, the Heldring girls were always kept under strict supervision when outside the confines of the institution.★

Janna "Jannie" Anderson (neé Arnoldussen) was 16-years-old in 1942, and came from a large family who had been living on the Island for over 100 years. Her parents, Johan and Daatje, lived comfortably at 25 Molenstraat in Zetten, close to the Linge Canal, where they raised livestock and grew a variety of vegetables and fruit. Johan was the local postmaster, while Daatje stayed at home with the children: "My parents enjoyed outdoor activities and often went walking in the parkland around Hemmen near the castle," remembers Jannie. "Along with my older brother Joop and sister Allie, we always had chores to do around the house and it was my job to milk the cows before and after school."

The Germans took over dairy production and issued local farmers with special containers to collect the milk. Every year each farm and eligible household was expected to deliver at least one cow for slaughter as Jannie recalls: "My father was no exception and made the

---

★ At one point Otto Heldring was taken hostage by the Germans, who used him along with many others as collateral against reprisals. Luckily Otto was released in September 1944, and was able to assist the Allies, who found the Heldring establishments, many of which were empty at that time, ideal for command posts and headquarters.

journey across the Rijn to the cattle market at Wageningen several times during the occupation. Things deteriorated to a point where you couldn't trust your neighbors, some of whom belonged to the Controle Dienst." Controle Dienst (CD, Control Duty) men were mainly local farmers, who either volunteered or were forced by the authorities to assess farming output and search private homes for undeclared food products. As experienced farmers, the CD men had a good understanding of crop yields and cattle farming and often turned a blind eye to any shortfalls. Dodewaard farmer Dirk van Tintelen recalls one particular incident concerning the Controle Dienst. "A neighbor came to me for help and we decided to play the system. My friend had a beautiful fattened calf due to be handed over to the CD, which we switched for my newly born runt. When the authorities visited my farm to collect, I told them that my animal had been still born and they went away none the wiser. After our small victory we butchered his beast and shared the meat amongst our families."

At 24-years-old, Frits van Schaik had worked in the shipyards at Dodewaard for almost ten years. Local resistance leader Menzo van Wely worked as an accountant at the same shipyard as Frits, who recalls:

> One day Menzo tentatively inquired if I would be prepared to repair weapons for his BS Group in Dodewaard. Most of the guns were German that had either been lost in 1940 or stolen by the resistance. To be honest this work was no less dangerous than any other underground activity as the penalty for being caught was still the same – death! Usually before being shot the unfortunate individual would be tortured to betray the names of his/her group. For this reason, I knew only Menzo and his brother-in-law Teunis "Teun" Meurs. Subsequently, I worked quite closely with Teun who lived in Hien.

Teun and Frits would often go together on recon missions to identify and record enemy positions. Most of the weapons repaired by Frits were taken care of by a Mr Koedood, who lived somewhere in Tiel. In the summer of 1942, Menzo asked Frits to go with him to purchase a rifle from local man Teunis van Eck, who lived in Dodewaard, as Frits recalls:

> Van Eck told us that he wanted 20 guilders for the weapon despite the fact that it was not available for us to see. Reluctantly, Menzo handed over the money and arranged for the gun to be collected a few nights later and taken to Tiel by another BS cell from Arnhem. What Menzo didn't know was that among the Arnhem group was a traitor who, when the rifle was delivered, betrayed everyone involved, including Mr Koedood and Teun van Eck. The following morning, unaware of the arrests, I stopped by Van Eck's house on my way to work. His wife became hysterical and told me what had happened and asked to see Menzo but when I got to the yard, I discovered that he had "dived" and gone into hiding. I was afraid that under torture, Van Eck would reveal my name but nothing more was heard from him. It was only after the war we learned that poor old Teunis had died in a concentration camp on May 12, 1944.

Initially during the occupation, Allied bombers only flew at night but as the war progressed, they began to attack railways and shipping in broad daylight. Shortly before the liberation, Frits van Schaik was travelling by train from Sliedrecht to Dodewaard when the engine was attacked by fighter planes in Geldermalsen and destroyed. "Like most trains all over occupied Europe, the last two wagons were fitted with AAA guns. During the attack the gunners were unable to return fire because they were beneath the roof of the station. Two people were killed and it took more than two hours before a replacement engine could be found. About 20 minutes after setting off from Geldermalsen, the new engine was attacked and badly damaged at Kesteren."

Johannes "Hannes" van den Hatert, a 21-year-old working on the railways at the time, recalls: "For the most part, if the Allied pilots saw that a train was not armed with AAA guns, they would circle overhead three times. This alerted the driver, allowing him time to stop, and for the passengers to leave the train, before the aircraft began their attack. I personally witnessed this happen on several occasions, near Kesteren."

The constant air attacks meant that food became scarce but the countryfolk were always able to covertly purchase vegetables, milk, and bacon from local farmers. The German authorities could be petty at times and would never tolerate the sale of unauthorized goods, such as apples and cherries. If caught, an individual – who after all was just trying to make a few extra pennies – could be fined and sent to prison.

As the air war intensified over the Betuwe, more aircraft were shot down. Others dropped their bomb loads over the Island after being damaged, in order to improve their chances of getting home. The Germans even ordered civilians to dig trenches along all main roads to protect their soldiers from air attack. A number of Allied planes came down, but one crash in particular stands out in the memory of the local population. On the night of June 25, 1943, a Royal Canadian Air Force Handley Page Halifax from 419 "Moose" Squadron, flown by Sgt George Neale, crashed at Indoornik, one mile north of Zetten. Crewman Sgt Ross McLachlan, who was 22-years-old at the time, recalls:

We were only on our third mission, when the plane was attacked near Cologne by two Focke-Wulf 190 night fighters. At first I wasn't aware that a fragment of cannon shell had embedded itself in my arm, until blood began to seep across the maps in front of me on my navigator's table. But at the time it seemed the least of my worries. As the pilot struggled to regain control the outer starboard engine disintegrated and then the inner caught fire. After jettisoning the bombs we descended to around 10,000 feet and circled, looking for a place to land. We assumed our respective crash positions and waited anxiously while Neale, using all of his skill, brought the aircraft safely down. As the plane lurched to a halt, George was thrown head-first through the escape hatch but amazingly was unharmed.

Overview of 'the Island' campaign,
October 3–November 27, 1944

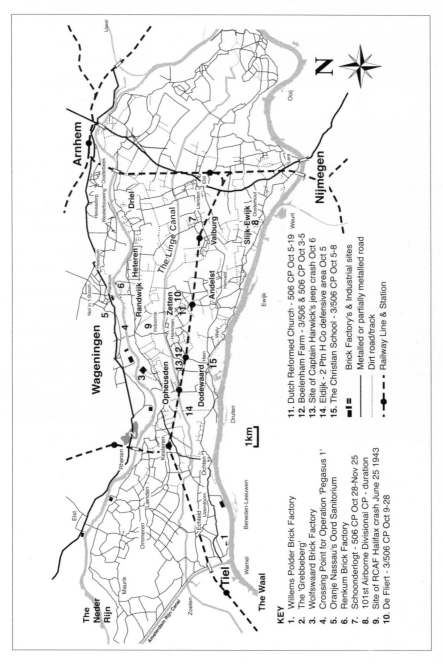

KEY

1. Willems Polder Brick Factory
2. The 'Grebbeberg'
3. Wolfswaard Brick Factory
4. Crossing Point for Operation 'Pegasus 1'
5. Oranje Nassau's Oord Sanitorium
6. Renkum Brick Factory
7. Schoonderlogt - 506 CP Oct 28-Nov 25
8. 101st Airborne Divisional CP - duration
9. Site of RCAF Halifax crash June 25 1943
10. De Fliert - 3/506 CP Oct 9-28

11. Dutch Reformed Church - 506 CP Oct 5-19
12. Boelenham Farm - 3/506 & 506 CP Oct 3-5
13. Site of Captain Harwick's jeep crash Oct 6
14. Eldijk - 2 Ptn H Co defensive area Oct 5
15. The Christian School - 3/506 CP Oct 5-8

■ ▪ ▪ Brick Factory's & Industrial sites
━━━ Metalled or partially metalled road
······· Dirt road/track
━ ● ━ Railway Line & Station

At first light the men said goodbye to each other and split into two escape groups leaving bomb aimer Sgt Bill Jaffray behind with McLachlan. At 0530hrs, after destroying any sensitive equipment and disposing of maps and documents, the two airmen walked west towards Hemmen, where they bumped into 15-year-old Bart Franken, who worked at the castle. Bart led the two men into a nearby orchard where several local people were already picking cherries. Now badly in need of medical attention, Ross was advised as to the whereabouts of the local doctor. After a breakfast of precious cherries, the two airmen headed into Zetten but soon became disorientated. Roelf Polman, a 16-year-old language student, was woken by English voices in the street and went outside to investigate: "Clearly the men were in trouble, so I agreed to act as their translator and went with them to Dr De Hully's place along Steenbeekstraat, near the Christine Hermine School. Once inside, Sgt McLachlan collapsed and had to be revived by Mrs De Hully, using a handkerchief soaked in cologne. The doctor treated Ross but was concerned about what the Germans might do if they found out. The Canadians agreed that it might be best if he telephoned a local policeman named Lassche, who lived next door to the school and immediately came over to arrest Ross and Jaffray."

Meanwhile, a large crowd had gathered outside the doctor's house and began taunting the pro-German Lassche with endless choruses of the Dutch National Anthem! The NSB constable barely made it back through the crowd to his house, where he telephoned the authorities. It was nearly an hour later, by which time Lassche had begun to fear for his life, that a couple of German soldiers arrived on a motorcycle and began to disperse the crowd with their pistols.

The local greengrocer, Willem van IJzendoorn, stepped out of the throng and approached the airmen as they were leaving Lassche's house. Nicknamed "the Krol" because of his height and stature, Van IJzendoorn handed a bag of oranges to Bill Jaffray and said, "These are the color of our Queen's house – good luck friend." Oranges like these were a rarity during the war, distributed once or twice a year to schoolchildren through local grocers like Van IJzendoorn. Strictly against regulations and at great risk, Van IJzendoorn had kept a small supply for his own family. Lassche, now sweating profusely, knocked the oranges from Bill's hand. The Krol picked up the citrus fruits and handed them back to Jaffray, and in doing so growled a threat at Lassche. Lassche did not react, knowing that if the Krol didn't tear him apart, the crowd surely would. With the two Germans doing their best to contain the situation, Lassche, closely followed by a growing mass of people, marched his two prisoners along Kerkstraat, passed the Dorpschool (today the Van Lingen School) and the Dutch Reform Church, to the bus stop on the corner next to the Hofman pharmacy. Waiting outside was impossible so the airmen were taken into the drug store through a back entrance, where they were held in the kitchen until the bus arrived to take them across the river to Arnhem.

Ross McLachlan concludes, "The crowd almost rioted as we departed with the policeman for the German Police HQ at Arnhem. Bill and I were only at the police station for a few hours, when George Neal and the rest of the crew were brought in. From here we were sent to Amsterdam for interrogation and eventually ended up in a POW camp [Stalag Luft 6] near Memel in East Prussia … all in all it was quite an experience." The Germans posted guards at the crash site, which became a local tourist attraction. Three weeks later, and much to the disappointment of local children, the aircraft was dismantled and taken away.

On September 17, 1944, Allied fighter planes attacked German antiaircraft sites in the Betuwe, as the first gliders passed overhead and began landing six miles away at Renkum and Wolfheze along with thousands of British paratroopers. One low flying plane was seen with a soldier trailing behind still attached to his static line! Several gliders and transport aircraft crashed in the fields around Zetten. One glider carrying a team of signallers landed on Dick-Jan Bakker's farm in Hemmen: "After unpacking their jeep and trailer the men drove to

Driel, where amazingly they actually managed to catch the ferry across the Rijn to Arnhem!"

Many local people thought that the war might be coming to an end but they were wrong as Jannie Arnoldussen recalls: "Living on the Island became a nightmare, so my dad dug an air raid trench in the backyard to protect us from the daily artillery and mortar barrages. At night, like many of our neighbors, we slept on mattresses in the cellar."

Frans Mientjes was seven-years-old at the time and came from a large family living in Valburg: "Before the liberation, the RAF accidentally bombed Nijmegen and over 800 civilians were killed. My 15-year-old brother Piet was studying in Nijmegen at the time and directly after the bombing the Germans established a hospital in his school. The older boys were sent by the Germans into the streets to collect the wounded. I'll never forget this but my brother told me that he went into a nearby park and happened to look over a small bridge onto the footpath below. On ground was the mangled body of what appeared to be a young girl, about ten-years-old, and lying just a few yards away was one of her legs perfectly intact, still wearing a rollerskate."

As liberation grew closer the Allies parachuted in liaison officers (LOs) to train the Dutch underground in resupply procedures. Before a supply drop could go ahead, the LOs sought permission from the landowner, who was nearly always a local farmer sympathetic to the cause. This was a dangerous business and if suspected, the farmer and his family ran the risk of being sent to a concentration camp and their property being destroyed. The Germans deployed air guards every night specifically to detect these clandestine operations. Between 2015hrs and 2030hrs every evening the BBC would broadcast regular coded messages regarding drops on Radio Oranje. A reception committee would mark the DZ with an assigned code letter, either by using small bonfires or by flashing a codeword in Morse. Shortly before the end of September, the RAF dropped a consignment of weapons close to Opheusden, specifically for the underground to use during the forthcoming Allied assault on the Island.

By 1944, Dirk van Tintelen had been assisting the Dodewaard BS for some time: "During this period, I was living in Kesteren at a local bicycle dealer, Bram van Ingen's place and slept in one of his outbuildings. Although we were armed with Sten guns it was always nerve-wracking especially after our commander, Van Zanten, was captured and executed."

Not long after Van Zanten's death, another resistance leader, Rijk van de Pol, and his wife Jans asked the BS for assistance. The couple lived in a large imposing four-story house on the northern bank of the Rijn, next to the railway viaduct at Rhenen. Allied intelligence wanted to know German strengths and locations around the Grebbeberg. The British had information that German troops were resting somewhere in the area. Dirk van Tintelen volunteered for the mission and after crossing the railway bridge reported to Van de Pol, before heading east over the Grebbeberg towards Wageningen.

As protection, Van Tintelen carried newly forged identity papers stating he was a devout member of the National Socialist Movement and a foreman in a local factory:

Walking along the main road over the Grebbe, I could see the enemy troops with their heavy equipment, concealed in the woods. The soldiers looked exhausted and much to my surprise didn't challenge me, until I approached the base of the hill, where I was stopped and searched by two men manning a machine gun.

I made up this elaborate story about wanting to see a sick relative in Wageningen. Slightly suspicious, one soldier went away, while I waited under the watchful eye of his colleague. The man returned with a couple of officers, who ordered me to repeat the story and I told it so well that I even began to believe it myself! As we were talking, I noticed several trucks pass by loaded with British paratroopers, most probably prisoners from the battle at Arnhem. The Germans seemed convinced by my tale but I wasn't allowed to proceed any further. Once out of sight, I started to run and didn't stop until I reached Rijk's house, who kindly poured me a strong drink, before signalling the British with my report.

Van Tintelen received another mission to smuggle a pair of Tommy guns by bicycle to the village of Zoelen. The submachine guns were wrapped in a set of overalls hidden in a tool bag. "About halfway, I ran into a German sentry and thinking the best form of defense is offense, calmly stopped and engaged the soldier in friendly conversation: 'Excuse me mate how far is it to Maurik – I'm due to start work there on the defense line.' After a brief chat the guard waved me on my way without even asking what I had in the bag. That evening when I returned to Kesteren, Bram told me that Rijk van de Pol had been arrested." Despite being badly beaten, Van de Pol did not reveal any information about the group and was later released as Dirk recalls: "Someone had betrayed Van de Pol, and we all suspected Driekus Romein, who'd been hiding at Rijk's house after absconding from labor work in Germany but we were unable to prove anything."

The following day the Germans began to search houses and farms in Kesteren. Dirk's group had received prior warning that a raid might be taking place but they had no idea that it would be so specific. When a patrol arrived at Bram van Ingen's farm, they made directly for the outbuildings where Dirk was living. In his haste to escape, Van Tintelen left behind a pillowcase containing personal letters and photographs, as well as his army discharge papers, all of which were found by the enemy soldiers.

"Bram and I went to see my older sister Areke ('Zus') in Lienden, where she lived with my brother-in-law, Henk ('Niek') Berends," remembers Dirk. "Still shaken from the raid, I asked if they would help move some weapons and put us up for a short while. At the end of September, Zus and Niek received word that the authorities were closing in." Bram and Dirk were fast running out of options and needed to act quickly or they could easily become trapped by the very place they were trying to defend. The two fugitives made up their minds and

embers of 1/506 look on as the British vehicles roll by. (Bill edeking)

A Sherman tank rumbles past the Philips Light Tower en route for Boschdijk. (P. Hendrikx)

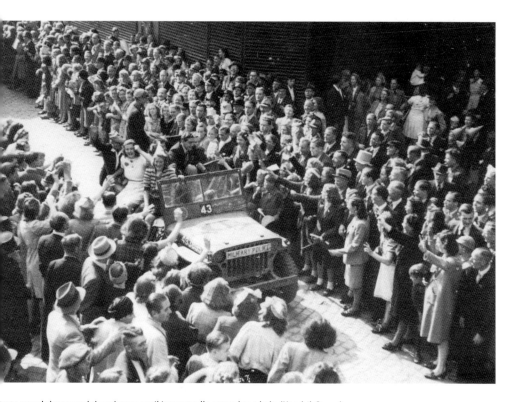

ense crowds hampered the advance until it eventually ground to a halt. (Hendrik Beens)

British Sexton self propelled gun and crew seen here in Frankrijstraat waiting for work to commence on the Bailey bridge over the Wilhelmina Canal at Son. (Piet van Heeswijk via Tom Peeters)

With the crowds now gone, members of the Machine Gun Ptn can clean weapons. The 1919-A6 machine gun had a two-leg swivel at the end of the barrel for dismounted use. Each 250-round box of ammunition weighed 25lbs. (J. J. M van Kruijsdijk via Tom Peeters)

Supply Sgt Ben Hiner posing at the Sint Josef Milk Factory situated along the river Dommel between de Wal and Paradijslaan, which became the main collection and distribution point for the regiment's supplies. (Ben Hiner)

During the night of September 18, Royal Engineers attached to the Guards Armoured Division constructed a Bailey bridge over the Wilhelmina Canal at Son. (John Reeder via D-Day Paratroopers Historical Center, St-Côme-du-Mont)

At 0615hrs the leading elements of XXX Corps crossed the new bridge and were finally able to make their way through on towards Sint Oedenrode and Veghel. (Foundation Remember September 1944 Collection)

Vehicles from XXX Corps on September 19, in Rechtestraat, trying to force their way through crowds outside a department store belonging to Vroom & Dreesman. (Tom Peeters)

3/506 leaving Eindhoven on September 19 along Grote Berg, heading west for Winterle in order to assess the possible enemy threat. (Tom Peeters)

ose members of the 506th not engaged on combat operations were tasked with policing the crowds along with local boy outs. In this photograph a paratrooper keeps people back as a Cromwell IV weighing 28 tonnes passes through Boschdijk route to Son. (Hendrik Beens)

eptember 19: people look on as American casualties are brought in to the RHQ Co command post at the Catholic Community entre. (John Reeder via D-Day Paratroopers Historical Center, St-Côme-du-Mont)

Later that evening the first flares burst over Eindhoven marking the target for the German bombers. (P. Hendrikx)

Stratumseind after the bombing, looking northwest towards the twin spires of St Catharina church. (Tom Peeters)

German prisoners of war under guard at the football fields near Son. (Mark Bando)

This staged photograph shows a group from 326th Airborne Engineers passing a burnt-out GMC truck along Hoog Straat in Veghel. The vehicle had been transporting gasoline when destroyed by a German Jagdpanther tank on September 23. (Currahee Scrapbook)

Defensive positions dug at Veghel by the 101st Airborne in Heilig Hart Square, close to the canal and industrial basin. (Erwin Janssen)

The Maria School on Kapelstraat in Uden became the 506th PIR regimental command post between September 22–23 and again from September 26–October 1. The school had previously been used as a home economics facility for young women aged 14 to 20. (John Reeder via D-Day Paratroopers Historical Center, St-Côme-du-Mont)

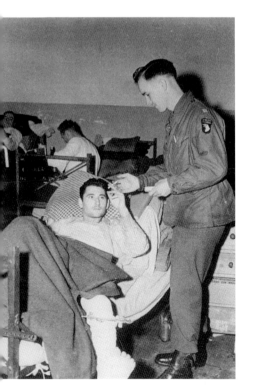

ABOVE, LEFT: September 23, Prince Bernhard of the Netherlands seen here with his deputy, Maj Van Houten, at the Ravens Huize Donck Hotel in Eindhoven. Now a restaurant, the hotel became the Prince's temporary HQ during the early stages of the campaign. (Tom Timmermans)

ABOVE, RIGHT: Col Sink and Maj Clarence Hester (regimental S3) far right, examining what appears to be a German Marder III, self-propelled gun, along Hell's Highway near Uden. (John Reeder via D-Day Paratroopers Historical Center, St-Côme-du-Mont)

Left: 506th Anglican chaplain Tilden McGee, seen here in a POW camp. Captured at Veghel, the Germans offered to exchange Tilden for a senior officer, captured earlier. Col Sink replied, "Hell no, we'll trade no battalion commander for a chaplain." (Mark Bando)

The railway bridge at Dorshout, over the river Aa, where H Co 2 Ptn fought off a ferocious and futile German attack on September 22, 1944.

ABOVE: The exact spot where John Purdie, Lloyd Carpenter, and Johnny Hahn were killed on September 25. The old Hell's Highway ran behind Van Genugten farm (seen here in the distance).

RIGHT: Don Zahn pictured in 1945 after receiving his battlefield commission. (Mark Bando)

Crew of a Royal Canadian Air Force Halifax bomber that crashed on the night of June 25, 1943, near Zetten. (L to R) rear standing: Sgt Ross McLachlan (Navigator), Sgt Reg Cleaver (Flight Engineer – RAF), Sgt George Neale (Pilot), Sgt Bill Jaffray (Bomb Aimer), Sgt Jack Griffiths (Wireless Operator – RAF). Front kneeling: Sgt Bill McLeod (Rear Gunner), and Sgt Dave Kenwell (Mid Upper Gunner). (Ross McLachlan)

The crash site at Indoornik, north of Zetten. (Rolf Polman via Ross McLachlan)

The brick factory on the river Waal where Dirk van Tintelen discovered the boat. (Dirk van Tintelen via Geurt van Rinsum)

Dirk van Tintelen in October 1944, after joining the Canadian Army at Beneden-Leeuwen. (Dirk van Tintelen via Geurt van Rinsum

October 2, 1944 – this picture taken by 1st Lt John Reeder shows the 506th PIR moving north through Grave while en route to the Island. (John Reeder via D-Day Paratroopers Historical Center, St-Côme-du-Mont)

...other wonderful photograph taken by John Reeder as the 506th reached the road bridge at Nijmegen. Note the smoke being ...eased to screen the crossing from enemy artillery. (John Reeder via D-Day Paratroopers Historical Center, St-Côme-du-Mont)

...t Lt Bill Wedeking (Machine Gun Ptn Commander) pictured ...ere in 1947 at Ashland, Wisconsin, after returning home ...om duty with the 11th Airborne Division in Hokkaido, ...pan. (Bill Wedeking)

Sgt Charles "Chuck" Easter, Machine Gun Ptn. (Tex Collier via Judy Gamble)

Pre-war photograph of Willem "Wim" de Bosch's house (seen here in center of picture with flat roof). Note the small footbridge spanning the drainage channel in front of the properties. (Bernard Florrisen – Opheusden)

81mm mortar team in action somewhere on the Island. (Currahee Scrapbook)

LEFT: Capt Jim Morton, the commander of 3rd Bn HQ Company. (Bob Webb Jnr)

MIDDLE: Pre-war picture of the Dutch Reformed Church on Kerkstraat, Zetten (opposite Dorpschool) which became the 506th regimental command post from the afternoon of October 5–19, 1944. (Geurt van Rinsum)

BOTTOM: Photo taken after the battle. A patrol moving along Dalwegenseweg towards the station passes a knocked-out PzKpfw II Aus F. The German reconnaissance tank had a top speed of 25mph and weighed 9.5 tonnes. (Mark Bando)

Another light reconnaissance tank lies upside down in the drainage ditch along Dalwegenseweg. (Bernard Florrisen – Opheusden)

Rocket attack from an RAF Typhoon aircraft somewhere on the Island. These ground-attack planes ultimately played a decisive role in breaking the German advance at Opheusden. (Donald van den Bogert)

decided their only option was to escape across the Waal, the southern bank of which had recently been liberated by the Canadians as Dirk recalls: "The odds of successfully crossing the vast river were remote but it now seemed inevitable that the only probable outcome if we remained would be capture, torture, and death, so what choice did we have?"

Approximately the same time as Dirk became a fugitive, the population of Kesteren was ordered to evacuate as the 363.Volksgrenadier Division began moving its forces into the area. "We cycled to another 'safe house' about five miles away at the 'Café De Vogelenzang' near the village of Echteld," recalls Dirk. "Although we had plenty of food, the owners forced us to sleep on planks above a stinking sewage pit. Not long afterwards, Bram disappeared and I never saw him again. A day or so later, I was sent to see a local farmer who lived close to the Waal. Mr Derksen explained that although he had helped a number of other people flee across the river, it was now virtually impossible due to the fact that the dijk had recently become the German main line of defense. However, he was able to pass on vital information regarding guard changes and patrol patterns."

Somewhat unexpectedly, the cattle which usually grazed on the flood plains along the riverbank had all been moved. On previous escape attempts, livestock were used as a cover story to get the escapees across the dijk. To make matters worse, the Germans had just instructed the civilians living in Echteld to evacuate their homes by the following morning.

The enemy had recently taken over a nearby farm and Derksen was nervous about two individuals who were already hiding on his property. One of the fugitives, Nico, came from Zeist, while the other had abandoned his family in Assen. After being introduced to the two men, Dirk immediately set about devising a plan of escape:

I had a kind of a premonition about finding a boat down by the river and that everything would be OK. Of course Nico and his buddy thought I'd lost the plot but I felt someone was watching over me and decided freedom was worth the risk. They were still unconvinced but we all shook hands and agreed that if I found a boat, then we would all escape together.

The "missing" cows gave me an idea and Derksen provided a stick and a couple of ropes, commonly used by cattle farmers when recovering livestock. Around 5pm, not long after setting off, I was stopped by a sentry, guarding the raised access road leading up to the dijk. The German was an older man and seemed slightly timid. As I was explaining, a *Feldwebel* [sergeant] walked over and demanded to know what was going on. After showing my false papers, I told both men that my dad was sick but a colleague had been kind enough to deliver his herd to "our" farm but two cows were missing. The soldiers listened intently and politely refused (thank goodness) when I asked them to help me look for the "absent" animals. As I turned to leave, they warned about the danger of Allied snipers and made it clear they couldn't be held responsible for my safety if I ventured any further.

Once Dirk crossed the metalled road over the main dijk, he was able to move unhindered towards the brick factory at Willems Polder. The factory was situated next to the river, one mile east of the Amsterdam Rijn Canal. Dirk reached the western edge of the brick plant and climbed over another dijk to reach the water's edge. Much to his surprise, he discovered an old rowing boat lying abandoned among the shrubs on the sand, anchored by a half-buried chain. "Although the oars were missing and the boat full of water, I still couldn't believe my luck. Lying on top of a nearby rubbish pile, I located an old clog and used it to bail out the water. Praying, I hauled the craft into the river and breathed a sigh of relief when it floated."

About 200 yards further along the bank was a dense group of tall willow trees that made for a perfect hiding place. Along the length of the river were dozens of breakwaters built at intervals to help prevent erosion. Each structure was around 100 yards long by about eight yards wide and had been laboriously created by piling thousands of boulders onto the bed of the river. One of these barriers was now in Dirk's way:

"As the boat was so heavy, my only option was to drag it around the breakwater. Along the way I picked up an old paddle, and the thought of just jumping in the boat and paddling away was hard to resist."

Eventually Dirk made it back to shore and hid the boat beneath the willows. He was tired and cold and had no idea of the time as his watch had become waterlogged. A storm was brewing and powerful gusts of wind conveniently masked Dirk's footsteps as he ran along the track leading towards the main dijk. Earlier, Van Tintelen had seen two enemy outposts on the road and realized he was now somewhere between the two. "Under cover of darkness, I followed an elevated pathway which finally brought me back to the farm around three o'clock in the morning."

The next day the Germans started evacuating Echteld, and many people were on the move to locations further west. As a result, security seemed more relaxed as Dirk recalls:

I used the opportunity to cycle over to the café at Vogelenzang, where there were suitable tools and raw materials to fashion a second paddle. When I got back to Echteld, it was completely deserted except for the Germans who were busy extending their defensive positions.

The two guys hiding at Derksen's farm were horrified when I told them how perilous our situation now appeared. The man from Assen got so worked up that he wanted to go home, Nico and I tried our best to change his mind but he wouldn't listen. That night I handed him my bike and quietly wished him luck. There was no time to hang about, and with Nico carrying the paddles we followed the same route that I'd used to return by the previous evening. Pistol in hand, it was my job to guard against any unwelcome intervention as we crossed the German defense line around 2am.

It started to rain and after about 30 minutes we reached the shore. Still fearful of ambush, we moved forward and carefully prepared the boat for launching. As we floated towards open water, the current became stronger and immediately pulled the small craft out into the river (which was nearly 350 yards wide at this point). Paddling furiously, my arms soon became weak and Nico tried to take over, but quickly got into difficulties as the boat began spinning out of control. For a moment we were afraid that the boat would be forced back towards the northern bank. Despite the pain, I took the oars and just as my strength was all but gone Nico spotted a breakwater. "Come on, come on, row faster don't miss it," he shouted excitedly. With my last reserve of strength, I propelled our small craft into the calmer water provided by the barrier.

It was pitch dark and still pouring with rain as we reached the beach on the southern shore. Stumbling through ditches and over barbed-wire fences, our conversation grew louder as we began to relax. We had been walking along a footpath for about 30 minutes, when I heard something and instinctively hit the ground. Moments later a couple of hand grenades detonated and two machine guns opened up from either side of the pathway."

When the firing stopped, I shouted the only English phrase I knew: "We are friends, it's OK." A green flare burst overhead and it was then that I realized Nico had been hit and severely wounded. Someone spoke to me in Dutch and after a brief explanation, I raised my hands and walked towards the soldiers, who were Canadians. After being searched and my pistol removed, I was forced at bayonet point to an old farmhouse. Mercifully, an ambulance arrived a few minutes later and took Nico away.

After a full body search, the soldiers took me by Bren-gun carrier to their HQ at Sint Josef School, in Beneden-Leeuwen. A lieutenant arrived holding a detailed map of "the Island" and asked me to show him our escape route plus any detailed information I had about the enemy positions. The officer seemed very interested when I told him that all the civilians from Echteld and Kesteren had recently been evacuated. Despite my obvious compliance, the Canadians kept me under guard. Later that same day, the officer returned with an interpreter, Wim Blijdeveen, who I happened to know. By coincidence, Wim was one of my neighbors from Dodewaard (my family lived in the suburb of Wely). I explained to him about the German positions and also mentioned that I'd previously worked in the Vink's cider and canning factory at Hien. By chance, Mr Vink was also on the south side of the river and thankfully was able to corroborate my story. Afterwards they told me I was free to leave but I had no desire to go anywhere and wanted to stay and fight with the Canadians. Wim kindly spoke to the commanding officer and it was arranged for me to have a medical exam.

The following day, a doctor passed me fit for service and also explained that Nico was now out of danger, despite the fact that a fragment from the grenade had almost penetrated his heart. After some basic marksmanship tests, the Canadians had a whip-round and provided me with a uniform and a pair of boots. The soldiers threw a bit of a welcome party and later that night I accompanied them on a patrol to the dijk. The lieutenant who carried out my initial interrogation came over and said that he had a little surprise planned for about 4am. I nearly jumped for joy as salvo after salvo of artillery pulverized the enemy positions across the river at Echteld and Kesteren. It was a good feeling to know that the co-ordinates for the barrage had come from the maps I'd drawn. I hope it gave the German grenadiers something to think about!

The tide begins to turn

A few days after Dirk crossed the Waal, the southern bank became the front line when the first Allied tanks crossed the bridge at Nijmegen and began to liberate many towns and villages along the river. It was not long before the Allies entered Dodewaard and forced the Germans out of the village westwards to Ochten.

Much of the predug defensive system around Dodewaard was utilized by British forces. Fighting intensified as the Germans tried in vain to envelop Dodewaard from Ochten, Kesteren, and Opheusden.

For several days British gun batteries located in Dodewaard fired on the enemy positions in Opheusden and Ochten. The accurate counter-battery fire from the Germans badly damaged Dodewaard, forcing the resistance HQ to move from the town hall to a large house in Groenestraat at Wely and then to the Vink's cider and canning factory at Hien.

Jaap van Schaik was 11-years-old and living in Hien when the British arrived: "Our house was in the middle of the British rest area and we spent a lot of time with the soldiers, who amongst other things taught us to throw a range of knives and daggers." Troops from the 7th Bn Somerset Light Infantry, 1st Bn the Worcestershire Regiment, and 5th Bn Duke of Cornwall's Light Infantry (DCLI) began arriving in the area as part of the 214th Infantry Brigade's advance and went into action on September 27, successfully pushing the Germans back from Opheusden and Randwijk. Jannie Arnoldussen happily recalls: "Before the attack, some of the Somerset boys were billeted in our barn at Zetten and being a vivacious 18-year-old blonde, the soldiers were always very pleased to see me." By the end of September, the resistance men from Opheusden, led by Stoffel van Binsbergen, amalgamated with the Dodewaard BS to arrest NSB activists, Quislings, and women known to have been fraternizing with the enemy. No harm came to the women who had previously had relations with the Germans, the *moffenmeiden*, who were sent to holding camps south of the Waal, to prevent them sharing further information, or point the finger at the resistence, should the Germans win the battle for the Island.

~ 10 ~

"Quiet as a church"
Opheusden – October 5–7, 1944

The 82nd Airborne Division had successfully completed their original mission to capture and keep open the bridge at Nijmegen over the river Waal – the gateway to the Island. During the early afternoon of October 1, 1944, the 506th PIR were alerted for a possible move to the city. At the same time in the Veluwe, the Germans evacuated the civilian population of Wageningen to Bennekom, Ede, and Veenendaal. The event should have rung alarm bells across the Neder Rijn but it seemingly went unnoticed by the British. The following morning, the 506th, along with the 321st GFA, 81st Antiaircraft Battalion, and B/326 Airborne Engineers, were moved by road from Uden to Nijmegen, across the now-famous bridge to support the 82nd for what was to become perhaps the toughest phase of the entire campaign.

When Gen Taylor relocated his CP to Slijk-Ewijk (called Slikkie Wikkie by the Allied troops), the men realized this was going to be a one-way ticket. The next day, the regiment replaced the British 214th Infantry Brigade (part of the 43rd Wessex Division) at Opheusden. The land around the small town of Opheusden was reclaimed floodplain consisting of open pasture and numerous apple and cherry orchards enclosed by deep drainage ditches and dijks. The Island campaign would soon become a succession of brief defensive stands, fierce fighting, and continuous out-flanking movements for the depleted and fatigued paratroopers of the 506th PIR, and ultimately would be some of the darkest days for 3rd Bn.

On October 3, due to a lack of transport the 506th was delayed in reaching its designated assembly area at Zetten. Eventually 2nd and 3rd

Bn took over the main line of defense (LOD) while 1st Bn went into reserve. The consensus among the British soldiers coming out of the line was that the area was quiet and there would be no action. Although the LOD was blocking the important western approach to the Island, the sector had been undeniably peaceful for the last week.

Maj Horton and his HQ staff moved into the spacious Boelenham farm, with Col Sink and 506th RHQ, just a few hours after the headquarters of the 214th Infantry Brigade moved out. The new command post and message center was conveniently situated one and a half miles southeast of Opheusden, close to the Hemmen-Dodewaard railway station. Built in 1927, Boelenham was owned and occupied by a middle-aged couple, Dirk and Jakoba Tap, along with their eldest son Arie. Adjacent to the farmhouse were several substantial brick-built barns, accessed via a long driveway from Boelenhamsestraat, the main road leading into Opheusden. Hidden behind trees on the eastern side of the driveway were the ruins of a small castle, complete with moat.

Almost every room on the ground floor was utilized by the Americans, except the kitchen which remained a living area for the Taps. Executive Officer Bob Harwick found a comfortable bed upstairs, in what had previously been a nursery of some kind. For the most part, the Tap family slept in a spacious cellar built under the western side of the property. The shelter was located close to the kitchen at the rear of the house and accessed through a small doorway that opened onto a steep flight of stone steps. The enormous vault was designed to store crops during the cold winter months, and offered the family ideal protection from the war.

The 5th Battalion, Duke of Cornwall's Light Infantry, was attached to the 101st Airborne as a mobile reserve. The commander of 5th DCLI, 39-year-old LtCol George Taylor, posted one of his lieutenants to the 506th as a liaison officer before setting up his battalion HQ in one of the large barns next to the farmhouse.

"When the third battalion moved into Opheusden, some of the vacating British soldiers were led away by a piper," recalls Bill Wedeking fondly. "The machine-gun platoon was ordered by Maj Horton to occupy the railroad station which also became our CP. A British tank was located nearby and the crew was having a pot of tea, so we decided to walk over and join them. The tankers liked our folding-stock M1A1 carbines because they were nice and compact, so we swapped one of our 'spares' for two German pistols."

The main railway building south of the tracks had been previously occupied by the stationmaster and his family. On the wall adjacent to the entrance was a large white panel emblazoned with "16" in black.★

"The CO also directed that one section of four guns, led by sergeants Garland 'Tex' Collier and Charles 'Chuck' Easter, be attached to H Company and the other section deployed around the station," recalls Wedeking. "Chuck had only recently taken over from Tom Simms, who'd been commissioned and posted to 2/506. Our fields of fire were very limited, except for the open space down the railway tracks and the area near the station. To supplement our firepower we also had a bazooka team and one .50 cal machine gun (from the 81st Antiaircraft Bn) working alongside us."

Willem "Wim" de Bosch, a 24-year-old living with his parents 200 yards due north of the station, had a couple of squads from the MG Ptn living in his barn. Wim's older sister, Dirkje, was more than happy to cater for the soldiers who included Dutch irregular, Leo Jeucken, who had been with HQ Company since Eindhoven. When Dirkje teased Jeucken about his stature, he jokingly told her "that being small was a positive advantage, especially when it came to dodging bullets!"

As the Germans were holding the high ground on the northern bank of the Veluwe, 2nd Bn moved north to the Neder Rijn, with Battery "F" from the 81st Antiaircraft Bn. They were to defend a wide front along the dijk from Opheusden to Heteren. The 3rd Bn took over a sector 2,000 yards long, facing west from the northern edge of

---

★ Station buildings were owned by the national network operator Nederlandse Spoorwegen, and numbered in ascending order along the line from east to west.

Opheusden, extending south through the railway station towards Dodewaard. "We had been made aware by the Dutch that the enemy were sending out two-man patrols into no man's land to check on our activities," recalls Clark Heggeness. "However, at the time we couldn't see or observe them from our own positions." Joe Doughty never forgot the parting words of a British major, as he handed over the CP at the Hervormde schoolhouse, on the northern edge of Opheusden. "It was something along the lines of 'Good luck Captain, I can guarantee that you Yanks won't hear a single shot fired in anger.'"

With G Company covering the northern flank, H Company minus 2 Ptn – who were in reserve around Boelenham farm – dug in at the railway station on the southern edge of town. I Company held a small pocket of land north of the Waal, and established a CP at the jam factory alongside the dijk at Dodewaard – where the company made full use of the extra "sugar rations."

Enemy activity increased immediately after the battalion took over, and the Germans made several unsuccessful attempts to cross the Rijn. This was followed by a series of sporadic artillery barrages that for the most part were directed along the front lines of 3rd Bn. "We were once again on British rations, which were absolutely dreadful," recalls Bob Harwick. "It was pitiful to see our GIs begging cigarettes from the Limeys. I had to look away, when I saw a Sherman tank pass by with a British crew, and heard one of our guys saying, 'Got any gum chum?'"

H and G Company were sharing the front line, as 1st Lt Alex Andros explains: "We were to tie in with G Company over on our right, whose line was about 400 yards west of the main road [Dalwagenseweg] that ran through town. I was working with Capt Walker to connect that line from G back to first platoon, who were behind us at the station. The position Walker initially suggested was completely open and flat with little cover to our front. This would have left us way too vulnerable, so I told him 'Either we move forward or we move back.' Walker decided on the former and I butted my guys neatly in with G Company, down to the railroad tracks." Andros' 3 Ptn were positioned along Smachtkamp, a dirt road that meandered from the northern edge of Opheusden down to a small railroad crossing at Parallelweg in the south.

The platoon was based in and around a small abandoned building designated "Blokpost 17," which had previously belonged to a signalman who controlled the nearby crossing point.* Cheap and functional, the compact two-storey building, built in 1882, comprised a kitchen and living room on the ground floor, along with a tiny cellar/pantry. A steep narrow spiral staircase led upstairs to an open-plan area, naturally lit by two skylights built into the low roof.

On the morning of October 5, the German 363. Volksgrenadier Division launched a ferocious attack in an attempt to break through and seize the bridge at Nijmegen. The vicious and uncompromising assault involved Infanterie-Regiments (IR) 957, 958, and 959 along with Infanterie-Fortress Battalion 1409.

At 0300hrs, enemy troops from IR 957 and IR 958 began probing the main 3rd Bn front line. IR 958 found a weakness along the southern side of the railway embankment, between 1 Ptn and 3 Ptn from H Company. Two hours later the Germans launched the first in a series of fanatical attacks along the "murder mile" that would last for nearly three days.

Before the battle, elements of the MG Ptn had been allocated outpost positions between 1 Ptn and 3 Ptn. Bill Wedeking was concerned that the first section, under Chuck Easter, which included corporals Fayez Handy, Andy Bryan, John Hermansky, and Nathan Bullock, had been deployed into isolated outposts far ahead of the main LOD without any proper infantry support. "In situations such as this, when my crews were attached to a rifle company, I had absolutely no control over what they were doing or told to do," recalls Wedeking. "Only on rare occasions such as this, were the guns actually deployed by the rifle platoon leaders themselves."

---

* An audible five-minute warning alerted the guard of an approaching train as it thundered over a series of electrical contacts located several miles away. The switches would trip a set of four alarm bells and red warning lights, located on either side of the crossing gates. It was the signalman's duty to manually lower the barriers to block vehicular access across the tracks. Depending on the geography of the line, it was not uncommon for a signal worker to have responsibility for up to three sets of gates.

Due to the lack of manpower in the first squad, Dutch teenager Leo Jeucken had volunteered to carry ammunition for Cpl Bullock, who was dug in about 50 yards north of Handy, on G Company's southern flank. Pvt Darvin Lee was next to Tex Collier and recalls:

Tex was sharing a slit trench with one of the airborne engineers who had been brought in to bolster our defenses when the first big barrage arrived [ahead of the main assault]. Cpl Andy Bryan and myself were only a few feet away in shallow shell scrapes, when the engineer was hit in the head by shrapnel and started screaming, "I'm gonna die – I'm gonna die." I calmly pointed out that I'd sustained a similar injury in Normandy, so there was no real need to panic. The guy calmed down enough for Tex and Andy to take him across to the temporary aid station [Blokpost 17] over by H Company. By the time they returned, the volume of mortar fire had increased and a shell exploded a few feet away from our exposed positions. We all commented how close it was and the last words I heard Tex say was something like "Yeah, but a hell of a way to go!" Another mortar landed even closer, covering me in debris, followed by another that exploded directly on top of Collier. His foxhole was covered by smoke and I called out to see if he was OK, but there was no answer. Crawling over, I could see that the back of his jacket was shredded and torn. As I lifted his head, blood trickled from Collier's mouth and it was then that I realized he was gone.

During the same barrage, Handy's gun, which was closest to the tracks, was knocked out and his gunner, Pvt Clyde Benton, hit by shrapnel. Pfc Morris Thomas stepped in on Bullock's gun, while Nathan helped Benton to the aid station. With enemy infantry advancing closer, Leo Jeucken crawled forward to help feed the ammunition while Thomas continued firing. Moments later, Thomas was wounded in the back and was forced to abandon his post. Leo bravely took over, and held off the enemy advance until mortally wounded by German small-arms fire. One of the men offered to carry Thomas over to the aid station, but he refused.

Moments later, Bullock returned and threw Thomas over his shoulder. Dodging bullets, he carried his friend to the aid station before heading to the rear with H Company. As the surviving machine-gunners pulled back, Andy Bryan took Collier's most cherished souvenir from his body – a 9mm German Luger pistol.

The Germans attack

On the night prior to the main attack (October 4/5), German patrols had fired submachine guns and flares along the LOD in order to solicit a response. The battalion had had strict orders not to return fire and reveal its positions. "I had kept my guys awake all night after a German fighting patrol tried to probe our lines," remembers Sgt Frank Kleckner, from H Co 3 Ptn. "It was so dark that we didn't even notice that the enemy were in the vicinity until they were within 30 yards of our positions."

Bob Stroud and his 1 Ptn were positioned several hundred yards behind "Blokpost 17," straddling the tracks at the railway station, with one squad led by Sgt Lou Vecchi to the right (north) and another led by newly promoted Sgt Hank DiCarlo on the left (south). Supported by Sgt Bob Martin's 60mm mortar squad, the platoon had established its CP in a heavily fortified concrete pillbox that had previously formed part of the Dutch Grebbe defense line in 1940.

During the night of October 4/5, 1st Lt Clark Heggeness and H Co's 2 Ptn were being held in reserve as Ken Johnson recalls: "At about four in the morning, we received an alert that we were about to be shelled. We managed to evacuate across a nearby road, just as the barrage began… A couple of rounds fell among us and I was no more than six feet away from Pfc Charles Stenbom, when he lost both legs in the blast. I can still hear the pitiful high-pitched scream that Stenbom let out, almost like an animal, it was truly terrible. From here we were hastily ordered forward to positions alongside the railway adjacent to Lt Andros."

The men quickly dug in along Eldijk, a 7 feet-high flood barrier to the west of Dodewaard that ran due south from the Linge Canal.

"The artillery we experienced that morning was unbelievable," recalls Johnson. "Pvt Bert Bailey was near the top of the dike when a shell exploded and blew his head clean off his shoulders. Still complete with helmet, Bailey's head rolled down the embankment and stopped at my feet. It was a horrifying experience staring down into his expressionless face, knowing that only minutes before we had been talking to each other."

Earlier, Heggeness had sent a patrol from the second squad forward to a small wooden footbridge along the canal, with instructions to hold it at all costs. Pfc Alex "Zanny" Spurr, a 22-year-old from Carbon, Indiana, recalls the disaster that then unfolded: "Close by was a well-constructed stone barn with walls four feet thick that became our CP. During the ensuing attack, the enemy managed to swim across the waterway and get behind the outpost." Hard hit during the assault, the patrol lost privates Nick Le Cursi and Randel Pettis, who were both replacements after Normandy.

Now virtually surrounded, the men had no choice but to take cover in the stone barn, where they had a field telephone wired back to platoon HQ. After a frantic conversation the patrol was ordered to delay the Germans for as long as possible, giving 2 Ptn time to withdraw and regroup with the remainder of the battalion. After an hour or so of heavy fighting, the situation became hopeless and, low on ammunition, the men had no alternative but to surrender. Spurr continues: "We abandoned our weapons and came out with our hands raised. After being thoroughly searched, we were taken to the German lines. Upon arrival our belts and the top buttons of our trousers were removed. An officer looked through all the mussette bags and took every blanket he could find but surprisingly never touched any of our spare clothing or rations. After interrogation we were held in what appeared to be an old wine store with a door at either end."

During their first night in captivity, Spurr and his friends were amazed to learn that one of the guards was a US citizen from New York. The soldier told the prisoners that he had been in Germany studying medicine when war was declared. "Over the next few nights we continued talking," recalls Spurr. "The man had a friend who had been slightly wounded and made it clear that they both wanted out of their current situation. We proposed that we could take him and his colleague back to American lines if he set us all free. The next night, when the guy turned up with his buddy, we knew that the plan was on. Using drainage ditches, we carefully waded back towards where we thought the Allied lines should be. After moving all night, it began to get light, so we decided to hide until the following evening. Finally we reached friendly forces and were directed to the H Company CP, where we explained to Captain Walker about our two German friends." Walker was pleased to see the team and congratulated them on defending the footbridge to the last round. He thought it was an incredibly selfless thing to do and made sure that the two 'prisoners' were well treated before promising to write everyone involved up for bravery awards. Spurr was later awarded the Distinguished Service Cross for his efforts.

Total war

On the level crossing next to the stationhouse was a flat-roofed wooden tool shed, which had been providing accommodation for Hank DiCarlo and his squad.

> As it was getting light, we heard gunfire coming from the direction of our observation post and realized something was wrong. A few moments later, privates Jack Grace and Jimmy Igoe came running towards us, shouting excitedly they had just killed two enemy scouts who had been trying to outflank them. Suddenly the area erupted with explosions and as the majority of our equipment and ammunition was still in the shed, we ran a relay race back and forth trying to collect it. Moments later, we began to see movement along the tracks and poked our LMG through the slit in the pillbox and opened fire. I saw several enemy soldiers fall before the rest spread out into the bushes and shrubs on either side of the railway lines.

Through his field glasses, Bill Wedeking saw enemy troops crossing the railway lines in front of his command post at dawn: "The .50 cal and my four MGs began firing down the tracks, forcing the enemy to stop and regroup. The bazooka team fired about eight rockets into an area where we thought the Germans were more highly concentrated. As the bazooka guys had only 12 projectiles at their disposal, we had to keep four back in reserve. About 0600hrs, Cpl Fayez Handy reported to the CP and gave me a few sketchy details of what had just happened to the four guns attached to H Company. As Handy was briefing me, I noticed that one of his hands was pouring with blood and he said, 'Look, Lieutenant, no finger!' One of our guys sprinkled some sulpha powder on the stump and bandaged the injured hand. We then instructed him to try and find the battalion aid station located at the northern end of the main street and he headed off but never came back. Roughly 30 minutes later, Sgt Charles Easter arrived and told me that all four machine guns had been destroyed and their crews annihilated."

Shocked by what he had just been told, Lt Wedeking sent Easter back to Boelenham farm with a runner to appraise Maj Horton of the situation and grab a hot meal. Wedeking recalls: "To be honest, I was seldom aware of where the battalion CPs were located and any contact was usually by runner. I later learned that after filing his report, Chuck was in one of the barns next to the CP when an artillery shell exploded through the roof, mortally wounding him. Upon hearing the news, I made Nathan Bullock temporary platoon sergeant and promoted him accordingly when it was confirmed that Easter had died on October 8, after being evacuated to Dodewaard along with battalion HQ." Ben Hiner witnessed the event and recalled. "I went over to tell Easter that it wasn't safe to remain in the barn but he was exhausted and had no intention of moving." After Chuck's death, his parents who lived in Cincinnati, Ohio, generously began sending care packages to the platoon.

Pvt Jim Melhus, MG Ptn, had been holding the line in a cherry orchard north of the station. At the centre of the orchard was a wooden platform about ten feet across and 30 feet high. While investigating the contents of a nearby barn, Jim discovered a pile of cord strung with tin cans, containing small pebbles that he thought would make an ideal perimeter defense. Tradionally these prefabricated lines were used by farmers to protect ripening crops from the local bird population, especially sparrows. Three weeks before harvest, usually in June or July, the lines would be strung from towers over the top of the trees and anchored to wooden poles situated around the edge of the orchard. During daylight it would be the farmer's job to keep watch from the platform and pull on the gathered cables to scare away any inquisitive birds.

After stringing 200 feet of "sparrow" cable across the front of his gun position, Melhus recalls:

Pfc Leonard Schmidt and Pvt Carl Pease were manning another gun 50 feet away to my left. We had been there since around 0230hrs and built our defenses in both primary and secondary positions. That night a couple of us were resting in a nearby building when we were alerted by small-arms fire.

One bullet smashed through a window and could only have come from the platform in the cherry orchard, so we knew the enemy was close by. Around 0500hrs, an unidentified patrol, responding in English, was discovered crawling along a ditch towards Schmidt and Pease's position. As Carl stood up to guide the men in (thinking they were Americans), he was shot in the head and died instantly. As the enemy hit us with mortars, one round struck my position and knocked out my ammo carrier [Timeteo Melendez] as we took cover. At least 12 rounds landed around our position, accompanied by intense rifle fire that cut through the tree branches above our heads. At that point we decided to move back and reoccupy our secondary position, and set the gun up as the enemy were trying to flank us over on the right. Just as I managed to get the weapon into action we were joined by some of the riflemen from H Company. Firing into the legs of the advancing German infantry, I saw several enemy soldiers go down before we ran out of ammunition. As we were about to be overrun, there was little choice but to spike both of our machine guns with hand grenades.

Melhus and Schmidt were furious with Cpl Lewallen, who was at the station, for failing to resupply them. After making their way back to the command post, the two gunners were astonished to find Lewallen huddled in the corner of the room. Grabbing firm hold, they dragged the corporal out of the building and ran towards town as Melhus recalls: "We owed him that at least and we were both in no doubt that he would have been killed if we'd just left him there." As they headed north along Dalwagenseweg, a shell exploded, peppering Lewallen's legs with shrapnel. Leaving Lewallen on the road, Melhus called for a medic and said goodbye.

Earlier, at around 0900hrs at the railway station, the noise from artillery and small-arms fire had become overwhelming. "Just up ahead on the same side of the tracks from our position was a row of houses and barns," recalled Hank DiCarlo. "Frank Padisak was concerned that these might be used as a means of approach so together with Joe Harris, I went forward with Frank to investigate. In the rush to clear the buildings, we almost shot each other with our Tommy guns; however we still managed to take out a couple of Germans as they ran out from behind a door of the last house. Rather worryingly we were now close enough to hear voices shouting commands in German, and realized that this had to be more than just a local thrust. At that point we dashed back across the tracks into a railway waiting room and made our way back to the CP."

Just before 1000hrs, after meeting with Col Sink and Maj Hester, Oliver Horton visited Lt Stroud at the station, in an attempt to assess the situation. A British Bren-gun Carrier and a Sherman tank had stopped on the level crossing, and the commander of the tank was now directing fire in full view of the enemy. About six German soldiers were moving towards Lou Vecchi trying to surrender when the crew of the carrier opened fire. Despite the fact that they were waving a white flag the men were all cut down and killed.

3rd Bn 506 PIR, Opheusden,
October 5, 1944

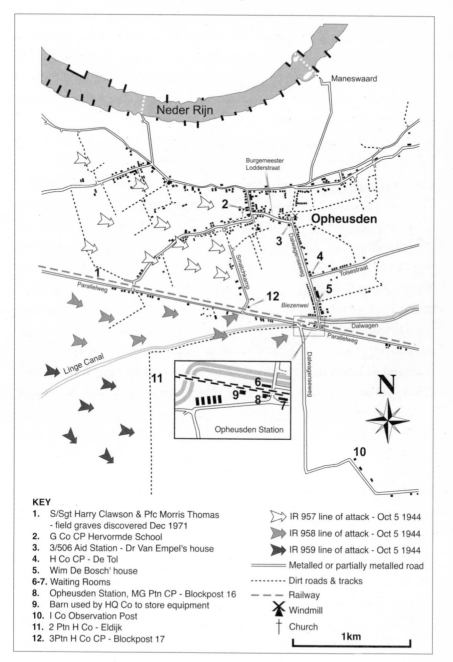

KEY

1. S/Sgt Harry Clawson & Pfc Morris Thomas
   - field graves discovered Dec 1971
2. G Co CP Hervormde School
3. 3/506 Aid Station - Dr Van Empel's house
4. H Co CP - De Tol
5. Wim De Bosch' house
6-7. Waiting Rooms
8. Opheusden Station, MG Ptn CP - Blockpost 16
9. Barn used by HQ Co to store equipment
10. I Co Observation Post
11. 2 Ptn H Co - Eldijk
12. 3Ptn H Co CP - Blockpost 17

⇒ IR 957 line of attack - Oct 5 1944
⇒ IR 958 line of attack - Oct 5 1944
⇒ IR 959 line of attack - Oct 5 1944
═══ Metalled or partially metalled road
------- Dirt roads & tracks
─ ─ ─ Railway
✕ Windmill
† Church

1km

"As we were preparing to pull back from the pillbox, Horton arrived and asked where we thought we were going," remembers Hank DiCarlo. "I respectfully replied that there was now heavy machine-gun fire coming down the tracks and that we would all be surrounded and killed if we stayed a minute longer. I couldn't believe it when the major stepped out from behind the bunker and was struck in the midsection by one of the machine guns that I'd just warned him about! We laid Horton down on the protected side of the blockhouse; there was nothing on earth we could do for him and he died a few minutes later. I looked at my watch and it said 10.20am."

Following Horton's death, Executive Officer Bob Harwick stepped up to take command. Harwick was highly respected by the men and despite the terrible circumstances, news quickly spread and his appointment was warmly received. Shortly afterwards, a jeep from B/326 collected Horton's body and took it to the regimental aid station at Dorpschool on Kerkstraat in Zetten.

"The battalion got into some of the meanest fighting, perhaps the worst we had ever encountered," recalled Bob Webb. "The whole thing seemed like it was a life and death matter for the Germans to break through. Our people were coming off the line really shaken, which was unusual." Webb's job at the time was to set up a battalion supply depot, with Ben Hiner, inside one of the buildings south of the level crossing along Dalwagenseweg. The 81st Antiaircraft Battalion was already there when they arrived, but were quickly persuaded to relocate. "It turned out to be a very handy place from which to service the troops during the early stages of the battle. The fighting was so intense that S/Sgt Roy Burger burned out three 81mm mortar barrels before completely running out of ammunition. Under heavy enemy fire, I loaded up a couple of trailers and made a run for Zetten to resupply him."

Local children Geurt van Rinsum, Cor de Ruijter, Adrie Hendriks, and Henk Arnoldussen (Jannie's younger brother) were "playing" close to the 81mm mortar battery at Hoofdstraat as Geurt recalls: "I was 13-years-old and totally fascinated by the American positions which were located next door to my house. Beside each mortar lay a pile of bombs in readiness for the two-man crew. When the command to fire was given each team worked in unison taking it in turns to drop the heavy shells into the tube. Firing at a rate of about 50 rounds per minute, it seemed to us that there was hardly a second when there wasn't a shell down a barrel."

During the barrage that followed, more soldiers were on hand to replenish the rapidly dwindling stockpiles of ammunition.

On other occasions we had always stayed nearby to the predug air raid trenches but this time decided to move closer for a better view. Suddenly we heard the all too familiar sound of incoming enemy artillery. The high-pitch whistling changed to a strange fluttering noise, as I ran with my friends toward the safety of the trenches. I threw myself to the ground as the first shell exploded, scorching my head, face, and legs, getting back up I continued to run until a soldier pulled me into a slit trench. I was lucky, as the blast ripped open the upper part of Adrie's leg down to the knee. I can still see him standing there screaming over and over again "I've been hit" as blood poured from the gaping wound, filling his clogs. Panic set in and I ran to my house, not realizing that Henk had also been hurt. Henk and Adrie were quickly evacuated with other casualties to the Dorpschool. Henk was treated and sent home but Adrie was moved to a hospital in Brabant for further treatment. It was months before his parents learned of his whereabouts and condition.

The quick and the dead

At the time of the battle, H Co's 3 Ptn had around 44 men at its disposal as Alex Andros recalls: "Sgt Charles 'Chuck' Richards' squad was on the right locking in with G Company. Sgt George Montilio's squad was in reserve, protecting our left flank, and Sgt Kleckner's first squad were way out front with the MG Platoon, and bore the brunt of the enemy assault. I had previously sent two guys to a house over on the southern side of the tracks to keep watch. Just before dawn, they came back and reported to Ralph Bennett that they'd seen a large number of enemy soldiers approaching from the west. More worryingly, the scouts· had also observed another group cautiously advancing behind the railway embankment towards us."

At daybreak Ralph Bennett was in a large tool shed located on the northern side of the railway junction at Smachtkamp, peering across the tracks with his field glasses. "It looked like the whole German army was coming our way in what seemed like one solid black mass," recalls Bennett.

A few moments later our artillery opened up but the Germans still kept coming. The two guys who had previously been on outpost duty moved forward with me along the edge of the embankment. We had only gone about 25 yards when we heard German voices coming from the other side of the tracks. I threw a grenade and scrambled across the railway lines and found myself pointing my TSMG at maybe a dozen or so enemy soldiers, standing in the wide waterlogged ditch that ran along either side of the embankment. The only way to describe what happened next was as if I'd clapped my hands to gain their attention. Simultaneously, the group lifted their heads and looked up towards me. We were so close that I could see the horror and panic in their eyes. Squeezing the trigger, I emptied an entire magazine into their faces and ran like hell back to our CP. Although I didn't realize it at the time, that one defining moment would haunt me for the rest of my life. When we got back to warn Lt Andros of the impending threat, he told me that Harry Clawson had been hit and I was now the new platoon sergeant.

While Bennett had been away, 1st Lt Andros and S/Sgt Harry Clawson were desperately trying to contact the battalion but signals corporal Franklin Stroble was unable to get his walkie-talkie to transmit. The three men were sheltering in a small orchard enclosed by deep drainage ditches when a shell exploded, killing Stroble and wounding Clawson. Half of

Stroble's face was missing and it was obvious to the others that he was dead. Andros was incredibly lucky to escape with nothing but a flesh wound and a dent in his steel helmet.

Pfc Dud Hefner ran across a makeshift bridge that spanned the ditch directly behind "Blokpost 17" and recalls: "Although we were still being shelled, I could plainly hear Clawson calling for help. Harry was completely blind and I placed his arms over my shoulders and carried him back to the CP."

Three or four men from Andros' platoon started firing from the corner of the Blokpost as the enemy tried to avance across the road junction. During the exchange of fire, assistant 3 Ptn leader, 2nd Lt Willie Miller, was seriously wounded in the neck. "The crossing soon became cluttered with enemy casualties and since we were in such close proximity, we began exchanging grenades back and forth across the embankment," recalled Andros. A small group of Volksgrenadiers got into the tool shed and started shooting as Gene Johnson remembers: "One of our guys fired a rifle grenade at point-blank range through the open door and took them out."

Pfc Spencer "S. O." Phillips was in Sgt Frank Kleckner's first squad and recalls: "Charles Hutchings and myself were on outpost duty about 100 yards in front of the LOD, when the Germans started another attack from the direction of the river. Hutchings took aim with his rifle and I told him to hold fire until the enemy was no more than 25 yards away from our position. We then pulled back to a house and took cover in the cellar as half a dozen artillery rounds destroyed the walls above our heads."

Part of the line held by G Co's 2 Ptn was also overrun, as Joe Doughty recalls: "During the bombardment my CP was hit, burying me in the rubble. I was lucky to escape reasonably unscathed except for a piece of shrapnel that narrowly missed my eye. The wound was serious enough for the medics to evacuate me to a hospital near Nijmegen and Ed Harrell took over the company in my absence." Shrapnel nearly severed Sgt Oscar Saxvik's thumb and severely damaged the nerve endings in his hand. "One of the medics wanted to remove it completely but I screamed like hell at him which thankfully worked. The doctors reconnected the digit but I had to have another operation after the war to fully restore function." During the battle two men from G Company, Pfc Andrew Cyran and Pfc John Androsky, were killed and Pfc Jim Hollen was captured.

On the northern side of town, not far from the G Company area, it had become impossible to safely maintain 3 Bn's aid station at Dr van Empel's house in Burgemeester Lodderstraat: "I was helping three other medics carry a dead soldier out the back door when a shell struck the front of the building," recalls medic John Gibson. "The terrific blast knocked all four of us to the floor. At the time there were a few wounded German soldiers lying on stretchers in the front room. Despite the fact that they were covered with debris, the explosion did nothing to shake them." After spending the best part of the day transporting casualties by road from Opheusden to Zetten, Assistant Battalion Surgeon Dr Barney Ryan was forced to relocate his entire operation to the Regimental Aid Station at Dorpschool.

One of the younger medics, T/5 Tom Call, was conveying wounded to Zetten, when he was killed: "Tom was travelling through a barrage in one of our jeeps when he slumped forward absolutely stone dead," recalls John Gibson. "The guys checked his body from head to toe but failed to find any obvious wounds. On further examination, Dr Ryan pulled down on an eyelid and found a tiny penetrating wound hidden by a fold in the skin. Incredibly a sliver of shrapnel had come over the windshield and under the rim of Tom's helmet, penetrating deep into his brain. There was no blood, nothing – we were all totally stunned by the incident."

Dorpschool pupil Geurt van Rinsum was watching the vehicles marked with red crosses ferrying injured to the school, which was only 500 yards away from his home: "Often the vehicles were so overloaded with casualties that they could drive no faster than walking speed. On one occasion a jeep drove past and I noticed a German sitting on the wheel arch with the lower part of his leg missing. Lying behind him on a blood-soaked stretcher was an American paratrooper with appalling injuries. Although virtually half of the poor man's face was blown away, somehow the soldier managed to raise a smile and wave as he was driven into the school. This shocking image is burned into my mind and is something that I shall never forget."

Holding the "murder mile"

Earlier, back at the railway station, Hank DiCarlo caught the eye of the battalion surgeon, Capt Stanley Morgan, as he was rushing towards the 3 Ptn positions on Smachtkamp. "Hey, DiCarlo, what in the hell are you doing here… I thought I took you off jump status?" Hank could only respond with shrug and a sheepish smile. Shaking his head before departing the doctor added, "Right now we have a lot of wounded who need my attention, but rest assured I will take care of you later."

At 0730hrs, Col Sink came forward with Regt S-3 Maj Clarence Hester to reassess the now critical situation on the "murder mile," just as Lt Andros sent his runner Pfc Elmer Swanson to look for stretcher bearers, who returned 20 minutes later with Dr Morgan and several members of the medical detachment. "At roughly the same time, Bob Sink arrived and wanted to know what the hell was going on," recalls Andros. "I told him frankly that we were getting our butts kicked, and he asked if we could hold on for another couple of hours while first battalion was being deployed!… With the enemy pushing forward on both flanks we both realized that it was impossible for 3 Ptn to remain any longer. After Sink's visit, I sent my radio operator Gene Johnson over to Chuck Richards with orders for him to pull out. Johnson returned almost immediately saying that Richards was being overrun and the Germans were now breaking through on the right flank." It was clear to Col Sink that immediate reinforcements were urgently needed to plug the gap, and at that moment the Airborne Engineers from B/326 were his only option.

Meanwhile, due to a lack of stretchers, the medics were unable to remove everyone from "Blokpost 17," and 3 Ptn medic, Pvt Irving Baldinger, was struggling with the more serious cases. As a result,

Dr Morgan and Cpl Walter Pelcher decided to stay and look after the remaining wounded until the detachment could return. When it became apparent that the medics would not be coming back, Morgan sent Pelcher and Baldinger back to Opheusden with the rest of 3 Ptn, opting to stay behind and look after Clawson, Thomas, Benton, and another injured machine-gunner, Pfc George Goins.

Very quickly things got intermingled as Frank Kleckner recalls: "I turned around and saw a German behind us about to take a shot at Pfc Charles Hutchings. My rifle was right alongside Hutchings' ear when I fired, and it was only then that he realized I'd just saved his life. Ralph Bennett's actions definitely saved my squad from being overwhelmed, because it kept the Germans on the opposite side of the railway embankment, so all I had to contend with were the enemy to our immediate front."

The following action was one of many conspicuous acts of gallantry that would be witnessed over the next two days by the men of the 506th PIR: "The enemy were attempting to envelop us and were now attacking from both the north and south," rememberd Ralph Bennett:

We were still being shelled like crazy and had been ordered to withdraw but it was my responsibility as the mortar sergeant to cover the maneuver. Lt Andros and a couple of the guys remained behind while I took a 60mm mortar tube off the base plate and stuck it in the ground.

There was a wooden cart stacked with bales of hay behind the signalman's house and Andros climbed on top to spot for me. Stripping off all the shell increments, firing blindly, I held the tube almost vertically within maybe five degrees of perpendicular and let the first bomb go. Open-mouthed we watched as the shell launched directly above our heads. Andros scrambled for cover under the cart as the round came down and exploded no more than ten yards away. But at least it gave me a starting point from where I was able to adjust and began dropping the other shells accurately behind the embankment.

Andros and Bennett could hear screaming coming from the other side of the tracks as Ralph recalls: "It fooled the Germans into thinking that the spot had been zeroed by artillery, which kept them from crossing the railway line. I only had enough shells to last me for about ten minutes but it bought some desperately needed time. Leaving me to cover the withdrawal, Andros said goodbye and headed back to Opheusden."

The bulk of B/326 Airborne Engineers, under the command of Capt Donald Froamke, were still in reserve at Boelenham farm when Col Sink ordered them west to support H Company. After about a mile, Froamke and his men came under enemy small-arms fire. The company was deployed into the Biezenwei, an open area of pasture west of Dalwagenseweg, where Froamke was killed trying to assist one of his men, Pvt Charles Wilber: "A bullet entered my chest and exited through my back and another hit my right leg just above the ankle. As the captain came to my aid, a shell exploded and hurled him high into the air, leaving my ears ringing from the blast."

Wim de Bosch was awoken early in the morning by incoming artillery: "My family were forced to take cover in the air-raid shelter behind our house. At dawn, I could clearly see a group of Americans crawling west through the Biezenwei behind our property towards Smatchkamp." At around 0900hrs, a paratrooper from B/326 Airborne Engineers stumbled passed the De Bosch family shelter, carrying Pvt Wilber. The soldier came over to ask Wim and his sister Dirkje if they could help take Charles into the house. After undressing Wilbers in the scullery, the brother and sister were shocked by the severity of his wounds as Wim recalls: "We made up some dressings before dragging the American, who was now shaking with shock, onto a bed in the back room, where my sister covered him with a blanket and placed a hot-water bottle at his feet. As Charles calmed down, he joked that this was the first time he'd ever been wounded. The other soldier decided to return to the fight and left his friend in our care. The artillery increased and in an attempt to protect Charles we covered him with more blankets.

The house was hit several times, forcing my sister and I to hide behind a mattress in the fireplace."

About an hour later, when Wim and Dirkje emerged they were nearly shot by another soldier who had come to see if Wilber was OK. After apologizing, the man went away to search for a medic. Dr Ryan arrived a few minutes later and sent a jeep to take Wilber to the Dorpschool. "Our property was occupied several times during the afternoon by the Americans, firing point-blank at the enemy, who were desperately trying to cross the Biezenwei," recalls Wim.

We had to consider my other sister Grietje, who was heavily pregnant, and my elderly aunt Mijntje, who had trouble walking, and by 4pm the Germans were almost upon us and we realized that it would be insane to stay any longer.

The noise of the continuous explosions shook the ground under our feet and the choking stench of cordite literally took my breath away. We could feel the bullets bouncing off the shelter and one narrowly missed me and embedded into the wall. The situation was now so desperate that we had to do something or be overrun by the Germans, who were now no more than 50 yards away.

I ran with my father to our barn on the main road, where we found our bicycles, plus a bakfiet belonging to a neighbor still intact. We brought the bikes to the shelter and loaded Mijntje and Grietje and as many blankets as we could carry in the bakfiet. A couple of my friends, Izak, Will, and Gerrit, who had been sheltering with us, pushed and pulled the heavy tricycle as we headed along Dalwagenseweg, in the direction of Dodewaard. Upon reaching the bridge over the Linge Canal, a bullet glanced off the frame of my bike. Moments later we passed a Sherman tank firing at regular intervals, and after travelling a further 500 yards, we seemed to be out of the firing line and headed for Hien.

From here the De Bosche family had hoped to follow the dijk road a couple of miles further east along the Waal to Herveld near Andelst, but were advised by some of the other refugees to remain in Hien. "We were taken to a crowded cellar belonging to the Van De Vrees farm, where later that evening we gathered outside to watch Opheusden burning deep into the night."

Tactical withdrawal

Earlier that afternoon in the southwestern sector near Dodewaard, the left flank of I Company came under heavy infantry attack supported by tanks, forcing Andy Anderson to call for support. Luckily the advance was thwarted by the 321st GFA and the British gunners from 79th Field Artillery Regiment. At around 1900hrs the enemy began to concentrate its attention on the southern flank of I Company, along the river Waal. Earlier in Dodewaard, Harold Stedman, Frank Lujan, and Wayman Womack were aiming their 60mm mortar fire onto a factory, where they could see troops from IR 959 gathering for a counterattack. After expending all their ammunition, Stedman and the others were forced to take cover in a nearby house: "We hadn't realized that the company had pulled back as the Germans had begun to push forward. The family who owned the house motioned for us to hide upstairs. Shortly afterwards, some German infantry entered the building but thankfully never ventured further than the ground floor. Soon after leaving the house we spotted a British officer lying in a nearby ditch and went over to help but he was already dead. Upon examining the body we couldn't find any trace of a wound. Some time later we learned from the medics that a tiny fragment of shrapnel had entered through the man's back and lodged in his heart. After seeing our colleagues maimed and killed in so many horrific ways, it made us realize just how little it could take to actually kill a human being."

Many people fled from the fighting in Dodewaard and took refuge in the stables and *deel* (integrated area connected to the house to keep cattle and store equipment) at the back of 12-year-old Clazien Hermse's house at Hien: "However, it wasn't long before we were forced to leave and made a run for Goedegebuure farm on the Waal dijk but almost immediately upon arriving we were sent back to Hien!"

Since around 0600hrs, the CP at Boelenham farm had been receiving attention from enemy artillery. At 0845hrs, Col Sink called for 1st Bn led by LtCol La Prade, along with a troop of British tanks and Bren-gun carriers from the Scots Greys, to gather in an orchard near the Hemmen-Dodewaard railway station in preparation for an urgent move into Opheusden. The temporary tank park soon became a target for the German artillery firing from Wageningen. At around 1400hrs, Boelenham took a direct hit, displacing the roof above the scullery, which injured lieutenants Alex Bobuck and Lewis Sutfin. Life for 51-year-old Dirk Tap and his family soon became a living hell as he recalled: "The intense shelling forced us to take cover in the cellar for the remainder of the day. That same evening, at least 18 people came to the farm seeking shelter after fleeing Opheusden."

Some time around 1500hrs, Gen Browning arrived at Boelenham to discuss the situation, and immediately advised the Americans to evacuate. A couple of hours later, Col Sink headed for the Dutch Reform Church at Zetten, opposite Dorpschool, as its tall steeple made a superb observation post from which to monitor the battle. Lying in the churchyard was the decomposing body of a German soldier, who had been killed by the British in late September, still clutching a bag full of religious objects.

Jim Morton went to Dodewaard and found a more suitable headquarters behind the dijk at the Christian School in Hien as he recalls: "In the meantime, 2nd Lt John Weisenberger, 1/Sgt Fred Bahlau, and S/Sgt Ben Hiner all volunteered to remain behind with the heavy equipment near Opheusden station until nightfall, when a truck could be sent to collect them, but there was a problem. One of the vehicles I planned to send was destroyed and the other overturned in a drainage ditch. In desperation, I sent a runner with orders for Lt Weisenberger to abandon the position but John and the others bravely decided to remain overnight and guard the equipment."

Back on the "murder mile" Bennett had run out of ammunition. "I wiggled the mortar out of the mud and threw the tube into a waterlogged ditch. Dr Morgan didn't want to leave when I told him it was time for us to go. Instead he said that the Germans would not do him or the wounded any harm, so I stood to attention, saluted, and told him that we would get back if we could." In a matter of minutes the aid station was overrun and despite his protests, Dr Morgan was marched with Goins and Benton to the nearby town of Ommeren. Although their injuries were not life-threatening, Clawson and Thomas were left behind. Morgan glanced back and saw a column of dense smoke rising from the signalman's house and thought of the two men being trapped inside.

By early afternoon Lt Andros returned to Opheusden and redeployed his men into the deep ditches along the western side of Dalwagenseweg: "After the withdrawal, there were only 17 of us left from 3 Ptn and three of those, including myself, were wounded." Meanwhile, Ralph Bennett was making his way along the irrigation ditches towards the northern end of Opheusden and recalls: "I remember seeing an abandoned .30 cal machine gun, with its top cover open, and assumed that the crew must have left in a hurry." Reaching Dalwagenseweg, Bennett could hear the sound of vehicles in the distance, and headed south to meet up with 3 Ptn at De Tol. The H Company CP in the old tollhouse was situated near to the railway station at the corner of Dalwagenseweg and Tolsestraat. Earlier one of the barns next to the house had been hit by shellfire and burnt down. When Bennett arrived, Capt Walker was nowhere to be seen, so he briefed Lt Andros and a couple of other officers about the German vehicles now trying to outflank the town.

It was getting dark when Andros sent Bennett back along the street to reassess the situation as Bennett recalled: "After what I'd just been through, it was something I could have done without, but I followed orders and selected four men to accompany me." At the same time, Frank Kleckner, George Montilio, and Chuck Richards occupied the orchard across the street and succeeded in temporarily pushing the Germans back from the Biezenwei. Meanwhile, keeping the apple trees on his left, Bennett headed north along Dalwagenseweg, towards the sound of the enemy vehicles. "As we got to the end of the orchard, I spotted a German sentry and cut the man's throat before deciding that it was too dangerous to go any further." Gene Johnson adds: "That night we were ordered to move to Dodewaard, but 1/Sgt Bolles told 3 Ptn to stay where we were and get some sleep and prepare for the following day."

Ben Hiner played a small but vital part in blocking the potential enemy armored thrust, when he advised one of the tanks from the Scots Greys of the impending enemy threat. The Sherman entered the town and knocked out a couple of light recon tanks along Dalwagenseweg, temporarily halting any further enemy armored movement.

"If only we had the tools"

Bobbie Rommel and his machine-gun crew had spent most of the day in a house on the southern edge of Opheusden, where they had established a fire position in the attic:

The owner of the property was badly wounded while climbing the stairs, when a shell exploded right outside the front door, covering the backs of his legs with shrapnel. The poor guy lost a lot of blood before the medics turned up in a jeep and hauled him away. That night the gun became so clogged with carbon that it actually stopped working. We were totally out of oil, and with nothing suitable in the house, we ran across the street and found something more suitable in a kitchen pantry. Tearing the gun down on the kitchen floor I coated the working parts with lashings of creamy butter and when the weapon was reassembled it functioned perfectly.

About the same time, Lieutenant Wedeking came over and offered us some rations back at the platoon area down by the canal. We had hardly eaten a thing all day so how could we refuse? As we were opening the ration packs, one of the guys noticed a group of civilians milling around behind the house opposite. It turned out there was a makeshift air-raid shelter behind the property and we went down inside to check that everyone was OK. It was full of old men, women, and children, so we gave them what was left of our meals. After nightfall another group of civilians turned up seeking permission to leave town, and it wasn't long after they'd gone when the Germans began to shell our positions. Luckily most of the projectiles landed in the mud along the canal bank and failed to explode. At that point we were ordered to move to a new location about a mile along the road towards Dodewaard where we dug in for the night.

Before the platoon moved out, Lt Wedeking ordered the removal of the breach block from the .50 cal machine gun, rendering it useless to the Germans.

After the "murder mile" had begun to stabilize, 1st Bn moved forward and recovered some of the ground that had been lost. During the later stages of the first day, Fred Bahlau found himself working alongside A Company near the railway station: "I ran towards this one guy who was firing a machine gun next to a dead German soldier and slid feet first into the body. Looking up, I suddenly realized that the soldier operating the gun was a buddy of mine from Michigan, Don Brinistool. Half joking I said, 'Jesus Christ … Brin, how's your mom and dad?' and between bursts, we had a brief conversation about home and family. Before heading into town, I distinctly remember shouting in Don's ear, 'You have got to hold the line at all costs so keep that gun burning.'"

By the time H Co's 2 Ptn got into Opheusden, most of the locals had abandoned their homes as Ken Johnson recalls: "I remember searching houses for stragglers and bizarrely finding a garage full of contraband black-market goods, piled next to a motorcycle that looked like it had just come out of a showroom. I loved big motorbikes and had owned a Harley Davidson before enlisting. Impressed by the Dutch bike, I said to one of the boys, 'How on earth can I get this home?' My friend burst out laughing and replied, 'After what happened out there today how on earth do you think you are gonna get yourself home let alone a darn motorbike?' Shrugging my shoulders, I couldn't help but ask if anyone had a spare set of spanners."

After 1st Bn moved into position, 3rd Bn withdrew under cover of darkness and reassembled at the Christian School in Hien. Bob Stroud recalled: "Along the way we came under mortar and artillery fire, and Pfc Glenn Sweigart was killed. Upon reaching the CP at the schoolhouse, we were ordered to return to our original positions due to some kind of admin error! On the way back we passed G Company, who had about 70 German prisoners they were escorting towards Dodewaard."

That night the entire 3rd Bn was ordered south of the railway, to form a defensive line 400 yards wide, continuing north into Opheusden, linking up with 1st Bn. Throughout the chaos of October 5, 2nd Bn's positions remained unchanged. However, the new order of battle followed a line from south to north, beginning with I Company along the Waal at Dodewaard. The main line of resistance (MLR) continued with one platoon from B/326 Airborne Engineers, H Company (with G Company in reserve), followed by C, B, and A Company, who were anchored up on the dijk next to the Rijn.

"Apart from Arnhem, Opheusden was probably the bloodiest battle of the entire campaign," adds Ralph Bennett. "The rifle companies lost a lot of guys and I was lucky to get most of mine out alive. Ultimately, one of the reasons why the German attack failed was due to accurate and effective counterbattery fire called in by the artillery observers attached to 1/506."

At some point after the signalman's house on Smachtkamp was hit, the Germans moved the bodies of Clawson and Thomas to a forward aid station on the southern side of the railway embankment, where they established a temporary cemetery. The corpses of the two Americans were then buried on the northern side of the tracks, to keep them separate from the German dead. Over the weeks following the battle the shallow graves were covered by floodwater and any external sign of their existence washed away.

When the morning comes

A vigorous and aggressive patrolling policy was maintained throughout the night of October 5/6 by all front line units, under a protective shield of harassing artillery fire. In the lull that preceeded first light on October 6, a heavy mist descended over the area. G Co 3 Ptn, led by 1st Lt Linton Barling, were moving westwards along the railtracks when they clashed with forward elements of II./IR 958. The enemy unit had moved into the station under cover of darkness, and were now threatening the MLR at the level crossing. Simultaneously, IR 957 attacked along the northern side of the station, pushing 1st Bn back 500 yards and pinning down H Company, who suffered two men killed from 2 Ptn – Pvt Jack Butler and Pfc Jose Hernandez.

The remainder of G Company were immediately released from reserve and sent to defend the tracks in an attempt to recapture the station. The 3 Ptn were somewhere in front of 5th DCLI, who were expected to be coming in from the right along Dalwagen on a flanking movement. Barling heard voices up ahead and, thinking they were British, moved forward in the fog to make contact. The voices turned out to be German and after a brief exchange of fire, the enemy displayed a white flag. As Barling passed the waiting room on the western side of the station, the door flew open and he was killed instantly by a burst of machine-gun fire.

At dawn, Ben Hiner was in one of the houses close to the southern side of the station along Dalwagenseweg. "I was peering west through the mist from a second-floor window, when I saw a number of soldiers eerily emerging from an orchard about 300 yards away." The advance party from IR 958 had found a gap in the lines, and were now moving in extended file – about ten feet apart – along the edge of the orchard in an attempt to outflank the town. At first Bahlau thought they were Americans, but then noticed the men were wearing long woolen overcoats. The roaring silence was shattered the moment Hiner opened fire on the gray-clad figures with his M1 rifle. Weisenberger and Bahlau were resting nearby in a large building belonging to the railway, and they immediately realized what was happening as Fred Bahlau recalls: "I was on guard behind a pile of battalion supplies outside the barn when I alerted Lt Weisenberger, who immediately ran over to support Hiner. However, the overwhelming weight of return fire forced them both back to the ground floor of the house."

The Germans made no attempt to clear Bahlau and Hiner's positions but instead circled around an adjacent building and crossed over Dalwagenseweg. "Using the nearest ditch we moved forward towards the building and managed to get behind the enemy who were now moving away from us," recalls Bahlau. "Using the ditch on the other side of the road we got close enough to throw a few grenades into the rear of the column."

"Lt Weisenberger's carbine jammed briefly, just as he jumped into the ditch with Bahlau," remembers Hiner. "I watched the rear as Fred engaged and captured five of the Germans. We then started to receive fire from a copse about 70 yards away. The guys continued firing from the ditch, as I scuttled around behind the trees and shouted for the enemy to surrender, which much to my surprise they did! The Kraut in charge wasn't being very co-operative, but soon changed his mind after I prodded him with my bayonet. For being so arrogant, we made him push one of his colleagues, who had been wounded, back to our original position in a wheelbarrow."

In total the three men had managed to capture 11 prisoners as Bahlau remembers: "Really they were just boys wearing brand-new uniforms who gave up easily. I guess we were lucky because this sort of thing would never have happened in Normandy." A brief look through the men's *soldbücher* (paybooks) revealed that the prisoners had originally been assigned to the 13. Infanterie Close Support Howitzer Company (ID 363). Once again the man pushing the wheelbarrow became argumentative, as Bahlau recollects: "The guy soon shut up when I gestured toward his throat with my knife, before hacking off his collar insignia as a souvenir!"

When the group returned to their original location they were glad to see that the long-awaited vehicles from HQ Company had finally arrived. After several trips through furious enemy artillery fire, almost everything, including the 11 prisoners, was successfully delivered to Hien. Lt Weisenberger remained at the battalion CP, while Bahlau and Hiner made one more journey back to the outpost, where they ran into Capt Harwick and 1st Lt Heggeness.

A couple of hours earlier, Col Sink had called Capt Harwick in Hien to report that a German raiding party had broken through the G and H Company front lines, ahead of another possible heavy attack, and asked him to investigate. Harwick called for a driver and jeep then tried to drive north, but artillery bursting across the open meadows along Dalwagenseweg prevented him from reaching Opheusden. Somewhere north of Dodewaard, Harwick spotted 1st Lt Heggeness, who happened to be in the vicinity with his 2 Ptn. Heggeness recalls: "The 'brass' wanted Capt Harwick to send out a patrol to assess the situation and capture an enemy soldier for interrogation and on the spur of the moment the boss decided to do this himself."

One of the sergeants from 2 Ptn suggested that Capt Harwick could take a small squad, park the jeep in "no man's land, then simply wait at a safe distance for a German patrol to come along and take the bait." This seemed ridiculous, and realizing that the enemy had been pushing down the railway lines towards Boelenham farm, Harwick decided it might be better to head towards Hemmen and asked Heggeness to go with him. The driver turned around and taking a more circular route, drove his two passengers to the farm, where Harwick intended to get an update from 5th DCLI, who were still occupying the old 506th CP.

Earlier, the owner of Boelenham farm, Dirk Tap, had been asked by the British to make preparations for his family to leave and recalls: "On hearing the news, the refugees who had been sheltering overnight in the basement fled towards Dodewaard. Around 1pm, artillery shells began to explode around the property and the cart that we'd been loading with our belongings was blown to smithereens. It felt like the world was ending as we scrambled out through the scullery door and returned to the cellar." Shortly after arriving, and concerned for the Tap family's welfare, Capt Harwick went into the kitchen to look for the family. As he moved through the scullery, towards the back door, a burst of automatic gunfire shattered a window to his left.

The British seemed totally unconcerned that the Germans were now only a short distance away from the house. Harwick thought better of the situation and ran to his waiting jeep. Thinking he could outflank the enemy, the anxious driver sped down the straight narrow driveway, and turned due west (right) along Boelenhamsestraat towards Opheusden.

Following the line of the railway tracks, the men had driven no more than 500 yards, when they ran into a patrol from II./IR 958 hiding behind a dijk, to their right, next to a large tree.

Capt Harwick yelled at the driver to "step on it" and ducked down. Initially the Germans seemed surprised but they soon came to their senses, and fired a volley of rifle shots, followed by several bursts from a machine gun. "At that moment, the world was just a piece of muddy road and fleck of green field as we cringed and reached 50 miles per hour," recalls Harwick. "I knew the jeep had been hit but we seemed OK, except the driver didn't attempt to take the slight bend up ahead."

As the jeep plunged into a drainage channel on the left-hand side of the road, Harwick and Heggeness were catapulted head first into the freezing water, losing their weapons and helmets. "Gagging on a mouthful of mud, I was acutely aware of a sharp pain over my left eye, as I struggled to stand," remembers Harwick. "Heggeness was already dragging the driver out from under the water." The unconscious, and unknown, soldier had been shot in the head, and what little life remained, ebbed away as he lay in Heggeness' arms. "We expected to be killed at any moment, and were sitting ducks as the enemy only had to come forward 50 yards to get a clean shot at us," added Harwick.

Initially the two officers moved west along the channel, which eventually fed into the Linge Canal. Clark remembers hearing German voices, "We remained motionless amongst the rushes and it appeared to me that the enemy were laughing at what had just happened. We could see their rifle barrels pushing back and forth through the reeds along the bank as they were trying to locate us."

After hearing the commotion, a patrol from 5th DCLI came up from Boelenham and attacked the Germans, allowing Harwick and Heggeness to make good their escape. Following the channel, the men crawled under a small bridge to the northern side of the road and waded southwest, until reaching the junction with Dalwagen. Here, a drainage pipe led back underneath the road and the men were able to crawl through the culvert and make their way to the safety of a nearby house before continuing to Opheusden.

By the time the two officers reached the outpost manned by Ben Hiner and Fred Bahlau, they looked like a bizarre pair of Halloween ghouls, as Bob Harwick recalls: "Our uniforms were shredded and torn and our faces caked with blood. My right leg had also been injured, but the first question anyone asked me was 'Where's the damn jeep?'"

Climbing the stairs of the outpost house, Harwick and Heggeness scanned the area from where they had just come through field glasses, but were unable to locate the crash site: "However, we did see plenty of enemy soldiers crawling around in the undergrowth to the west. Capt Harwick immediately got on the radio and called for artillery but incredibly, due to insufficient ammunition, none could be made available, so we called up our own 81mm mortar platoon only to be told the same thing!"

Fred Bahlau recalls the event from his perspective:

Capt Harwick thought that there might be a slim chance that the driver was still alive. He also wanted his maps and reports that were tucked into the doors of the abandoned vehicle. After being told the rough whereabouts of the jeep, Ben Hiner and I volunteered to mount a rescue mission in the vehicle that we'd previously been using to move the equipment for HQ Company.

I drove like hell along the canal, and eventually found Harwick's jeep on its side. As we stopped, the enemy opened up, hitting our vehicle several times. Jumping into the murky water, Ben and I managed to reach up inside and grab Harwick's papers. Floating facedown, the driver was obviously dead, so we recovered the body and headed back to Opheusden. The captain was in tears when he saw the lifeless driver and needless to say blamed himself for the soldier's death.

Afterwards the two NCOs were finally able to return to Hien, where Capt Morton was anxiously awaiting news. Morton recalled: "Hiner and Bahlau actually apologized for their absence, despite the fact that they had collected Capt Harwick's papers and brought me 11 POWs!" Hiner and Bahlau were awarded the Silver Star (with oak leaves for Bahlau) for the conspicuous gallantry they both displayed on October 6. The Tap family eventually escaped from Boelenham farm and were able to find shelter at a cousin's house in Andelst.

Later that afternoon the Germans forced 1st Bn back to the eastern edge of Opheusden, where they were ordered to form a skirmish line with 5th DCLI. Col Sink and the commander of 5th DCLI, LtCol Taylor, decided that a combined attack might be the best course of action. The main thrust would take place along Burgemeester Lodderstraat, west towards the church. The British would sweep south of the road and 1st Bn to the north, jumping off near the windmill (where 1st Bn had previously established an aid station).

The 30-minute meeting took place in an orchard behind what had previously been the H Company CP at De Tol, BrigGen McAuliffe sat in while LtCol Taylor issued his orders to B and D Company, 5th DCLI. Brigadier Hubert Essame, the commanding officer of 43rd Wessex Division, arrived to express his concerns about the apparent lack of British and American artillery. McAuliffe explained that the 321st GFA would do their best to support the counterattack, despite the fact that they did not have enough ammunition readily available for the mission. To make matters worse, the artillery officer for 5th DCLI had been wounded which meant that 5th DCLI had no forward observer available for the forthcoming attack.

The British moved out along Dalwagenseweg, using the deep roadside ditch for cover. Following an inaffective artillery preparation, both units began to advance and after about 300 yards came under devastating enemy 88mm cannon fire. Although delayed, D Company, 5th DCLI, decided to stop and reorganize near the windmill.

With everyone now on line, the attack recommenced, signaled by a single whistle blast from the Americans. The British were then targeted by several enemy machine guns located in a ditch adjacent to the road. The two leading platoons swept forward firing from the hip and hurling grenades, until all six enemy gun teams were neutralized. It was then that the Germans blanketed the area with artillery and mortar fire and their riflemen began to exact a devastating toll on the stranded British infantry.

LtCol Taylor was forced to commit his reserve platoon, whose leader Lt Durden managed to regroup the shattered remnants of D Company. Despite this, the Germans were able to infiltrate around both flanks, making it almost impossible to evacuate the wounded. At one point the German commander allowed the casualties to be removed and taken to the windmill. The American medics working at the mill soon became overwhelmed with the number of British and American casualties. Meanwhile, back at De Tol, Col Sink and LtCol Taylor decided to regroup and try again.

At 1600hrs, the Cornishmen from B Company, 5th DCLI, led another attack, this time through the orchards and houses on the southwestern side of Opheusden into the area of the Biezenwei meadow. The German mortar fire controllers had the location marked and recorded, and rained a continuous barrage of shells onto the British as they swung around into position. Small-arms fire rippled along the line as the Allied troops closed with the enemy. At one point the Germans brought in a self-propelled gun but the crew were forced to withdraw. Elements of 1st Bn, supported by a troop of tanks from the Scots Greys, were fighting for control of the railway station where the Germans had sited an antitank gun close to the canal bridge.

Cpl Bobbie Rommel's machine-gun section was now attached to 1st Bn, and they were struggling on the southern edge of town under the weight of their equipment:

> Cpl Don Gallaugher tripped and broke his ankle, which was all we needed. Shortly afterwards a British soldier walked past and surprised us all by saying, "Good morning chaps, lovely day, isn't it?" The man then headed off in the direction of the enemy lines leaving us to scratch

our heads and wonder if the Brit had actually been a Kraut. Moments later we came under enemy artillery fire and were forced to take cover in a roadside ditch, when a couple of British tanks arrived to support us. The commander of the first Sherman started hollering from his turret, "Hey Yanks, get moving – you'll never kill anybody hiding in that damn ditch will you?" Bang – a split second later an AT round hit the tank, badly wounding the commander. As we were carrying the casualty to the nearest collection point, the ungrateful SOB didn't say a single word, not even a "thank you," in fact he couldn't even look me or any of the other guys in the face.

Later that day the four of us came under shellfire and found cover in a nearby culvert that ran underneath an elevated section of road. We couldn't stay there for long and realized that our only means of escape would be through the mud-filled drain. The first two guys made it out the other side but as Andy Bryan and I followed, an enemy machine gun opened fire.

The weight of my .30 cal gun helped me gain some extra traction, as I ran like hell across the waterlogged ground. Upon reaching my colleagues, I screamed, "Where's Andy, where's Andy?" One look at their faces gave me the answer. The guys had seen him slip in the mud, before being riddled with bullets as he struggled to get back on his feet. It was the only time I ever cried, Andy was like a little brother to me.

Before he was killed, Bryan had given Tex Collier's Luger to Darvin Lee for safekeeping. Most of the men in the platoon were beginning to believe that the pistol was bad luck, but Darvin disagreed and defiantly kept it as a souvenir.

"The next morning one of the rifle companies reported a six-man enemy patrol in an adjacent field and asked for machine-gun support," continues Rommel. "I went over and one of the non-coms asked me to open fire. I wasn't going to waste my ammo on such a low-level threat, because we were down to less than 200 rounds for each gun. The sergeant begrudgingly blasted off a couple of shots from his M1, scattering the

Krauts in all directions – it seemed to me at the time that we were fighting like a bunch of Indians in the Wild West."

Reinforcements and relief

Technically the overall situation on October 6 had not been helped by the superb observation afforded to the enemy from positions across the river at the Grebbeberg and Wageningen. The fact that the Germans were still advancing when the joint Anglo-American attack began only added to the confusion. Luckily a squadron of RAF rocket-firing Typhoons happened to be overhead on a mission to destroy the ferry slipways on the Rijn at Maneswaard. Orders were received that if any potential targets could be marked with red smoke they would be neutralized by the fighter-bombers. The ensuing air strikes proved so successful that the Germans were forced away from the western edges of Opheusden.

After the windmill was virtually cut off, the casualties there were evacuated by jeep to Zetten via a back route. Soon afterwards it was decided to relieve 5th DCLI – which had lost 70 men killed and wounded – along with 1st Bn, and replace them both that evening with 3/327 GIR. Before returning to Slijk-Ewijk, Gen Taylor visited 5th DCLI to thank them personally for their efforts. Col Sink later went on to say: "These troops attacked on schedule with vigor and determination under the command of LtCol G. Taylor, in the face of withering enemy fire. Their courage and ability was an inspiration. The gallantry of the British officers and the men was outstanding and instilled in the men of the 506th PIR the highest regard for the fighting ability of the British Infantry."

At around 0100hrs on Monday October 7, a battalion of enemy soldiers launched another attack along the railway lines between 3rd Bn and 3/327 GIR (who were now defending the area north of the station). The German force from II./IR 958 overran the positions along the tracks, forcing 3rd Bn to tactically withdraw in order to shorten the line and contain the assault.

Around 350 enemy soldiers broke through, and advanced north of the Linge Canal towards Hemmen. By first light 1st Bn were resting in an assembly area near Boelenham farm, when they spotted the force moving towards them. Fighting alongside 1st Bn was Frits van Schaik and members of the Dodewaard resistance, who played an important part in repulsing the attack. Over the next 30 minutes, nearly 100 Volksgrenadiers were killed and wounded in a nearby apple orchard, while 231 were taken prisoner.

Wim de Bosch witnessed the aftermath of the battle of the apple orchard and recalls:

On October 7, we cycled north from Hien to the dijk trying to reach Opheusden, but were turned around by the Americans at Blauw-Hekke farm [Blue Fence farm]. On the way back we passed another farm, *De Ster* [the Star], where a terrific battle had just taken place. As we were picking our way through the bodies lying scattered along the road (now called Gesperdensestraat), we could see many more in the ditches and a nearby field. The German infantry had been gathering in the orchard when they were obliterated by Allied artillery and mortar fire. Much to our amazement we watched as an American paratrooper nonchalantly prepared some food on a small stove no more than six feet away from the torso of a German soldier.

At around 0830hrs, elements of II./IR 958 were stopped south of the railway tracks by 3rd Bn and the glider infantry, who fortunately on this occasion had full mortar and artillery support.

By nightfall 1/327 GIR relieved 3rd Bn and 506th PIR's involvement at Opheusden came to an abrupt end. Despite the lack of ammunition on October 6, Col Sink acknowledged the contribution made by the 321st GFA when he said: "The support provided during the three-day battle was efficient and the work of the forward observers superb. The fire missions were prompt and accurate to within 100 yards. LtCol Edward Carmichael and his entire regiment deserve the highest credit for a duty well performed."

The 3rd Bn moved to an assembly area southeast of Zetten located around a large farm called De Fliert. During the clean-up operation, around 200 bodies (mainly German) were collected and buried in a temporary cemetery on the western side of Opheusden.

Frits van Schaik was now working full-time in the resistance and over the previous two days had acted as a guide to evacuate the civilian population from the town. "My group was based at Vink's cider factory and after the battle worked alongside the British, who took over the signal house at the station. One of my jobs was to identify any enemy soldiers hiding among the refugees, trying to infiltrate the area. Any suspects were ordered to repeat the phrase '*Misschien gaan wij morgen schaatsen in Scheveningen*.' This was an old trick that we'd learned in 1940, which meant 'Maybe we are going skating tomorrow in Scheveningen.' Strangely the Germans could never say this sentence properly because the 'Sch' was almost impossible for them to pronounce." Although the German Infanterie-Regiments 957, 958, and 959 suffered devastating losses during the three-day battle for Opheusden, they were not going to relinquish their foothold on the Island without further bloodshed.

∾ 11 ∾

"Welcome to the meat grinder"

The battle of the Island –
October 1944

After the hell of the previous few days, 3rd Bn was placed in regimental reserve around Zetten, along with 1st Bn. Over the following week, both units were debriefed and reorganized, given showers, and issued new clothing before catching up on some much-needed rest. But it was not long before military routine kicked in with inspections, continuation training, and a regular fitness program.

As the 101st Airborne Division began to establish its forces on the Island, the role of the resistance groups started to diminish. However, the Dutch irregulars still played a vital role in reconnaissance. The road bridge at Nijmegen was the only serviceable link between the Island and the Allied troops in the liberated areas south of the river Waal. It was vitally important for the enemy to try and cut the connection, denying the Allies a staging area from which to launch an attack across the Rijn.

The Germans did everything they could to destroy the bridge and on several occasions even used frogmen. In late September, a group of German underwater demolition men had been compromised while attempting to float mines towards the bridge using the strong currents in the Waal. On another occasion, a resistance group saw three frogmen surfacing close to one of the shipyards downstream from Nijmegen. When the resistance men shouted at the divers to come ashore they immediately submerged but it was not long before they reappeared on the surface due to lack of oxygen. Warning shots fired by the Dutchmen forced the divers to shore, where they were arrested and handed over to the military. Shortly afterwards, steel antisubmarine nets were hung across the river detering any further demolition attempts.

On October 9, Capt Harwick and the battalion staff moved to a new CP situated one mile southeast of Zetten, in a beautiful farmhouse called De Fliert. Next to the property was a huge four-story barn that conveniently shielded the house from direct enemy artillery.

Bob Harwick recalls his first impressions of the building. "When we moved in I was surprised to find a pile of clean towels still neatly stacked in a linen cupboard. The place was very luxurious and we ate our meals on a beautiful antique walnut conference table in the front room." Despite the apparent safety, Harwick slept on a bed of straw inside a large fireplace in the scullery at the back of the house. "For once my engineering degree actually came in useful, when I fashioned a 'bedside' lamp from a pair of old batteries, a length of wire and a bulb in a tin can. After carrying a panel from my parachute all the way from Eindhoven, I finally gave it to a local tailor, who transformed it into a scarf for my wife Eileen, whom I playfully called Pat."

Before the Americans arrived, De Fliert's owners, Dirk and Grietje den Hartog, had been harboring Max Nathan, a six-year-old Jewish boy from Arnhem. As cattle traders, the Den Hartogs were well aquainted with the Nathan family who ran a successful chain of butchery shops in the Veluwe. In 1941, the Nathans not only trusted the Den Hartogs with their son, but also their life's savings of 1,000 guilders, knowing full well that one day they would be stripped of their assets by the Nazis and deported.[*] During the battle for Opheusden, most of the Den Hartog family fled across the Waal, leaving Dirk and his 17-year-old son Geurt to look after the farm.

Although the abandoned property occupied by Bobbie Rommel and the MG Ptn was not up to the same sumptuous standards as

---

[*] Max Nathan survived the war and used the money given to the Den Hartogs to start a new life in Israel.

De Fliert, at least it still had an intact kitchen and sink: "As a mark of respect, I insisted that every pot and pan we used during our stay was washed up and neatly stacked on the draining board."

Cpl John Hermansky had been wounded in Normandy and was now showing signs of battle fatigue. "Opheusden had clearly taken its toll on John," continues Rommel.

One day when we were playing cards, an enemy shell exploded outside and a fragment of shrapnel flew through the window, bounced off the table and embedded itself in the wall just above our heads. Hermansky leapt to his feet and we found him in a terrible state, curled up under the stairs sobbing and shaking by the back door. Kneeling down, I placed my arms around him and tenderly whispered that everything would be OK. After a few moments John composed himself and returned to the game. Nobody said a word; we realized that he needed to let go and wished we could find the courage to do the same. I had no idea at the time it would take me another 50 years to come to terms with my own experience.

Hermansky was not the only person coming to terms with recent events as Ken Johnson from H Co 2 Ptn recounts: "Private Jose Tellez Jr went completely mad and began to scream before opening fire with his TSMG on members of our platoon. Luckily Tellez was wrestled to the ground and subdued before he could do any real harm. The poor guy was removed from active duty on a section eight [mentally unstable] and we never saw him again."

The old timers learned that the enemy never fired one shell at a time as Bob Webb explains. "For instance, a mortar makes a 'wump' sound when fired and there would be a delay between the first (fired for effect) and the corrections that followed before the main barrage arrived. Another particularly horrible device was the *Nebelwerfer* or 'Screaming Meemie' as we named them. The Nebelwerfer was a rocket launcher that fired multiple projectiles high into the air giving off a terrifying noise. They would always take you by surprise and on some nights we'd get maybe 30 of these things launched at us. At times it was like being under siege." The Germans also began to operate their new vengeance weapon, the V-2 rocket, one of which came down in a meadow along the banks of the river Waal at Wely. Webb continues, "We were puzzled when vivid orange zig-zag patterns started appearing in the sky. The phenomenon lasted for about six weeks and turned out to be the vapor trails from the new rockets, launched against London, illuminated by the sun in the stratosphere."

On Saturday October 14, 2nd Bn was finally withdrawn from its positions along the Rijn and 3rd Bn assigned to replace them. At 1100hrs 3rd Bn occupied the dijk between Opheusden and Heteren, along with the regimental demolition platoon, while 2nd Bn (less 3 Ptn) moved into divisional reserve at Valburg.

Situated along the foreshore northeast of Opheusden were two factories that had been producing bricks since 1870. The battalion soon discovered that its new home was behind the main dijk, overlooking the brick factory at Wolfswaard. The higher ground on the Veluwe, especially near Heveadorp at Westerbouwing, provided the enemy with a commanding view across the Rijn, allowing them to target any daylight movement with devastating efficiency. Subsequently the area between the factory and the dijk, which was also the main line of resistance, became a "no man's land" that could only be patrolled under cover of darkness. "That first night a haystack situated about a quarter of a mile away to our rear was hit by artillery and caught fire," remembers Ken Johnson. "The Germans crossed the river and infiltrated behind our lines, using ditches that ran perpendicular to our positions. Camouflaged against the backdrop of the blaze the Germans got close enough to kill Cpl Gordon Laudick before we even realized they were there."

Previously the Germans had dug a tunnel through the wall of the dijk and the battalion utilized the earthwork to gain safer access to the factory at Wolfswaard, where an OP had been established to monitor

Wageningen as T/5 Teddy Dziepak (I Co 1 Ptn) recalls. "Squad leader Sgt Jimmy Sheeran, who returned to the company just before we jumped at Son, quickly became familiar with the set-up. One night Jim led me and five other guys up a steep flight of stairs to the second floor. As we reached the top it was pitch black and Jimmy said, 'Now be careful fellas, there's a narrow walkway about three feet wide with no safety rails, so put your hand on the shoulder of the man in front of you and follow me.' We couldn't see a thing and blindly shuffled along, terrified that if we stepped off the gantry, we would almost certainly fall headfirst to our deaths." Sheeran led the men to a small room overlooking the river and settled them down on what he said was a pile of soft sand. At first light the men were not amused to discover that there was no walkway and they had just spent the night wallowing on a pile of blackened brick dust and were now covered from head to toe in soot!

Each OP team would spend three days at the factory observing any vehicle traffic or troop movement on the main road between Rhenen and Wageningen. On occasion the tedium was broken by a little ad hoc swimming practice as Hank DiCarlo recalls: "Some of our stronger guys would swim across the river at night to plant Hawkins mines along the road and in the morning we would take bets on what type of vehicle would be blown up first. The British Hawkins mine was the size of a large tobacco tin and made one heck of a bang when it exploded."

Pvt First Class George McMillan (I Co 2 Ptn) was first on the scene when 16-year-old Willemien Taken was wounded. Willemien (Willy) had rowed across the river from Wageningen to look for her family and found three aunts sheltering in the factory at Wolfswaard. Many local families had chosen to seek refuge here from the shelling and were now living inside the large ovens built into the walls of the factory. Life soon became routine and often the Americans and the Dutch would share evening meals.

One afternoon, while pegging out washing, Willy was hit by a burst of enemy machine-gun fire. McMillan, Pvt Jim Collins, and Pvt John

Jacobs stopped the bleeding and calmly administered first aid before contacting Dr Barney Ryan by radio for help and advice. Capt Ryan was still in Zetten at the Dorpschool, and did not think that the teenager's wound was life-threatening so decided to wait until nightfall before evacuating her. In the meantime, it was McMillan's job to look after Willy: "The doctor told George not to give me anything to drink but keep my lips wet with a damp sponge. As darkness fell, the doctor arrived with a four-man stretcher team, who carried me beyond the dijk to their waiting jeep. We stopped in Randwijk and hid from a passing German patrol. Subsequently, Dr Ryan decided it would be safer to spend the night in the cellar of a nearby farm, before proceeding to the hospital at Slijk-Ewijk the following morning." At the time the facility at Slijk-Ewijk comprised three large tents and was operated by A Company, 50th Field Hospital, who had previously worked with the 506th in Veghel.

The 321st GFA were using a small office on the upper level of the second brick factory, two miles further east, near Randwijk, as their observation post. A row of three windows, each about five feet in width, conveniently overlooked the northern riverbank, as forward observer William "Jay" Stone recounts: "One night my buddy and I were lying on a pile of old mattresses when we noticed a group of Germans in freshly dug foxholes. Each time one of them stuck his head above the ground we called in a barrage of mortar fire. This wasn't an isolated incident and we never really understood why the Krauts seemed to have no clue that we were right there on top of them?" All the factories along this stretch of the river were important to the enemy and therefore were spared from direct artillery fire. The German commanders believed that they would one day recapture the Island and resume brick production in order to rebuild some of the more heavily bombed German cities.

In an attempt to keep warm as the weather worsened and winter rain began to set in, the men made small "tactical" fires from sand, lightly soaked with gasoline, as Harold Stedman recalls: "Our faces soon became coated in a thin layer of soot that made everyone's teeth look pearly white." Because rations were so poor, many of the men began to show signs of scurvy, due to a lack of vitamin C. The rations situation became so acute that Col Chase instructed Fred Bahlau to "acquire" a supply of fresh beef using any means possible, and the resourceful Bahlau came up with a simple but brilliant idea: "After dark we drove out into the fields towing a trailer, whereupon one of my guys would restrain a cow, while I struck the beast with a sledgehammer, square on the forehead. A third member of the team would then slit the animal's throat as it fell onto its front legs, and before the poor creature had time to fully collapse, we quickly pushed it into the trailer and drove off – job done."

But despite the cruel and demanding environment not everyone was so blasé about killing the local livestock. Harold Stedman was milking one of the cows grazing behind the MLR, when the Germans opened up with artillery. Harold ran for the nearest foxhole, dropping his helmet full of fresh milk, just as a shell exploded nearby, killing the cow he had been milking, or so he thought. "When things calmed down, I noticed the cow wasn't dead, in fact the poor creature was the only animal out of a herd of maybe 30 to survive and was now desperately trying to stand. She was making such a pitiful sound that the only humane thing to do was shoot her. Afterwards, I cut the loins out of the carcass and divided them up among the guys for them to cook. The following morning, to my absolute horror, I discovered that the animal was still alive and had no choice but to shoot her again."

Ken Johnson's squad came across a farmhouse with a large pigpen containing a sow and about a dozen piglets. "My buddy jumped over the fence and grabbed one of the offspring, which instantly began squealing for its mother. Despite being hungry I asked him to put it back. The guy flatly refused, until I told him that he had a mother who loved, cared, and prayed for him just like the little critter he was now holding in his hands. I guess conscience got the better and he kissed the piglet on the forehead before placing it back in the pen with its brothers and sisters."

Cowboys and Indians

From time to time the British directed a battery of low-intensity spotlights across the river. The heavy cloud base common at this time of year allowed ambient light to reflect downwards onto the enemy held ground. The artificial "moonlight" lit up the area in front of the MLR, effectively silhouetting all German movement on the northern bank. One night in the I Company sector, Harold Stedman was just finishing his stint on OP duty in an old building close to the river: "There was about 300 yards of open ground between the dike and the outpost line of resistance [OPLR]," recalled Harold. "From our OP we had a direct radio link to whoever was manning the 60mm mortar. At the first sign of movement or noise out on the river the guy on duty would call for a parachute flare. If an enemy patrol was trying to cross, the OP would then call in a fire mission from the mortar team before alerting Andy Anderson... Around midnight, I rode back to our RV on the company bicycle to where Frank Lujan was waiting. Handing Frank the bike, I told him there was nothing happening, and headed off to my foxhole." Lujan never returned from his shift and a couple of days later, Stedman heard via "Arnhem Annie" that his best friend had been captured and executed.

The German radio station hosted by "Arnhem Annie" entertained the Allied troops by playing swing and big band music, intercut with propaganda and calls for the Allies on the Island to surrender. One of Annie's more popular lines was "Just bring a toothbrush, overcoat, blanket and come across the river where you will be treated like kings." In a cheeky response, A/506 actually sent a patrol across the Rijn and left a toothbrush, coat, and blanket with a short note labelled for the attention of Annie. It later transpired that Frank Lujan was not executed, and after the war he told Stedman that a party of around 15 enemy soldiers had captured and taken him back across the river: "The Germans 'liberated' Frank's jumpboots before marching him all the way to a prison camp in East Prussia."

Shortly after Lujan's abduction, Harold Stedman was helping a wounded colleague to the company aid post when he came close to death: "On the way back, I heard [a noise] and decided to crawl up the embankment when something else suddenly gained my attention! Looking down, I was shocked that my hands were now between the trigger wires of an 'S' mine, known to us as a 'Bouncing Betty.' When tripped, the partially buried German anti-personnel mine would launch into the air and explode, showering the area with high-velocity steel ball bearings. Carefully raising my hands, I slowly backed away but it was a miracle that the thing didn't go off."

Bob Webb was working with a colleague down by the river in the G Company area and recalls an equally sticky moment:

We entered a house and walked right in on four isolated enemy soldiers [probably from 10th Naval Training Battalion or 26th Security Battalion], who surrendered without a fight.

Before we could do anything, two SS soldiers [most likely from 5th SS Panzer Grenadiers], presumably from the same patrol, entered the room and forced us to squat on the ground, hands on heads against the wall. Things really started to look bad when one of the SS men, a sergeant, started to argue our fate with the other soldiers. Help was at hand when a couple of G Company guys burst in and took control. Five of the enemy soldiers instantly put down their weapons and took a step back except for the SS sergeant. The tension began to mount as we speculated what might happen next and much to our relief, the sergeant surrendered.

Evacuating the Island

Between October 19 and 21, the Allies ordered the evacuation of thousands of the women and children from Dodewaard, Hemmen, and Zetten, while villages further east, such as Andelst and Valburg, were evacuated at a later date. By and large most of the families were put on boats and sent across the Waal as Frits van Schaik recalls: "My parents, who came from Dodewaard, filled a wheelbarrow with as much food and clothing as they could carry and walked to the embarkation point at Slijk-Ewijk."

Clazien Hermse recalls the evacuation of her family from Hien: "At the time my dad remained behind because the authorities wanted the men to help round up abandoned livestock. The rest of us, including my mum and brother, were driven by the British to Slijk-Ewijk, where we crossed the river and were sent to the Albertijnen Klooster [convent] at Heesch, near Nijmegen. Here we were allocated small rooms, called cells, that had previously been occupied by monks. Sleeping on straw-covered floors, everybody soon became infested with fleas and lice. After being disinfected with DTT, we were moved to Tilburg where the factories could provide more space for the growing numbers of refugees."

Because he was already a refugee, Wim de Bosch's evacuation was slightly different as he briefly recounts: "As we were being transported by cart to Andelst, there was a restriction of two bicycles per family and after crossing the Waal we were driven in a convoy of British trucks to Neerbosch en Nistelrode, near Eindhoven."

Zetten was the last village in the immediate battle area to be evacuated, as Jannie Arnoldussen recalls.

After boarding American and Canadian army vehicles, we were transported to the cloister at Heesch. The following day we moved a further 50 miles southwest to the Van Arendonk shoe factory in Tilburg. My mother had just been given a pile of blankets and allocated a space on the factory floor, when she bumped into her brother, who was living with his wife above a local café, and he kindly invited us to stay with them. The evacuation was a difficult time for everyone, and we survived on a diet of horsemeat, soda crackers, and soup provided by mobile kitchens. But life still went on and and rather bizarrely in December, I got a job working for the Hema Company.★ making Christmas decorations!

★ Hema "Hollandse Eeheidsprijzen Maatschappij" or Holland Uniform Prices Company was a chain of cheap department stores.

After arriving at a wool factory in Tilburg, teenager Daan Viergever and his family (also from Zetten) were taken to a private house by local boy scouts, who helped carry and unpack their belongings as Daan recalls: "Our hosts were Kees and Cor Beers, along with their 22-year-old daughter Corrie. I instantly fell in love with the gorgeous raven-haired beauty, who was always listening to the Philips Corporation radio station 'Horizon Nederland' which broadcast dance-band music and news from 'free' Eindhoven."

Bandit country

On October 21, 3rd Bn were preparing to hand over control of their sector to 1st Bn. H Co's 1 Ptn and 3 Ptn were asked to remain and help support a forthcoming mission to rescue a group of British paratroopers from the Veluwe. Three separate five-man night patrols were sent across the river to Wageningen, one of which was led by Alex Andros from 3 Ptn with Capt Bill Leach (Regt S-2). Leach needed intelligence on enemy troop strength, possible OPs, and a Nebelwerfer position, which had been causing problems along the MLR.

The team would be crossing the river underneath an intermittent barrage from a pair of 40mm Bofors antiaircraft guns, belonging to the 81st Antiaircraft Battalion. Andros selected four men, Sgt George Montilio, Mike Eliuk, Jim McCann, and S. O. Phillips, and recalls, "I was amused to learn that the regiment had very unimaginatively hidden several small rubber rafts in an old boathouse down by the river, especially for the patrols to use. After safely crossing the Rijn, we left big Mike Eliuk (who was one of our strongest guys) to guard the dinghy, and headed across a wide flood plain towards the tree line."

While crossing the open ground, Montilio and Andros heard the click of a rifle bolt and stopped dead in their tracks. "It was obviously someone on outpost duty but we weren't sure if we should change our route or even go back," recalls Andros, but I decided to hell with it and we carried on. Although Wageningen was quiet, we spotted a couple of mortar positions and several 88mm gun sites in the distance. Before moving westwards into the suburbs we stopped for a short period to observe three enemy soldiers laying communications wire.

The abandoned mansions in this part of the town were clearly occupied by the Germans, as we could see the odd sliver of light emanating from some of the cellars. We tried to stay off the main drag but ended up climbing over dozens of garden fences, which really slowed us down, so reluctantly we returned to the road. After carefully retracing our steps to the river, we were relieved to find Mike Eliuk waiting patiently by the boat. Paddling back we were just approaching the southern bank, when our own forces opened up with rifle fire and hand grenades. Realizing the mistake they quickly stopped, but it was lucky that none of us was hurt!

Capt Leach woke Col Sink when the patrol reported to Regimental CP at the church in Zetten. Bleary-eyed he thanked the men for a job well done and told them to go and get breakfast. "Mike Eliuk and I spotted a bottle of brandy and some glasses on a table in the back room of the CP," recalled Spencer Phillips. "We poured ourselves a drink and were just about to take a sip when Sink walked in. Although the old man gave us a fierce look, he never said a darn word as we gulped down our drinks and saluted."

∽ 12 ∽

"Operation *Pegasus I*"
The rescue of the British Paras – October 22, 1944

Second Lieutenant Ed Shames had recently taken command of E Co's 3 Ptn and was assigned to outpost the dijk between Heteren and Randwijk, despite the fact that the remainder of the 2nd Bn was now in divisional reserve. The platoon CP was located three miles away to the west in the ruins of a fruit-processing factory in the Drielsche Zeeg area. Uncompromising, "the Mutiny Platoon," led by a rumbunctious senior NCO, had earned itself a ramshackle reputation with its own code and ethics, but things were about to change. "I was informed word had gone around that some 'hard-ass' former first sergeant was taking over and the men were intent on showing me who was boss," recalls Ed. "On my first day I called a meeting at the factory. Twenty percent of the platoon failed to turn up including the platoon sergeant. I made it clear that we would reconvene the following morning and expected 'ALL' repeat 'ALL' to be present."

The next day everyone was in attendance except for the sergeant. "It was clear that this guy had no place in my world," remembers Ed. "I spoke passionately and frankly to the men and informed them that I was replacing their former leader with 25-year-old Sgt Paul 'Hayseed' Rogers. I had noticed Paul previously during my role as operations sergeant and was impressed by his quiet countryboy honesty and military professionalism."

Looking around the room Shames continued, "As you know we have been designated as 'Regimental Patrols Platoon.' I'm not sure that this is any kind of an honor as most likely we will be getting the garbage and the danger that goes with it. I'm gonna bend the 'rules' governing night-patrolling and from now on everytime we go out, I'll be going with you … this is the way it should and will be."

The members of 3 Ptn seemed to appreciate Shames' sentiment and he could feel the atmosphere in the room changing in his favor. "I am a perfectionist, and although it is not always possible to attain, we will bust a gut trying. There are two reasons for this. The first is to accomplish whatever mission we are given and secondly, if we understand our role inside and out, then we will have a better chance of getting home and it is my job to get you home. I didn't come here to be loved but I would want you to respect me … if I earn it. Likewise, I expect you to prove yourselves as soldiers and individuals – if not you'll be out of here before you know it!"

The patrol sector for 3 Ptn was a large area from the fruit-processing factory, to the windmill at Heteren, to the brick factory near Randwijk. At the time Ed Shames was lucky to have Pvt Robert McArdle as his runner. McArdle was a resourceful man who could beg, borrow, and steal virtually anything as Shames fondly remembers:

We had an abundance of cherries and 29-year-old "Mac" turned out to be brilliant at trading them for all manner of other goods and supplies. Because of the distances between OPs, "Mac" managed to procure a step-through moped that I used to check on the defenses like some kind of crazed commuter. We called the windmill in the east of our sector [owned by the Aalbers family who were corn dealers from Heteren] "Fire at Will" due to the heavy shelling it constantly received. During my first week with the platoon, I remember riding on the "putt putt" to drop off Cpl Walter Gordon for OP duty at the windmill, when the Germans opened up with an 88 from across the river. The rounds were landing all around as we hurtled along the dike towards the mill. All the while Gordon was shouting in my ear at the top of his voice, "God dammit sir you're gonna get us both killed like this!" All we could do was grit our teeth and laugh like lunatics, as I squeezed the last ounce of speed out of the bike.

On the night of October 15, a man swam across the river and came ashore directly opposite one of the listening posts in the 3 Ptn sector. "A couple of my people near the brick factory challenged the guy, only to be told that he was a British paratroop officer with an important message for Second Army," recalled Ed Shames. "Initially I found it hard to believe because the river at this point was much wider, extremely fast-flowing and bitterly cold. I explained who we were and after a short 'interrogation' the British officer requested a meeting with Colonel Sink."

The swimmer was LtCol David Dobie, commanding officer of 1st Bn, the Parachute Regiment. Thirty-two-year-old Dobie had been captured at Arnhem on September 19, along with his adjutant, Maj Nigel Grove. Wounded by shrapnel, both men were taken to a German military hospital at Apeldoorn from where Dobie made good his escape. After being picked up by the Dutch underground he joined around 80 British paratroopers who were being hidden in private dwellings around the town of Ede. At the time Ede was full of refugees, who had been evacuated in early October from Wageningen, making it easier for the British to blend in. Several weeks later an escape plan was hatched during a meeting with Brig Gerald Lathbury, commanding officer of the 1st Parachute Brigade, at a safe house in Ede, where the brigadier had been recovering from wounds previously sustained at Arnhem.

There were now around 2,500 enemy troops stationed in the area, belonging to the ID 363 who had established a headquarters in the town. It had originally been intended to re-equip the paratroopers to enable them to fight a guerrilla war until the Allies crossed the Rijn. A Belgian Jedburgh agent, Gilbert Sadi-Kirschen ("Captain King"), whose team (codenamed "Claude") parachuted with the 1st Airborne Division, had arranged airdrops of weapons, ammunition, rations, and uniforms via his Special Forces radio link to London. However, with the Island offensive now in stalemate, Lathbury decided that he had no choice other than to evacuate the small airborne force to protect the lives of the local population, who would be at serious risk if the British remained.

Lathbury and his officers were well aware of a service telephone line from the PGEM power station in Ede to Nijmegen but preferred to use Sadi-Kirschen's secure radio link to the UK. However, when the need arose for more expedient communications, Lathbury turned his attention towards the telephone at the power plant. It did not take long for the brigadier to decide that Dobie, with his natural ability to improvise, would be the best man for the proposed escape. On October 14, after several intensive briefings, Dobie, accompanied by his Dutch guides, said a few last farewells and headed for the Rijn. Before leaving Ede, the colonel agreed a time with Maj Allison Digby Tatham-Warter (CO, A Co 2 Para) that two nights hence they would talk via telephone from Nijmegen.

Shortly after arriving at Sink's CP in Zetten, Dobie was dispatched to XXX Corps HQ in Nijmegen. During the two days that followed, the telephone link between Tatham-Warter and Dobie played a crucial role in shaping events. LtGen Sir Brian Horrocks visited the 506th CP during the morning of October 18. Initially, Sink was not overly optimistic when asked about the possibilities of rescuing the British. But because Dobie had come ashore in the E/506 sector, he naturally asked Col Strayer for assistance. Coincidentally, Strayer and Dobie were no strangers and had worked together in the UK during exchange visits.

From his CP at Lonkhuyzen farm (opposite Hemmen Castle) Strayer and Regt S-3 Maj Hester met with the 2nd Bn company commanders and intelligence staff. Later that evening Ed Shames was ordered to Lonkhuyzen, along with 1st Lt Fred "Moose" Heyliger (1 Ptn), and 1st Lt Harry Welsh (2 Ptn). "Heyliger and Welsh collected me in a jeep from the canning factory and drove to Strayer's CP, where he was waiting for us in the cab of a 6 x 6 truck. The colonel said very little about what we were doing or where we were going during the long journey towards Nijmegen. It was dark by the time we reached our destination which, as I recall, was a large barn. As we entered the dimly lit building, I was surprised to find around 70 people sitting on benches and folding chairs. For the most part they were British but we also noticed some Polish troops and eight or nine Americans."

A couple of British soldiers came from the rear carrying a wooden platform. Ed jokingly whispered to Welsh that Strayer had inadvertently invited them to some kind of floorshow! "We stood to attention as a British brigadier walked in and stepped onto the podium. He told us to sit and relax, then without any formal introduction explained, 'Gentlemen, at this precise moment several trucks are en route from Belgium, carrying 25 collapsible canvas boats, destined for the river Maas here at Grave.' So at least we now knew where we were!" The brigadier was most likely Sir Harold Pyman, the British Second Army Chief of Staff whose headquarters were in Grave. He continued, 'I have called you here tonight to discuss the possibilities of mounting a mission across the Rijn to bring back a number of our paratroopers, who have recently escaped the fighting at Arnhem. Colonel Strayer, as part of your battalion is currently holding the section of river in question, we would like some of your men for the job … what do you think?' Strayer nodded his head and the brigadier continued, 'The operation will not be without risk, so we'll need three of your very best senior NCOs and 17 other ranks from E Company to support our forces by forming a bridgehead on the northern bank of the Rijn, near Wageningen.'"

Sir Harold outlined some of the logistics, such as boat handling and the pair of Bofors antiaircraft guns that would fire 40mm tracer shells across the river to guide the evaders to the waiting craft. "There was no question that the British had come up with a top-notch plan but there was one thing that worried the hell out of me," remembers Shames:

How could they even think to send only enlisted men, on what could quite possibly be a suicide mission, and not have any officers with them? To me it went against all facets of duty and honor.

When the brigadier finished his briefing, he asked if there were any questions. I shot out of my seat with my hand raised as Strayer looked over and sneered under his breath, "What the hell do you think you are doing?" After introducing myself, I asked, "Sir, if the operation is that important, surely one of us should go with them, and also why are our soldiers leading the patrol and not yours?" The brigadier ventured hesitantly, "Are you volunteering for this patrol, Lieutenant?" "No, Sir, I don't volunteer for anything," which brought a big laugh from all present but I didn't see any humor in what we were discussing. As the laughter died down, he asked again if I was volunteering for the job – "I s'pose I am Sir, I s'pose I am."

Looking at my colleagues, who were still shaking their heads and grinning, the brigadier asked if maybe they would care to join me? Somewhat reluctantly, Heyliger and Welsh agreed although I wasn't popular for forcing them to volunteer, but I'm glad they did, because Moose and Harry were both reliable people and superb officers. On the other part of my question, the Brigadier said that he planned to work closely with 2nd Bn specifically in the sector patrolled by my platoon. Directly after the meeting we went back to our outfits, and as Heyliger was the most senior, he was chosen to lead the mission. Although every one of my men wanted to participate, I would not let Paul Rogers go on this or any other patrol that followed. It became a standing joke between us that he wasn't up to my standards, but in all seriousness, I needed to know that if anything ever happened, he would be able to take over.

After much thought, I picked cpls Walter Gordon and Francis Mellett, Pfcs Walter Hendrix, Gerald Flurie, Wayne "Skinny" Sisk, Robert "Popeye" Wynn, and Pvt Lester Hashey. Welsh and Heyliger selected ten of their people [Sgt Robert Mann, T/4 John McGrath, T/4 Charles Rhinehart, T/5 Ralph Stafford, Pfc Bradford Freeman, Pfc Ed Mauser, Pfc James McMahon, Pfc Silas Harrellson, Pvt John Lynch, and Pvt David Pierce] for the mission now codenamed Operation *Pegasus I*.

The next day, Heyliger, Welsh, and Shames returned to Grave with their men, where Royal Engineers from the 43rd Wessex Division were on hand to teach the boat-handling skills required on the river Maas, which had a similar current to the Rijn. "Being from Norfolk, Virginia, I had pretty much grown up with rowing boats," recalls Shames, "but the flat wooden hulls on the British variety proved particularly challenging. That afternoon we practiced for four hours and another 12 the next day and soon realized that once on the river there was absolutely no margin for error." The men were put through their paces by the sappers and rehearsed until everyone knew exactly what was required.

Assault training also took place during this period. Shames' men were to form a semi-circular bridgehead about 75 yards wide on the northern bank of the Rijn, with a machine gun on each flank as Ed explains: "Corporal Mellett was in charge of one .30 cal and it was his job, if we were ambushed, to provide interlocking arcs with the other gun, giving us time to withdraw and form a skirmish line along the riverbank."

Meanwhile, using the telephone at the PGEM power plant in Ede, Maj Tatham-Warter was able to communicate with David Dobie in Nijmegen to further develop the plan, now set for the night of Monday October 23. It is likely that Dobie advised Tatham-Warter to utilize the same route that he had previously taken down the shallow valley between Renkum and Wageningen towards the river.

Much to the amusement of Digby Tatham-Warter, the final evacuation point was given the codeword "Digby." The signal indicating that the group had reached the river was to be a red torch, flashing a "V" for victory sign. During their third communication, Tatham-Warter announced that the Germans were planning to evacuate the nearby town of Bennekom on Sunday October 22, so it would make sense to bring the operation forward by 24 hours and maximize the inevitable chaos.

On October 21, to get things moving, Dobie and his intelligence officer, Lt Leo Heaps (a Canadian who had also recently escaped from Arnhem), moved into Strayer's CP at Hemmen. This left Tatham-Warter in the capable hands of SAS major Hugh Fraser and intelligence officer Maj Airey Neave.

hicle checkpoint and traffic control, close to 101st Divisional HQ at Slijk-Ewijk. (Donald van den Bogert)

routine patrol from the 502, after the battle for Opheusden, passing through the Hemmen-Dodewaard station near elenham farm. (Donald van den Bogert)

Members of the 321st Glider Field Artillery Regiment calling in fire control orders from their dugout control post in Hemmen. (Tom Peeters)

Three members of the 506th PIR dangerously expose themselves to engage a stranded enemy patrol. (Currahee Scrapbook)

...andwijk – one of the last surviving traditional brick factories on the Rijn. The set of windows visible in the roof were used by ...he 321st Glider Field Artillery Regiment as an observation post. Bricks are still made here today by hand in the traditional way ...sing wooden moulds.

...he commanding view offered to the Germans from the high ground at Westerbouwing south across the Neder Rijn onto the ...land. Note the railway bridge at Driel seen here on the far left.

Photograph taken looking southeast towards Zetten as members of the 101st Airborne Division cross the bridge over the Linge Canal along Wageningsestraat, heading for positions along the Rijn. (Donald van den Bogert)

Tunnel previously dug by the Germans through the main dijk wall near Wolfswaard. (Currahee Scrapbook)

LEFT: View across the Neder Rijn from the observation post used by 321GFA in the brick factory at Randwijk.

MIDDLE: 2nd Lt Ed Shames (left) and S/Sgt Paul Rogers in a photograph taken at Saalfelden, Austria 1945. As a joke Paul is wearing Ed's cap to show who really wore the trousers in 3 Ptn E Co. (Karen McGee via Sara Shames Ehret)

BOTTOM: The windmill known as "Fire at Will" located in the 3 Ptn sector at Heteren, pictured here in 1939. (Donald van den Bogert)

Heteren, de Molen

LtCol David Dobie, CO of 1 Para, 1944. (Imperial War Museum via Bob Hilton)

LtCol Robert Strayer, CO of 2/506. (Currahee Scrapbook)

Photograph taken midway across the Neder Rijn close to where the *Pegasus 1* boat crossing took place.

d Shames standing on the southern bank of the Neder Rijn
n October 2007, contemplating the success of Operation
egasus 1.

Pfc Frank Lujan (I Co 3 Ptn) was taken prisoner by the
Germans and is pictured here at Camp Mackall, North
Carolina. (Colleen Holt)

andgoed Schoonderlogt (meaning country house) near Valburg, became the 506th PIR command post from October 28–
November 25, 1944. When the British first arrived on the Island they famously knocked out several German tanks at a crossroads
near the farm complex. (John Reeder via D-Day Paratroopers Historical Center, St-Côme-du-Mont)

Landgoed Schoonderlogt (right) today. (Geurt van Rinsum)

The primary school on Kerkstraat at Andelst (municipality of Valburg) that became the 506th regimental aid station during the latter part of the Island campaign. (Bernard Florissen – Opheusden)

ovember 1944, Regimental Surgeon Maj Louis Kent (left) and medic T/4 Paul Miller standing outside the aid station in Andelst. John Gibson via John Klein)

A knocked out Tiger tank remains as a stark reminder of the fearsome tank battle that took place between the Germans and the British around Valburg/Elst on September 21, 1944. (Donald van den Bogert)

Wrecked British vehicles were scattered throughout the area – an American team are seen here attempting to recover a previously abandoned truck. (Currahee Scrapbook)

Maj Lloyd Patch took over command of 3/506 from Maj Robert Harwick on November 21, 1944. This photograph was taken in Austria after Patch had been promoted to lieutenant colonel. (Bob Webb Jnr)

View north along the top of the railway embankment, where the Germans had their positions, looking across the river Rijn towards Oosterbeek. The Germans blew up the bridge on September 17, 1944.

Members of the 506th trying to repair a flood-damaged road near the regimental command post at Valburg. (Currahee Scrapbook)

This picture most likely shows 1st Bn preparing to leave Lienden en route for Mourmelon-le-Grand, France, at 0600hrs on November 26, 1944. 2nd Bn departed the day before from Valburg. (Donald van den Bogert)

This enemy Stug III 75mm self-propelled gun was knocked out by a member of C Co 501 PIR using a British Piat antitank weapon as it emerged through the archway of the railway bridge at Driel on October 5, 1944. (Geurt van Rinsum)

On November 12, 1944, S/Sgt Ralph Bennett received his Silver Star from LtGen Lewis Brereton (CO of the First Allied Airborne Army). The 60mm mortar sergeant won the award while covering the withdrawal of H Co from Opheusden on October 5. (Ralph Bennett)

An aerial photograph taken near Driel in early December 1944, clearly showing the extensive flooding caused when the Germans demolished the dijk and flooded the Island. Note stranded ship top centre. (Geurt van Rinsum)

Regimental bar at Camp Chalons, at Mourmelon-le-Grand. Duty corporal Bob Hoffman (H Co 1Ptn) poses for the camera while dishing out drinks. Lofty T/5 Don Baker (RHQ Company) is seen (left) behind the soldier being served by Hoffman. (Currahee Scrapbook)

Pfc Jim Melhus (left) and Pvt John D. Figuerda on leave in Paris in December 1944. Note the white boot laces, made from parachute rigging lines. (Jim Melhus)

T/5 Johnny Gibson (3/506 Medical Detachment) and T/4 Dave Marcus (RHQ S-3) glad to be alive and enjoying themselves in Paris. (John Gibson via John Klein)

delst, December 1944. A jeep is photographed being driven through floodwater along Tielsestraat near to the Leigraaf Canal. onald van den Bogert)

ar damage, Kerkstraat, Zetten, in 1945. (Jannie Anderson)

Jannie Anderson (née Arnoldussen) sitting on the front gate outside her home at 25 Molenstraat, Zetten 1945. Note shattered buildings in background. (Jannie Anderson)

Jannie posing with her family and friends on a Sherman tank abandoned near her house on Molenstraat. (L to R) Ali Poves, Aunty Jannie, Jans Teunissen, Jannie, Henk Arnoldussen and dog (Henk was wounded during the battle of Opheusden), Fred (a British soldier), and Alie Arnoldussen (front kneeling). (Jannie Anderson)

Hoofstraat, Zetten 1945. Local people patiently standing in line waiting for parcels from the Ministry of Food. (Jannie Anderson)

Preparations across the Rijn

Preparations were now underway across the Rijn. Maarten van den Bent was a resistance worker living in Renkum, and well aware of the risks he and his colleagues were about to undertake. Two weeks earlier his brother Simon had been captured and executed by the Germans. During the evening of October 21, Maarten made a final recon with Maj Tom Wainwright (OC Supply Company 156 Para) and Dunkirk survivor CSM Robert Grainger (D Co 10 Para). After checking the road near the empty sanitorium at Orange Nassau's Oord, the three men visited a nearby dairy farm belonging to Jan Peelen.

Peelen was a friend of Maarten's, whose local knowledge had been invaluable to the preparations. At the same time, Hendrikes van der Pol (alias "Flip") and Maj Tatham-Warter (codename "Dr Peter") were looking around Peelen farm for a suitable final assembly point. Leaving Wainwright and Grainger at the farm, Maarten and Jan headed north through the woods towards a large hotel, Nol in 't Bosch, to scout a shorter route, and afterwards waited along Molenweg for Van der Pol and Tatham-Warter to arrive. After a brief discussion they all agreed the troops would leave the road at a nearby bend, which offered clear views in either direction. At 2015hrs, after a brief map-orientation session, Grainger and Wainwright changed into their military uniforms in the cellar of Peelen farm before heading off to reconnoiter the route to the river.

On Sunday afternoon, together with the commander of the Ede resistance, Dirk Wildeboer (alias "Bill," who had previously arranged civilian clothing and ID cards for many of the soldiers), Tatham-Warter, and Brigadier Lathbury met up with Maarten van den Bent, to give him the go-ahead for the operation. Before going home, Maarten was briefed by Capt Tony Frank (2IC, A Co 2 Para). Frank told him to expect an additional group of around 40 armed and uniformed British soldiers (led by Maj Tony Hibbert and Dutch truck owner Piet Kruyff). Hibbert's group would be arriving from Oud Reemst, near Arnhem, and it was to be Flip's job to make sure the two lorries arrived at Molenweg on time.

About 90 men (including 30 airborne medics) came in during the day, guided predominantly by nurses from the Red Cross and local boy scouts. Dressed as civilians, the soldiers spent the evening at a central rendezvous point, operated by Tony Frank, in a copse opposite the sanitorium at Dennenrust. Later that same evening a wagon delivered weapons and uniforms to Orange Nassau's Oord.

Maj Tatham-Warter asked Maarten van den Bent to meet the vehicles that were expected to arrive around 1900hrs. Disguised as a lumberjack, Maarten returned to Molenweg where he was horrified to see two men waiting in a parked car. The occupants were part of a local neighborhood watch scheme and their presence forced Van den Bent to relocate to another position further down the road. Not long afterwards, Jan Peelen arrived, carrying an old axe, and reported to his colleague that the vehicle had gone. As the area now seemed clear the two men began to chop and stack wood as they waited for the two lorries from Oud Reemst to arrive.

American security measures

In the meantime, along the southern bank, members of H Co's 1 Ptn and 3 Ptn were assigned outpost positions across a two-mile front maintained by 1st Bn. The first OP (to the west) was next to the brick factory at Wolfswaard. The second was centrally located opposite Wageningen by the ferry crossing and a third situated 900 yards further east on the dijk near Randwijk. Hank DiCarlo recalls, "For a couple of nights before the operation, the two Bofors antiaircraft guns, about half a mile apart, fired tracer shells across the river for several minutes every hour. The tracer was marking the left and right parameters of the embarkation area [Digby] and as long as the escapees kept within these limits, they were heading in the right direction. It was hoped by firing the Bofors on a regular basis that it wouldn't arouse suspicion or alert the enemy when the time came to evacuate the British."

By Saturday night, all the boats had been placed under apple trees in the 3 Ptn area adjacent the river. Night routes were laid out using engineer tape and additional artillery placed on alert, ready in case anything went wrong. Before being deployed S/Sgt Ralph Bennett reported to the H Company CP at Normaalschool on Hoofdstraat in Zetten, for a final briefing about the operation. "I took about 15 guys from my platoon and distinctly remember somebody lightheartedly playing a piano after the meeting. The night of the operation was so cold that I urinated in my own trousers trying to keep warm."

Throughout the evening of October 22, constant enemy mortar and artillery shells were landing immediately behind the operational area. A barrage of rockets fired from a Nebelwerfer battery hit the new Regimental CP, located at Christine Hermine School in Zetten, seriously wounding three men.

Back on line, Pvt Ed Petroski, a replacement from H Co 1 Ptn, was making a large amount of noise as he fiddled with his poncho, trying to stay warm and dry, as Hank DiCarlo recalls: "Our platoon sergeant, Frank Padisak, leaned towards 'Petro' and quietly growled 'If you shake that thing one more time, I'm gonna kill your god damned ass.' We all muttered our approval and for the rest of the night Petroski remained as still as a statue."

The point of no return

Back on the northern side of the river, as the paratroopers from Oud Reemst were arriving at Molenweg, a platoon of German soldiers pedaled by on bicycles: "Luckily we were partially hidden from view and the Germans disappeared into the darkness completely oblivious to what we were doing," recalled Maarten van den Bent.

A group of about ten resistance men were also on board the trucks, including Charles Douw van de Krap (a Dutch naval officer) and two recently escaped Russian POWs... Shortly before midnight, just as we were preparing to move out, Tatham-Warter began to worry about Peelen's ability as a guide. It was never my intention to take over but, keeping Jan by my side, I moved the group down hill in single file through the woods, onto a track densely lined with tall pine trees. We soon reached Jan's cattle barn, where the soldiers were issued weapons and changed into military uniforms [previously transported from the Orange Nassau's Oord Sanitorium by Peelen on his three wheeled bakfiet].

At this point the column split into four groups. Flanked by two smaller sections, the main body with Brig Lathbury, Tatham-Warter, and Tony Hibbert followed the advance party led by Maj Wainwright and CSM Bob Grainger. Maarten van den Bent moved through the meadows west of Oranje Nassau's Oord, with Wainwright's group, crossing the elevated main road from Wageningen to Renkum. "As we were negotiating the dijk, Grainger and two other men fell headfirst into a ditch and started to giggle," recalls Maarten. Maj Tatham-Warter was not far behind and whispered something along the lines of "For Christ's sake shut up, where the hell do you lot think you are?" "Everyone who was close enough to hear just had to laugh making the situation ten times worse," recalls Maarten. "Things had calmed down by the time we traversed a small bridge, and crawled across the open meadow area to the brick factory alongside the river [as the Bofors guns began firing]... According to Major Wainwright, this was a critical point between two German observation posts. Moving downstream towards the collection area, somebody was spotted by an enemy patrol, but, surprisingly, after a brief exchange of automatic fire they withdrew."

Upon reaching what they thought was "Digby," Tatham-Warter and Wainwright sent a signal across the river but failed to detect any response. To make matters worse the next burst from the Bofors was not due for at least another 30 minutes. Thinking they were either in the wrong place or the mission had been cancelled, Tatham-Warter was weighing up his options, when a Canadian accent spoke out from the darkness. "Are you people by any chance looking for some boats?" The voice belonged to Leo Heaps, who was with Heyliger and Welsh. At that moment, Tatham-

Warter could have exploded with joy but instead calmly confirmed that "indeed they were the people looking for the boats."

Earlier, Airey Neave and Hugh Fraser had joined Col Sink and LtCol Strayer and the southern shore party down at the riverbank. Nearby, Ed Shames and his men were anxiously awaiting the order to embark. "I did my best to remain calm but kept regurgitating bile, which during the course of the mission actually damaged the fillings in my teeth."

Shortly after midnight, a red flashlight was seen across the river, blinking the "V" sign that signaled the start of the operation. The Americans quietly carried their boats into the water and proceeded to paddle, while enemy artillery flashed somewhere in the distance, silhouetting the men as they rowed across. Leo Heaps and David Dobie joined the first phase and were with either Heyliger or Welsh.

Because of the strong current, a couple of the wooden framed craft collided during the slow and deliberate five-minute crossing. "Upon reaching the northern bank I began to set up my defensive bridgehead," recalls Ed Shames. "Moving away from the river together with Walt Gordon, we placed the men in a wide semi-circle about ten to 15 yards apart, with the two machine guns on the riverbank protecting our flanks. Cpl Gordon and I then took up prearranged positions at the apex and waited... We had expected to meet one of the Dutch resistance workers, but there was nobody to be seen, so Heyliger and Welsh went forward with their teams and disappeared into the woods. While we were waiting for the search party to return, I sent Cpl Gordon around to check on the men."

Tension began to mount when, as a diversionary tactic, British artillery started to shell enemy positions east of Arnhem. About ten minutes later much to everyone's relief, Heyliger and Welsh reappeared with Brig Lathbury and his men. Immediately a signal was flashed across the river for the other boats, crewed by the sappers from the Royal Engineers, to come across.

Once inside the bridgehead, it took about 30 minutes and several trips to evacuate all 149 people (including approximately 130 British paratroopers and seven American airmen). At around 0120hrs, Ed Shames was told by a British officer: "All present and correct, last man sir." (Strictly speaking he was not the last man as one of the Russians had dissapeared during the journey.) With that the signal was given for the perimeter to implode and exfiltrate back to the river. "We were the last to leave," recalls Ed. "I had two American airmen in my boat, one of whom was a pilot called Clyde. From my perspective, the patrol went like clockwork both in its planning and execution. We had suffered no casualties and I believe to this day that it was one of my proudest moments in World War II."

When they reached the southern bank, the British were ecstatic and shook hands enthusiastically with the Americans before being led away for a debriefing. S/Sgt Ralph Bennett was behind the dijk, near the ferry and watched the returning boats. "After everyone was safely ashore we pulled back to create a protective shield. I talked to a couple of the Paras as we were walking back to the collection point [Strayer's CP] who told me that they'd had a rough time and that the German tanks during the battle at Arnhem had smashed through anything and everything in their way." After arriving at Lonkhuyzen farm, each man was given a cup of coffee laced with rum and a complimentary carton of cigarettes before being taken by truck to Nijmegen. Unfortunately, as he was leaving Hemmen, Tony Hibbert's legs were crushed, when the jeep on which he was sitting, collided with another vehicle in the pitch darkness.

The following day Col Sink officially commended Heyliger, Welsh, Shames, and each of the enlisted men for their aggressive spirit, courage, and devotion to duty. Brig Lathbury sent a special message via the BBC to Dirk Wildeboer stating: "Message for 'Bill,' everything is well, all our thanks." CSM Robert Grainger was awarded the Bronze Star by the 101st Airborne Division, and Maarten van den Bent, along with several other members of the resistance, including his murdered brother Simon, were given the Medal of Freedom by the US government in 1947.

~13~

"Our work is nearly done"

Driel –
October 26–November 27, 1944

On October 23, 1st Lt Moose Mehosky reported to Col Sink, who had just relocated his regimental CP to the Christine Hermine School in Zetten.* Many local families had been sheltering in the school before the evacuation, but the only people living at the school when the 506th arrived were the headmaster, some of his administrative staff, and one of the teachers, Miss Mattie de Raadt. Tragically one week later, Miss de Raadt was critically injured by shellfire and died in hospital at Nijmegen on November 1.

Capt Harwick welcomed Moose, who had recently been released from hospital, and informed him that Rudolph Bolte was dead and Bob Stroud was now in charge of his old platoon. The following night, two nine-man patrols were ordered across the river to assess the current enemy situation after Operation *Pegasus*. Before being posted to 1st Bn, Moose was asked to lead one of the patrols, from I Company, which included Harold Stedman, Jim Brown, Glenn Cosner, and Joe Madona.

The idea was for the team to rendezvous with a local resistance guide at an appointed time and place near Wageningen, as Harold Stedman recalls: "During the incursion and much to our surprise, we heard music and followed the sound to a house on the edge of Wageningen, which was guarded by a single enemy soldier... After

---

* The school on Steenbeekstraat had previously been a home economics academy for young women and incorporated a Huishoud School (or Finishing School) for girls aged 12–14.

carefully surrounding the building, it soon became clear to us that a group of Kraut officers or maybe senior NCOs were inside having a party. The plan was for Madona to walk confidently towards the sentry and when challenged, deal with the guy, while the rest of us shot up the building and threw grenades through the windows. Joe got to within 20 feet before the sentry said anything and at that moment we shot the hell out of the house and everyone in it. Despite one of our guys being slightly wounded, we all made it back across the river in time for a tot of rum."

On Thursday October 26, the regiment was assigned to defend the northeastern sector of the Island at Driel. Two days later Col Sink handed over to the 501st and relocated his regimental CP to Landgoed Schoonderlogt, a complex of three beautifully appointed farmhouses, three-quarters of a mile northeast of Valburg.

The largest house, owned by the Mom family, became Col Sink's CP, while another became a headquarters for 2nd Bn. Close to Schoonderlogt were several batteries of 105mm guns, belonging to 321st GFA, ready and waiting to support the 506th PIR.

At the beginning of November, 3rd Bn were being held in reserve at the tiny hamlet of Lienden, while the medical detachment was sent to nearby Valburg as Johnny Gibson recalls: "One of the local girls, Eve de Wort, lived across the street from the aid station and often helped with some of the basic nursing duties. She was a lovely-looking lady and her presence on the ward really broke up the monotony, especially for the patients."

Bob Harwick who had recently been promoted to major recalled: "Scattered around Lienden and Valburg were quite a few burnt-out British trucks and a wrecked café [Café Mientjes] that had a sign outside advertising Amstel Bieren. We were told that an Allied tank had ripped the side of the café clean off during the heavy fighting that took place around here in late September… The bar was still intact although it had become a desk for one of our supply guys and the dining area out back was now filled with hundreds of cases of rations." In early October, the

501st PIR had discovered that the cellar was full of wine and consumed every last vessel during one particular hazy evening binge. At the time, the owners had fled the fighting, as Frans Mientjes recalls: "When my dad went back to the café to check on our property, he found that all our valuables had been stolen and 150 bottles of communion wine belonging to my uncle, who was a priest in Utrecht, had been consumed. The commander of the 501st, LtCol Ewell, charged the soldiers with being drunk and disorderly and ordered them to give back all the jewellery, which ironically was later stolen by the British in 1945."

The town of Valburg had remained relatively untouched by enemy action. However, the Heilige Jacobus de Meerdere (Holy Jacob the Superior) Catholic Church was badly damaged by artillery, after the British had established an OP in the tower on September 30.

Wednesday November 1, 1944, was "All Saints' Day" and the locals made their way along the mud-covered main road to give thanks at the church. Maj Harwick attended the service and recalled:

> The hum of prayers in Dutch sounded odd at the time, but the serious faces of the civilians and the candle gleam on the gilded altar gave proof of one international tie – a reverence to God, in this mad time of suffering and hardship. I sent my prayers out to my mom and dad, which was something that I'd done since Normandy. Any time we passed a church, time permitting, denomination immaterial, I would always offer a quick prayer home. My devotions were no longer words merely to be recited as part of some ephemeral thought. They became a heartfelt tie to my family in the hope that fate would somehow be kind to me. As the service ended and the congregation began to leave, my guys picked up their weapons, put on their helmets, and once again became soldiers.

For some time, the enemy had been sending propaganda leaflets across the Rijn, packed into specially modified artillery shells. The projectiles gave off a peculiar sound as they exploded, alerting the men, who liked to collect the literature for souvenirs. At times, the rhetoric levelled at the division could be quite amusing as Bob Harwick recalls. "To have been really effective, the doctrine should have promised a ten-day leave or tour of Berlin with spending money, a big warm bed with clean sheets, beer and spirits, and the feminine touch. If the Krauts had gotten our people to believe that, then I would've had to post a dozen guards to prevent the men from swimming the river!"

As a response, 1st Lt Alphonse Gion and M/Sgt Herman Coquelin from the regimental Interrogation Prisoner of War team (IPW) made a broadcast in German across the Arnhem-Elst railway embankment at Driel on the night of November 2. The embankment, called the Schuytgraaf by the Dutch, was over 50 feet high and marked the boundary at that time between 2nd Bn and the Germans, who were now holding the ground on the eastern side of the tracks. Earlier a patrol from F Company had sent 22 men across the mound, capturing two prisoners, who revealed much of the information used by the IPW team in the following broadcast:

Calling all German troops, we know that you admit the cause is hopeless and that the war is definitely lost. Your continued resistance prolongs our heavy serial bombings of military targets in your cities and the unavoidable death to your families. You can see yourself the thousands of planes going every day into Germany. The German High Command fully realises that their safety depends on their ability to keep you firmly entrenched in your positions. Do they care if your families must suffer as long as they themselves are deeply sheltered in the earth? Most of you are classified "for limited service only," you had been promised that you would only be employed to man fortresses because of your physical defects, and not used in the front lines. What happened to these promises?

Every morning many of you go on sick call and doesn't the medical officer send you away saying, "Don't worry, we are going to be relieved soon?" But where is this relief going to come from? Ask your company commanders or Major Hohmann – they do not know themselves. You have two choices: these are (1) complete, eventual annihilation if you continue to resist the Allied cause, or (2) come into our lines and we promise you good treatment, cigarettes, and three full meals a day. If you continue your resistance you will always regret having caused unnecessary misery to your family and friends.

Lay down your arms now and save yourself this regret. Now is the time to make the decision. It is much better for you and your family to lose small compensations and petty feelings of pride, rather than suffer death for yourself and families. Come into our lines now with your hands held high over your head. If possible hang a white cloth on the front of your blouse. If you do that our troops have been told not to fire at you. Now our shells will fall on your company and battalion CPs. Come now while your officers are deep in their holes. Your relief is here but come to us within the next hour.

When the barrage from 321GFA began at 2130hrs, a number of enemy troops tried to desert but were shot by their own NCOs. However, four soldiers did actually make it across the embankment, and revealed amongst other things, that they had been fighting for fear of the greater danger of not fighting.

Bloody, muddy Island – life on the MLR

All three battalions were deployed around Driel (where the 1st Polish Parachute Brigade had landed on September 21) on a regular basis with each rotation lasting four days. The first stint for 3/506 began at 2350hrs on November 3. The battalion was deployed into a wide area of farmland west of the imposing railroad embankment that led to the now demolished bridge, which had previously spanned the Neder Rijn near Oosterbeek and Arnhem. "We spent the daylight hours in the cellar of a farmhouse [De Laar – no longer in existence] about 500 yards west of the embankment," recalls Hank DiCarlo:

At night we ran contact patrols with the British 50th Infantry Division, now on our right flank to the south, situated in some empty houses. The Krauts had dug in along the top of the mound where they had sited a number of automatic weapons. The rest of the company was over to our left (north) down by the river, quite close to the jam factory northwest of Vogelenzang. Damn good thing too, because jam was the only thing that made the British biscuits we were eating remotely edible.

Lieutenant Stroud paired up the guys that were left in 1 Ptn and sent them out every 90 minutes on the contact patrols, including Don Zahn and myself. The nights were cold and wet, and we regularly froze in our tracks when enemy flares burst overhead.

On one occasion, because it was getting light, we stayed over with the Brits and watched their snipers pick off a couple of Krauts, after they had injudiciously exposed themselves against the skyline along the embankment.

Ken Johnson recalls a similar incident but with a somewhat different outcome. "I spotted a German soldier standing in broad daylight on top of the railroad bank and, more for my own amusement than anything else, called for artillery. The Kraut was like a jack in a box darting from one foxhole to another as the shells began to explode around him. After the barrage, I took a look through my field glasses to survey the damage and watched the same soldier still moving about completely unharmed – it was the craziest thing."

Around this time Helen Briggs from the American Red Cross renewed contact with the 506th PIR: "I was now stationed in Paris and assigned to a hotel at the Gare de l'Est railway station, when I decided to restart the 'Poop Sheet.'" The "Poop Sheet" was a monthly current affairs bulletin that Helen had originally produced back in the UK for the battalion. Thinking it would improve morale she mailed a copy to each platoon but seriously misjudged the opening article: "Rather naively I reported on a Red Cross detail that was stationed with me at the hotel, who had brought back some juicy fresh steaks while driving supplies inland from the beaches." Helen never imagined that her battalion would be malnourished and for the most part living in foxholes full of freezing brackish water. The men were not impressed with the newsletter and half jokingly sent a letter back, thanking Briggsey for the wonderfully printed toilet paper!

Despite the fact that most of the machine guns lost at Opheusden had now been replaced, the MG Platoon only had ten men left out of an original strength of 40. Lt Wedeking's CP was located in a small abandoned farmhouse near the railway bridge, as he recalls: "By then most of the civilian inhabitants living in Driel and immediate vicinity had been evacuated to Valburg. Despite having fresh water from a hand pump at the CP, we still used purification tablets to make sure it was safe to drink. We supplemented our rations with vegetables dug from the farmhouse garden, while the surrounding orchards gave us a plentiful supply of semi-frozen pears and apples. Without proper infantry support, radio, or telephone as usual we felt totally isolated, although at one point I did have a British officer from the Royal Artillery attached to me as an observer."

One evening a British radio truck arrived at the farm and parked next to the house, which did not bode well for the platoon as Jim Melhus recalls: "The crew were making far too much noise and their light discipline was atrocious. We knew that the enemy would also be taking an interest so one of the guys went over and had a 'polite' talk to the crew who made a pathetic apology and drove off. As predicted, two minutes later, the German observers working from the church tower in Oosterbeek brought down an intense artillery barrage narrowly missing the CP."

"All of our MGs (Cal .30 M6) were located each night with listening posts to guard against enemy combat patrols," recalls Bill Wedeking. "The guns were placed in position during the early hours of darkness to preclude enemy observation. Cover and camouflage discipline had to be maintained at all times, especially during the recent bad weather when the ground was more easily scarred."

On the last night of deployment, John Hermansky from the MG Ptn was severely wounded by random shellfire. Bill Wedeking was there at the time and recalls:

> I was leading a three-man patrol in column formation to position one of our machine guns and a listening post near the dijk down by the river. John was about 30 feet behind me, when an enemy shell landed just over on my right. Part of the blast was directed towards John, penetrating his chest and abdomen with shrapnel. Fortunately, the machine gun he was carrying absorbed most of the impact, which undoubtedly saved his life… Fumbling around in the darkness, we immediately dusted Hermansky's wounds with sulpha powder and administered a shot of morphine. Although John was still able to walk, he was in a great deal of pain and losing a lot of blood. Back at the CP we bandaged his wounds properly and tried to make him as comfortable as possible. At first light we left the farm and slowly made our way toward the 506th area and sometime around 1100hrs, were challenged by troops from the Second Army.

After a brief meeting with a British officer, the men were evacuated to the 101st divisional area at Slijk-Ewijk, from where Hermansky was taken to a medical facility in Nijmegen.* As Bill remembers: "Afterwards I was asked to report to Col Sink, who was disturbed that my platoon had been committed to such a foolish task, especially with the limited personnel we had at our disposal. Much to my surprise, Sink then decided to send us all to Brussels, for some much-needed rest and recuperation!" It seems that Wedeking was not the only person needing a break. A few days later, after leaving Bob Strayer in charge of the Regiment, Sink also headed to Brussels for three days' leave.

---

* The next time Wedeking saw Hermansky was at Le Havre in July 1945, where the corporal was working as a military policeman at the gang plank of a US Liberty ship, loading men from the US 4th Infantry Division returning to the USA.

Due to the lack of serviceable communications equipment out on the line, Bob Webb took it upon himself to liberate four German switchboards and link them to an assortment of telephones he had acquired from Philips in Eindhoven.

Each portable exchange was connected to a company via four totally separate W130 communication cables. The theory being that if three cables were damaged, there would always be one line still serviceable... We ended up with around 23 miles of cable and a telephone in virtually every foxhole. A system like this was almost unheard of, and for tactical reasons we rigged each phone so that the ringing tone was barely audible. Any trooper could buzz our main switchboard and we were able to patch him through to just about anyone in the battalion. This was extremely useful when the Germans sent over their recon patrols and the rifle companies were able to observe and report back via the network. Using this method we knew exactly where and when to intercept them.

On November 7, Col Sink showed the system to Gen Taylor who was on a regimental visit with MajGen William Miley, from the newly formed 17th Airborne Division. Sink was more than enthusiastic about Webb's handiwork and pointing at the switchboards respectfully asked Gen Taylor who he would like to talk to: "We have Bn HQ, Co HQs, Ptn HQs, and OPs, so come on, who do you want to talk to?" Thinking Sink was pulling his leg, Taylor sarcastically replied that none of electrical gadgets in front of him were on the regimental Table of Equipment. Sink just smiled and asked Webb to patch the general through to I Company (who were now down to fewer than 50 men). One of the sergeants answered the phone and was totally astonished to find that he was speaking directly to the divisional commander!

Two weeks later when the 2nd Bn Seaforth Highlanders (152nd Infantry Brigade) were about to take over, Webb contacted their Communications Officer, and was told in no uncertain terms that the

"Jocks" would be using standard radio equipment: "It was sickening to think that after all the hard work we had put into creating the system, the British were just going to rip it out and throw it away."

After the visit, Col Sink and Maj Harwick went to Valburg, where they had been invited to dinner by the headmaster of the local Catholic school. Despite the circumstances, it would seem that Mr Bruil and his wife put on quite a spread as Bob Harwick fondly recalls:

> It was a magical evening, the like of which we hadn't seen for a very long time. A perfectly set table with white cloth, napkins, silverware, and a first course of thick soup, pot roast, fresh string beans, potatoes, applesauce, and wine.
>
> We soon got to talking and the conversation began to center on what the Dutch really thought of the American soldiers. It was clear that we didn't make the same impression on them that the British did. Rather surprisingly over the past few weeks I'd been asked several times, if we really were all gangsters! Up on the Island the people weren't exactly hostile but compared to the British we were definitely not perceived as gentlemen. We both tried our best to make a positive impression and the following morning as a sign of goodwill, Col Sink assisted the Bruils by arranging to transport food and supplies to their relatives in Nijmegen.

By November 9, 3rd Bn were replaced on the MLR by 1st Bn, and withdrawn to divisional reserve at Valburg. Unbelievably, as if there was anything left to steal, the Inspector General from SHAEF and 101st Assistant Commander, BrigGen Higgins, decided to inspect both 2nd (who were in reserve at Lienden) and 3rd Bn for "looted" goods.

On Sunday November 12, Harwick's men were sent to Nijmegen where they joined the 82nd Airborne Division for showers and recreation, which for the most part consisted of listening to the divisional band playing groovy dance numbers. In preparation for Paris, everyone wanted to practise their "snow job d'amour" on the few local women, who were most definitely not available or interested. One member of HQ Company, Pfc Dewy Rex decided to dress up as a woman and took over a room in a nearby building. One of Rex's chums spread the word that a gorgeous girl was charging for sex and anyone who was interested should act quickly if they wanted a slice of the action. Of course each person who fell for the gag went away and told his buddies about the "girl" upstairs which perpetuated the joke for a good couple of hours before the bubble finally burst.

Now a corporal, Bob Webb was only too happy to scrub away the dirt and grime of the last few weeks. "I spent the afternoon washing my stinking clothes, showering, and getting my boots halfway clean in readiness for an awards parade headed by Major General Brereton and Major General Ridgway." During the ceremony 1/Sgt Fred Bahlau, S/Sgt Ralph Bennett, and S/Sgt Ben Hiner received their Silver Stars from Gen Brereton. Afterwards, Ralph witnessed the first appearance of the new German Me 262 jet fighter. "A number of our aircraft were chasing this one unidentified enemy plane, when it gave off a small puff of smoke and disappeared into the distance. After seeing the V-2s we began to wonder what else the Germans were capable of developing."

On November 21, 3rd Bn returned to the line for its last four-day rotation with a new commanding officer, Maj Lloyd Patch. Bob Harwick had replaced Patch as commander of 1st Bn, and his departure marked a turning point for the men, as Hank DiCarlo recalls:

> We knew we were being relieved in a few days by the Scottish, so the guys didn't want to take any more silly chances. Night patrols became extremely unpopular and the bad weather only increased our desire to be elsewhere. Even the Germans seemed to be cutting back on their patrol activity, which did make us suspicious but pretty soon it would no longer be our problem. Over the last two weeks, the excessive rainfall had caused water levels along the Rijn to rise alarmingly, and the subsequent flooding forced the MLR at Driel to be withdrawn by almost 500 yards.

There was a rumor that the enemy might take advantage of the flooding by demolishing part of dijk wall in their sector, and as a precautionary measure we were briefed on Operation *Deluge*, the army's plan to evacuate all Allied troops to the higher ground.

For Thanksgiving, Col Sink issued a heartfelt message to the regiment that read:

> You soldiers may wonder, from your environment of cold and rain, from your foxholes and your barns, what there is for which one should be thankful – let me name a few things. We should be thankful that we are Americans, and that when we finish the Germans and Japanese, we will have an America to which we will return, an America unchanged in ideals, undiminished in opportunity, and undamaged by the sweeping destruction of war.
>
> Those of us who have seen the bondage and suffering of the peoples of Europe should give thanks that our loved ones have been safe and free. We should be thankful for this splendid regiment. The success attained by it is a tribute to its ideals and our belief in its cause. With honor and gratitude to those of our comrades not by our side, we should be thankful that we are here to carry the torch for them and to do our job, with honor to them and credit to ourselves.
>
> These are some of the things for which we should be collectively thankful. Let each man add to this his personal blessings. With profound humility, should we offer our gratitude to the God of battles, let us, in giving thanks, resolve that the inspiration of the past is the light of our future. May each of you, on this day of Thanksgiving, consider well the thoughts mentioned above and take comfort from them.

When Teddy Dziepak from I Company came out of the line he took off his boots and was horrified to see that his feet were purple and hideously swollen. "The following morning, because I couldn't get my boots back on, I borrowed a pair of clogs and shuffled over to the first aid post, where they diagnosed me with trench foot. My condition was so acute that the medics evacuated me back to the UK, where I spent the next five weeks in hospital."

As the flooding grew more widespread, it became obvious that the population of Valburg and Andelst would have to be evacuated. For this the authorities created a secondary plan and codenamed it Operation *Noah*. In Valburg, during the morning of November 25, as the advance party from 506th Regimental HQ was moving into the vicarage belonging to the church of the Holy Jacobus, Operation *Noah* was in full swing. Hundreds of women and children were being sent across the Waal to reception centers in north Brabant. Seven-year-old Frans Mientjes was part of the exodus: "Shortly after arriving at the Philips factories in Eindhoven, my sister Annie and I were placed with the Friederich family, who lived in the Centrum district on Vondelstraat. The rest of my family were split up and sent to Netersel and Bladel." Because of the intense overcrowding caused by the earlier evacuations from Dodewaard and Zetten, around 6,000 refugees living in Tilburg and Eindhoven had to be relocated to Geertruidenberg (NBr) and Aat (Ath) in Belgium.

During the early hours of the morning of November 25, 3rd Bn handed over control of the 506th sector to 2nd Bn Seaforth Highlanders, from the 152nd Infantry Brigade. At long last, after 71 days of hell, the regiment was being sent to a rest camp in northeastern France, at Mourmelon-le-Grand near Reims. The 3rd Bn formed the rear echelon with RHQ and followed 24 hours later behind 1st Bn and 2nd Bn, as Hank DiCarlo recalled: "Because there was a security issue with the bridge at Nijmegen, we marched four miles to the Waal and crossed the river in motorboats, before being loaded onto British trucks and driven to Mourmelon. It was dull and drizzling with rain when we arrived at 1000hrs the following morning [November 28]. Our first impressions of Camp Chalons were not reassuring but we had dry billets and proper beds, which were immediately put to good use as we crawled in and slept, slept, slept."

~ 14 ~

"Club Mocambo"

Camp Chalons –
November 28–December 20, 1944

Situated outside of the garrison town of Mourmelon-le-Grand, Camp Chalons had been used by the French Army as a barracks and training area since 1857. The surrounding countryside still clearly showed the scars of the battle of the Marne 26 years previously. Adjoined to an airfield, the camp had been used by the Germans as a parachute school and tank depot.

"A belated Thanksgiving dinner was held and shortly afterwards we received mail and our barracks bags," recalls S/Sgt Ralph Bennett. "Once again the B bags had been torn open and all the souvenirs we'd collected from Normandy were gone. I later found out that the bags belonging to the officers were kept in a separate area and had remained untouched – RHIP, 'rank has its privileges.' There were new people arriving from the UK and as a platoon sergeant it was my job to get them assigned and squared away. We all thought, for us at least, that the war was over, so getting weapons into the artificer's [armorer's] for repairs and re-equipping the guys seemed pretty low on the list of priorities." In most cases the battalions set up a training company to give replacements a week to ten days of orientation instruction. "Mourmelon gave us a chance to stop being 'mud sloggers' and start being soldiers again," recalled Bob Webb. "Close-order drill, class 'A' uniforms, spit and polish, to be honest, for once it was a welcome change." A handful of thrillseekers, like Pfc George McMillan from

I Company, volunteered for Pathfinder duty and were sent to Chalgrove in Oxfordshire to begin their training.

The camp became synonymous with reconstruction and cleaning as the men were expecting at least three months' rest in their winter quarters. The first week was marked by incessant rain, which soon turned the ground around the camp into thick mud. In desperation, gravel was "borrowed" from local roads, and bricks recovered from ruined buildings to create proper company streets and sidewalks.

The NCOs started on the business of housekeeping with enthusiasm, as Capt Jim Morton recalls. "We cleaned, scrubbed, and shined, and even employed an artist to make up some fancy signs. On the walls of the barracks the men painted scrolls bearing the names of our comrades who had fallen in Normandy and Holland. Athletic equipment was requisitioned and football and boxing teams were organized." Everyone was looking forward to the football game scheduled in Reims for Christmas Day, between "the Screaming Eagles" from the 502nd and "the Sky Train" representing the 506th.

Miss Polly Baker from the American Red Cross arrived to open a new club, which was nothing compared to what 1/Sgt Fred Bahlau had in mind for the NCOs from HQ Company as he recalls. "I found a circular bar about 15 feet in diameter in a deserted Air Corps club and aquired a variety of fixtures such as mirrors and glasses. We then built a number of tables and chairs and 'borrowed' a few tins of gray and maroon paint from the airfield. With a yellow parachute draped from the ceiling and subdued lighting, 'Club Mocambo' became the smartest spot on the camp." As a finishing touch the communications section kindly fashioned an electric sign, which Bahlau suspended over the entrance. With morale sagging, the club proved invaluable in rebuilding comradeship and esprit de corps amongst the NCOs. "Mocambo" became the only company NCO club in the division and was often frequented by guests from other units. On one occasion at the club, Darvin Lee (MG Ptn) bumped into Grady Collier and was able to present him with the Luger pistol taken from his younger brother's body at Opheusden. Grady was a first sergeant in the US Army 9th Air Force and happened to be working at the airfield with the 826th Aviation Engineer Battalion.

Despite the distractions of "Club Mocambo," the only real topic of conversation on everyone's lips was Paris. It was planned to send the regiment to the queen of European cities one company at a time, and it was not long before a 72-hour pass policy was introduced. But not everyone got to see Paris. Instead many received 48-hour passes to Reims or Mourmelon, which made Fayetteville in North Carolina look positively Presbyterian by comparison. "A few of the married soldiers, who included Maxwell Taylor, received 30-day passes back to the USA," recalled Bob Webb. "I couldn't imagine doing that and then having to come back to the European theater of operations!"

Bob Webb and Jim Melhus were among the lucky ones who made it to Paris as Webb recalls: "I went with my buddy Sgt Bill Pershing, and stayed in a beautiful hotel and drank champagne. The American Red Cross arranged tea dances in the afternoon and I met a girl called Renée, who invited us to her home the following day for lunch. In the past her father had been a head waiter in England and spoke perfect English. He took a cork out of a bottle of cognac and threw it in the fireplace as a welcome gesture. We were on best behaviour as her family were so gracious." Jim Melhus had a slightly different experience,

I was paired up with Pvt John D. Figuerda, a recent replacement in the 81mm Mortar Platoon. We had so much back pay that I was able to afford a beautiful gold ring encrusted with rubies and diamonds! After arriving in Paris we headed to the red-light district at Place de Pigalle, where we came across two girls, about 14-years-old, being hit on by GIs. The girls were clearly a little out of their depth and needed help so we hired a horse-drawn carriage to take them home. One of the girls, Odette, lived across the other side of the river Seine, along Boulevard du Palais and we soon found out that her father didn't like Americans, so we decided not to hang around.

On Sunday 17 December, as most of the enlisted men were going on leave, many officers, like 1st Lt Clark Heggeness, were writing letters of condolence to families of the men who had been killed. However, the letter Heggeness wrote to Rudolph Bolte's widow Erma was slightly different:

My dear Mrs Bolte, I hope you have not lost confidence in me for not answering your letter sooner but in the rush of things in Holland, I misplaced your V-mail and just found it. I'm back in France now, it's so wonderful being away from all that mud and shells and everything that goes with the front. Rudy was one of my best friends. He and I were room mates in England, and we went all through the Normandy campaign together.

It takes a lot of fortitude for a man his age to volunteer for parachute duty and all the extra rigors of jumping. I always will take my hat off to him, going through everything all us young kids do. Mrs Bolte, we'll always miss Rudy, when he died he left a gap in the ranks I know no other officer will be able to fill. We jumped near Eindhoven on Sunday afternoon, September 17. The next morning Rudy was crawling through a field, leading his platoon when he was killed. I wasn't with him right at that time but about 300 yards away. Almost everyone cried when they found out, that's how much everyone, men and officers alike, thought of him. I don't know if Rudy told you or not but he was not supposed to make this jump.

War seems so unjust and so many of the real guys "get it" and those who seem so ungodly always come through okay. Sometimes I wonder why they are not dead and guys like Rudy can't live. Rudy thought the world of you and the girls. Whenever he had the chance he always first thought of buying the girls a souvenir of the place he happened to be. He always told me about your daughters, the things they did and how dearly they thought of him. He was truly a great guy and one of the finest friends I've ever had. I know it's hard to realize he's gone, how extremely difficult it is to accustom yourself to his last [letters]. I only hope that what he has written is some small comfort to you and the girls. If there's anything I can do, please don't hesitate to ask me.

For the last couple of days, the news broacasters had been vaguely uneasy about a German threat in Belgium. In the early morning of December 18, word filtered down from regiment to prepare for the worst. On the Sunday before Christmas, while many were still on leave in Paris, the Germans broke through towards the port of Antwerp. Field Marshal Von Runstedt's thrust into the Ardennes had begun and his Tiger tanks advanced over 60 miles in three days, jeopardizing the entire American front.

Helen Briggs was in Paris at the time and recalls: "The MPs collected all the paratroopers who were on leave and held them at the Red Cross Club at Gare de l'Est, until they could get transportation to Reims." Back at Camp Chalons, the regiment awoke early to discover that instead of prelimary rifle practise, it would be going back to the war. There was no briefing or preparation as Clark Heggeness recalls: "On December 19, we loaded onto enormous open trailer trucks outside the divisional headquarters bound for an unknown destination." In the panic the men were woefully under-equipped and most did not even have enough ammunition to make up a basic M1 load.

In the twilight of the afternoon, the 506th PIR rolled northeast across the battlefields of World War I and through the bitterly cold wooded hills of the Ardennes forest until finally on the morning of December 20, they detrucked in a small village close to the border with Luxembourg. Although the rumble of artillery could be heard in the distance most even then did not know where they were. It was a strange way to start an operation which would prove to be yet another courageous chapter in the history of the 506th Parachute Infantry Regiment – the defense of Bastogne.

Epilogue

On December 3, 1944, under cover of darkness the enemy demolished a section of the main dijk about a mile behind the railroad bridge at Driel. The massive explosion ripped a 150 feet wide gap in the embankment and flooded the land east of the railway between Elden and Elst. Seeping through culverts and drainage ditches, the floodwater soon found its way across the Island, forcing the British and Canadian forces, and the few remaining civilians, to migrate along the river Waal towards Zetten and Dodewaard. However, the Germans had an unexpected surprise when the territory held by their own forces near Opheusden also became inundated with water.

At the time, Frits van Schaik and his resistance group were based at Oosterhout, near Nijmegen, and he recalls: "Reinforced by members of the farming community, our job starting from Dodewaard was to gather and move as many animals as possible eastwards to Lent, which was not far from Nijmegen. Because of the extreme flooding, we were forced to herd the animals along the railway embankment that led directly into Lent from Valburg, a distance of about six miles."

Hemmen farmer Dick Bakker remembered: "Amazingly all our horses found their way back across the flooded areas to the farm, where we promptly tied them together and took them to Valburg. Soon afterwards, I was evacuated to Belgium and reunited with my family." The evacuated livestock, now numbering thousands, were moved to an enormous farm in Brabant where, five months later, many were slaughtered in order to feed starving cities such as Amsterdam and The Hague after they were liberated.

In January 1945, while the 101st Airborne was still deployed around Bastogne, Zetten was virtually destroyed when the Germans counterattacked against the British on the Island. The vicious tank and infantry battle raged in the snow for several weeks until the Germans finally gave up and withdrew.

Dirk van Tintelen, who had joined the Canadians after escaping from the Island, recalls: "It was a very emotional time for me, to be so closely involved in the liberation, especially in places like Rotterdam. On several occasions as we [were] liberating some of the coastal towns and cities, the girls would rush over thinking I was Canadian, only to be completely confused by the fact that I was actually Dutch!" The Germans finally capitulated on May 5, 1945, eight months after the 506th PIR first went into action on the Island. Ironically the surrender was signed in Wageningen at the Hotel de Werald.

Zetten was the first village to be declared safe for the population to return to, as Jannie Arnoldussen recalls:

Zetten was a wasteland of destroyed and damaged buildings and most of the houses in our street were gone. The front wall of my parents' barn was full of holes, but at least the house was still standing, despite the basement being flooded. Everything had been looted, even our pots and pans, and I was horrified to find human hair and bloodstains splattered across the floor and walls of my bedroom.

I visited my friend Bets den Hartog's house and found a German jackboot with part of the leg still inside. Despite the supposed cleanup, the threat from unexploded ordnance was still a problem. A close friend stood on a landmine and was blown to pieces and I can still remember seeing the parts of his body hanging from a nearby tree. In another village two little boys were killed in a similar way. It was a terrifying time, but slowly the mines were cleared and the community was rebuilt.

I managed to get a job working in an office for the district of Valburg. One day my sister came to visit we were standing outside talking, when two Canadian soldiers from the First Special Service Force drove by on their motorcycles. My sister and I were both wearing dresses made from white parachute silk, which caught the eye of the Canadians. I became very close friends with one of the men, James Anderson, who two years later invited me to Canada, where we were married on January 2, 1948.

Two weeks after Zetten was declared "safe" the people from Opheusden, Dodewaard, and Hien were allowed to return. As they passed through Andelst, many began to notice signs in English stating "Whisky Route," which led straight to the Vink's cider factory at Hien! Some like Dick Bakker managed to get home earlier as he recalls: "I wangled my way back to Hemmen with a merchant who lived at Zetten. The farm was a total mess and I counted over 1,500 shell craters around the property. Incredibly the Germans had built a massive wooden bunker inside our barn which was surrounded by a deep drainage pit full of stagnant water."

Food was still in short supply and many locals had to stand in line for grocery parcels delivered by the Ministry of Food while others received assistance from charities such as the International Christian Organization. The fighting might have been over, but the effects of the war would be felt by these communities for some time to come.

In total during *Market Garden*, the 101st Airborne Division lost over 900 men killed, nearly 4,000 wounded, and 1,000 captured or missing. Between 1945 and 1966, the bodies of 27 American servicemen missing in action at Opheusden were discovered and given proper burials; however, the remains of S/Sgt Harry Clawson and Pfc Morris Thomas were not discovered until 1971. When exhumed, they were each found to have a complete set of dog tags, but only Thomas' skeletal remains revealed any sign of fractures associated with being crushed. Capt Donald Froamke's body was recovered in 1945, perfectly preserved in the boggy marshland of the Biezenwei, and still carrying a map case and silver-plated fighting knife. At the time of writing the remains of Tex Collier and Leo Jeucken have never been recovered, but maybe one day in the future they will be found and returned to their families. Looking back on the campaign, MajGen Maxwell D. Taylor was quoted as saying, "In my prejudiced view, if the operation had been properly backed from its inception and given the aircraft, ground forces, and administrative resources necessary for the job, it would have succeeded in spite of my mistakes or the adverse weather, or the presence of the 2nd SS Panzer Corps in the Arnhem area. I remain Operation *Market Garden*'s unrepentant advocate."

Perhaps the last word should go to one of the enlisted men, Pfc James Martin, from G Company:

> All the airborne troops did a magnificent job throughout *Market Garden*. The problem in my opinion was not [LtGen] Dempsey, it was General Montgomery for not moving the troops up the highway quickly enough. They always said that it was 'A Bridge Too Far' but I refute that. The British paratroops had a long ride over and were dropped about six miles from their objective and therefore lost the element of surprise. The British and Poles did not get the back-up support as promised. That stalled everything. The Germans had almost unlimited artillery and armor – so where was the tactical air support… High-value troops like paratroopers should never be kept in purely defensive positions where there is no strategic objective to be denied to the enemy. The worst part of the whole thing was the fact that all the fuel and supplies for this operation were taken from Patton, who was furious. The idea of trying to maintain a supply line on 30 miles of road through enemy-held territory seems to me to be pretty foolhardy, especially without proper tactical air support.

To this day *Market Garden* remains a controversial operation, hotly debated by historians and veterans alike. But what cannot be disputed is the unquestionable courage and determination of the Third Battalion, 506th Parachute Infantry Regiment.

Bibliography

Listed below are works that I have consulted during my research. To their authors I offer my sincere thanks.

Books and Papers

Burgett, Donald, *The Road to Arnhem* (Dell Publishing, 2001)

DiCarlo, Hank and Westphal, Alan, *Currahee Scrapbook* (506 PIR, 1945)

Gutjahr, Major Robert G., *The Role of Jedburgh Teams in Operation Market Garden* (thesis presented to the US Army Command and General Staff College, 1978) c/o Tom Timmermans

Heaps, Leo, *The Grey Goose of Arnhem* (Futura Publications Ltd, 1976)

Koskimaki, George, *Hell's Highway* (101st Airborne Division Association, 1989)

Liddell Hart, Sir Basil Henry (editor-in-chief) and Pitt, Barry (ed.), *History of the Second World War Part 17, Civilians in the Front Line* (Marshall Cavendish USA, 1973)

Margry, Karel, *De bevrijding van Eindhoven* (*The Liberation of Eindhoven*) (September Festival Foundation,1982)

Mehosky, Ivan Paul, *The Story of a Soldier* (Rutledge Books, Inc., 2001)

Norton, G. G., *The Red Devils (From Bruneval to the Falklands)* (Leo Cooper, 1984)

Rapport, Leonard and Northwood, Arthur Jr., *Rendezvous with Destiny* (Infantry Jounal Press, 1948)

Sigmond, Robert and Van den Bosch, Cees, (ed.) *Escape across the Rhine, Operations 'Pegasus' I and II, October/November 1944* (Airborne Museum Hartenstein, 1999)

Taylor, George (compiler), *The 5th D.C.L.I in N.W. Europe, 1939–45*

Van Hout, Jan, (ed.), *Aangeboden Door De Gemeente Eindhoven, Herinneringen Aan September 1944* (*Memories of September 1944 – Presented by the Municipality of Eindhoven*) (self-published, 2004)

Reports and personal letters

442nd Troop Carrier Group After Action Reports Operation: "Linnet," "Comet" and "Market" (1944)

Air Support Requests 101st A/B Division 20–26 September 1944

Eindhoven Fire Brigade Reports 13–19 September (1944), c/o Tom Timmermans

First British Airborne Corps Operation "Market" Report on Airborne Medical Services (1944)

Headquarters 506th PIR "After Action Report" – Operation "Market" (1944)

Headquarters 506th PIR Citation "Dorshout Bridge" (1944)

Headquarters 506th PIR Citation "Operation Pegasus I" (1944)

Headquarters 506th PIR Statistics: 17–26 September (1944)

Headquarters 506th PIR Unit Journal for Operation "Market" (1944)

Headquarters IX Troop Carrier Command Operation: "Linnet," "Comet" and "Market" (1944)

Holland Recollections H/506, October 1985 (tape recording), c/o Pat McCann

Marshaling Area in England and Holland from 14–19 September 1944 by Captain Derwood Cann (1948)

Memoire of Maarten van den Bent "Pegasus I" – Airborne Museum Hartenstein, c/o Dan Viergever

Pegasus Memorial Battlefield Tour Guide, 12 September 2008, c/o Daan Viergever

Personal letters of Fred Anderson, c/o Kathleen Anderson

Personal letters of Alex Andros, c/o Aaron Walser

Personal letters of Willem de Bosch, c/o Bernard Florissen

Personal letters of Harry Clawson, c/o Aaron Walser

Personal letter of Bart Franken, c/o Ross McLachlan

Personal letter of Henricus van Genugten, c/o Tom Timmermans

Personal letters of Robert Harwick, c/o Bob Smoldt

Personal letter of Sam Hefner, c/o Aaron Walser

Personal letters of Clark Heggeness, c/o John Klein

Personal letters and information of Darvin Lee, c/o Judy Gamble

Personal letters of Willemien Loedeman (née Taken), c/o George McMillan

Personal letter of Joe Marshall, c/o Judy Gamble

Personal letters of James Morton, c/o Fred Bahlau

Personal letter of Rolf Polman, c/o Ross McLachlan

Personal letter of Robert Radmann, c/o Daan Viergever

Personal letters of Helen B. Ramsey (née Briggs), c/o Bill Wedeking

Personal letters of Dirk Tap, c/o Willemien van Steenbergen

Personal letters of Doug Wilber, c/o Bernard Florissen

Tactical Operations of the 101st A/B Division 17–27 September (1944)

Tactical Study HQ XVIII Corps Airborne Operation "Market" (1944)

Tape recordings of interviews with Robert Webb (1980s), c/o Bob Webb Jnr

Report on the last flight of Halifax – JD214 and her crew by Joop Siepermann

Wartime memoire of Landon Kenneth Cozad

Interviews

As noted in the Introduction a number of people were interviewed in the course of my research and these are used extensively throughout the book. The individuals interviewed are listed below in alphabetical order:

Jannie Anderson

Fred Bahlau

Sam Bailey

Dick Bakker

Manny Barrios

Ralph Bennett

Frits Berens

Derwood Cann

Landon Cozad

Henk de Jong

Mario "Hank" DiCarlo

Jo van Dongen

Joe Doughty

Bob Dunning

Teddy Dziepak

Bill Galbraith

John Gibson

Kenneth Glassburn

Johannes van den Hatert

Piet van den Heuvel

Jenny and Jan van Hout

Ben Hiner

Ken Johnson

Hendrik de Jong

Jos Klerkx

Wim Klerkx

Walter Lukasavage

James Melhus

Frans Mientjes

George McMillan

Ross McLachlan

James Martin

Wan van Overweld

Johannes Peerbolte

Judson Wright Pittam

Clazien van Rinsum

Geurt van Rinsum

Bobbie Rommel

Albert Roxs

Frits van Schaik

Jaap van Schaik

Seymour Shapiro

Ed Shames

Ray Skully

Harold Stedman

Noud Stultiens

Dirk van Tintelen

Bill Wedeking

Daan Viergever

Glossary

BAR	Browning Automatic Rifle
BS	Binnenlandse Strijdkrachten
CD	Controle Dienst (Control Duty)
CP	command post
DCLI	Duke of Cornwall's Light Infantry
DLM	Dutch Liaison Mission
DZ	drop zone
GFA	Glider Field Artillery
GIR	Glider Infantry Regiment
IP	Initial Point
IPW	Interrogation Prisoner of War team
IR	Infanterie-Regiments
LKP	Landelijke Knokploegen (National Paramilitary Group)
LMG	light machine gun
LO	Landeljke Organisatie (National Organization)
LOD	line of defense
Med Det	medical detachment
MG	machine gun
MIA	missing in action
MLR	Main Line of Resistance
NCO	Non-Commissioned Officer
NSB	Dutch Nationaal Socialistische Beweging (National Socialist Movement)
OD	Orde Dienst (Order Service)
OP	observation post
PAN	Partisanen Actie Nederland (Partisan Action Netherlands)
P/F	Pathfinder company
QRF	Quick Release Fastening
RHQ	Regimental Headquarters
RVV	Raad van Verzet (Council for the Resistance)
SFHQ	Special Forces Headquarters
SHAEF	Supreme Headquarters Allied Expeditionary Force
SOE	Special Operations Executive
TAC	Tactical Air Force
TCG	Troop Carrier Group
TSMG	Thompson sub-machine gun
XO	executive officer

Index

INDEX

Praise for *Tonight We Die As Men*

"A product of original research and an important contribution to the literature... An amazingly detailed glimpse into the tragic experiences of this heroic parachute battalion."
Mark Bando, author of *101st Airborne: The Screaming Eagles at Normandy*

"It will be hard to find a better book about a single airborne battalion in World War II... The two British authors take the reader back to Toccoa, Georgia ... then on to airborne training at Fort Benning and Camp Mackall. They also flesh out the personalities mentioned in the book so that by the time the regiment is in England and preparing for its baptism of fire in Normandy, the reader has developed a fondness for each trooper."
Mason Webb, *World War II History*

"Ian Gardner and Roger Day have set out to tell the story of the 3rd Battalion of the famed 101st Airborne Division 506th Parachute Infantry Regiment. The objective of the battalion was to capture and secure the two wooden bridges built by the Germans over the Douve River east of Carentan ... Despite the successful achievement of this important objective by the 3rd Battalion, accomplished with heavy losses, the authors found that little had been written about the battalion. In fact, they call the 3rd a 'forgotten battalion,' as opposed to the 2nd Battalion of 'Band of Brothers' fame."
James C. Roberts, *Washington Times*

"The most comprehensive, factual World War II history I have ever read. The reader is given a vivid account of the day to day life of the combat soldier in Europe. I appreciate the fact that I have met some of these men personally and now I am more aware of what they went through to defend our freedom."
Lamar Davis, Stephens County Historical Society, Tocca, GA

Available now as an e-book from iTunes